Breaking the Mould

Also by the author

An Accidental Diplomat (New Island, 2001)
The Casting of Mr O'Shaughnessy (New Island, 2002)

Breaking the Mould

A Story of Art and Ireland

Eamon Delaney

NEW
ISLAND

BREAKING THE MOULD
First published 2009
by New Island
2 Brookside
Dundrum Road
Dublin 14

www.newisland.ie

ISBN 978-1-84840-056-6

Printed in Ireland by ColourBooks

New Island received financial assistance from
The Arts Council (An Comhairle Ealaíon), Dublin, Ireland

10 9 8 7 6 5 4 3 2 1

To Fiona

Contents

Acknowledgments

I have many people to thank for their encouragement and help in writing this book. Most especially I want to thank my immediate family and extended family. I also wish to thank the many people who knew my father and helped with information. They include Arthur Reynolds, Campbell Bruce, John Montague, Waki Zöllner, the family of Wolf Mankowitz, Michael Kelly, Mick O'Dea RHA, Patrick and Mary Rooney, Susan Moylett and Barry Devlin.

I especially want to thank Jacquie Moore at the Office of Public Works, Sunniva O'Flynn at the Irish Film Archive, Susan Kennedy of the Lensmen Photo Agency, Mairead Delaney at the Abbey Theatre, Irene Stevenson at the *Irish Times* photo archive, and John Bowman who helped with radio material and was always encouraging. I am also very grateful to those who have allowed me to quote from their writings: Roisín Kennedy, Judith Hill, Aidan Dunne, Des Geraghty, Seamus Heaney, Peter Murray, Joanna Shepard, James Ryan and Roisín Higgins.

A big thanks to those at the Irish Museum of Modern Art who did such great work in getting *Eve* erected: Hugo Jellett, Enrique Juncosa and Christine Kennedy. Also to those at Adams Salesrooms for their sensitive work in restoring related sculptures: David Britton, Jane Beattie and James O'Halloran, and to Ian Whyte of Whyte's Auctioneers. Along the way, I am beholden to those who provided help and kind hospitality including Anne Cleary and Denis Connolly in Paris, Maimi Scanlan and Bridget Rooney in Phibsborough and all at the wonderful Tyrone Guthrie Centre in Annaghmakerrig, County Monaghan.

For many years, I have been based at the *Business and Finance* group, from where *Magill* magazine has been published, and it has been a great privilege to have such companionship, not least the continuing support of publisher Ian Hyland. I am also very grateful to Barbara Galvin for legal advice. I make my living through writing and, as a freelancer, I want to especially thank those who have supported me over the years: Frank Coughlan at Independent Newspapers, Caroline Walsh at *The Irish Times*, Ros Dee and Paul Drury at the *Irish Daily Mail* and John Burns at the *The Sunday Times.* Also, Shay Howell at RTÉ. I also want to thank the editor of RTÉ's *Sunday Miscellany*, Clíodhna Ní Anluain, since some of the material grew out of that programme.

And, of course, I wish to thank my publishers, New Island, especially the redoubtable Edwin Higel for keeping the faith and Deirdre O'Neill for doing a wonderful job with the editing. One is always grateful for their enthusiasm and judgement. I am grateful too to Gráinne Killeen for handling publicity.

Lastly, of course, I am beholden to my dear wife Fiona, who not only provided constant encouragement and support but who read an early draft and suggested a crucial change in the book's construction. To her, always love and affection, as well as to my son, Ciaran, for amusing and distracting me on the floor as I tried to finish the project.

Eamon Delaney
Dublin

Introduction

My father was a sculptor. He lived in a house in the West of Ireland, facing the Atlantic Ocean. The fields around the house are full of his sculptures, bronze shapes and spiky stainless steel trees and constructions. The house is empty now and surrounded by ferns, where once it echoed to the sound of industry and children, as is the adjoining workshop and studio. But there is still sculpture about, inside and out. As ever, the sculpture lives on, jangling in the sea breeze.

When he went into a nursing home in a nearby town, I rescued from the house some photographs, papers and two scrapbooks. One was a big red book like a church register with newspaper cuttings of my father's career in the 1960s and 1970s. The other was a smaller scrapbook, recording his emergence in the 1950s. They shed a light on a lost world, with pictures of social scenes long departed, many of them in titles which no longer exist: the *Dublin Evening Mail*, the *Sunday Review*, *Hibernia*, and all of the *Irish Press* group. The material propelled me into writing this account. I remembered much, but there was much that I didn't, and so I would write myself into remembering. It would not be an exhaustive account, looking up records and files. I would simply work with what came to hand and make enquiries. It would also be a chance to write about art, and especially sculpture – that most important but neglected art form.

I would also write about my relationship with my father and how it was transacted through the world of art. I was living in Paris and would walk through the Tuileries garden, with sculpture on either side: large outdoor works by David Smith, Henry Moore and Giacometti. It was like meeting old friends. It made me want to write about sculpture, and its effect, and the atmosphere of my childhood. Paris was also where Eddie first represented Ireland abroad. After Paris, he got married and soon I was born. It was the same with me. After Paris, I went back to Ireland hoping to meet someone special. And I did, and in the most romantic fashion. I just walked into a café near the Liberties in Dublin one day and there she was: the love of my life. Within months I was preparing to get married, and soon a child was due to be born.

I was thus further stimulated by the impending birth of my son and the simultaneous decline of my father. It would be like Bill Viola's *Triptych*, with one generation passing out of life as another passes into it. The hope was that I could finish the book before my son was born and my father passed away. My main source has been the big red scrapbook, made by Hely's, the famous stationers, which readers of Joyce's *Ulysses* will remember being advertised by four men walking around Dublin with the company's name spelt out on their hats, HELY – one letter per man. They are like an art project: moving sculptures, walking through the city that my father peopled with his statues, and which the rest of us have peopled with our lives and memories.

The impulse to write about sculpture was strengthened by a visit shortly afterwards to Israel, and the Museum of Modern Art in Tel Aviv. Inside, were works by Lehmbruck and Barlach. Outside, in the Mediterranean sunlight, there was an amazing sculpture garden, with an outdoor café. I only wished my father has been well enough to travel. Many of his works have ended up in Israel, after all. But by now he was in a nursing home and unlikely to ever leave. Not even to go down to his studio, a short distance away, by the sea, and which he always said was 'waiting for him'.

In this way, I re-encountered my father and the lives of my parents as well as the emerging modern Ireland of the time. It was like big toys out in the open air, just the way Eddie always wanted sculpture to be.

CHAPTER 1

'Gentlemen, You Have a Country'

The earliest memory I have – that is, the earliest memory that I can date (it was 1966 and I was 3 years old) – was of the Big Man going over our house in a wooden box. Thomas Davis, founder of the Young Irelanders, and now 2 ton of bronze, was on his way to placement in central Dublin as part of the 50th-anniversary celebrations of the 1916 Rising. Too large to fit through the door or gate, the rebel had to be hoisted by crane over the lane of fishermen's cottages in Dún Laoghaire where we lived, watched by all the neighbours. I had the day off school, with a toothache, from St Joseph's Orphanage and School. We were not actually orphans, but we often used the full name of the school to make people feel sorry for us. The Big Man was leaving and now we were waving him goodbye.

After him came Wolfe Tone, a year later, also sculpted in our backyard. He went up over the roof too. The founding father of Irish Republicanism, whom the British tried to hang in 1796, was off to emplacement in St Stephen's Green, now 10-foot tall and backgrounded by a series of granite columns which, in a habit of the city's wits to nickname public monuments, was quickly dubbed 'Tone Henge'. In 1971, it was blown up by Loyalist paramilitaries – the first Northern-related bombing in Dublin. Anxious to get at the symbolic core of Irish Republicanism, and emulating the Republicans who were always attacking monuments, Ulster

Loyalists had two years previously attacked Tone's grave in Bodenstown. This time they put the explosives up inside his codpiece; a variation, perhaps, on Brendan Behan's line that 'all the problems of Ireland came from the balls of Henry VIII'.

In the newspaper photos of the time, so exciting for us at school, only the legs remain. The statue had to be made again. 'There's a few things I didn't get right the first time,' my father said with a wink, ever the wag. He also said that the statue's arm would now move outwards, with the other tucked in, just as if Tone was marching – marching back to life. Some detractors said my father, Edward Delaney, was 'paid twice' for the job; others that he blew up the statue himself. Tone's torso was shattered and the Shelbourne Hotel opposite received part of his hand.

In our childhood, we were surrounded by such statues and masks: strange, headless figures and skeletal animals. In the darkness, our surroundings looked like Picasso's *Guernica* with jagged silhouettes and upheld arms. For years, we slept with the death mask of Austin Clarke, the poet, hanging over our bed. He was the nice white-haired man who was smoking a pipe in Colman Doyle's photo book *The People of Ireland* (on the reverse page to my dad, coincidentally – bookish meditation versus rugged, plaster-spattered physicality). He was also the author of 'The Lost Heifer', which we were studying at school, and the wonderful ghost story about running around the Black Church three times at midnight and meeting the devil.

Except this was not quite Clarke's death mask but a version of the original taken in wax, which had been allowed to melt and then cast in bronze. The melting did not happen suddenly, but over the course of time, hanging near the fire, so that the face looked as if it had truly sagged with age and contemplation. Another version had his whole face folded over like one those surrealist images, or the famous 1960s cartoon poster by Robert Crumb, *Stoned Again*, with the character's head sliding through his hands.

The proper bronze original was put in the lobby of the Abbey Theatre, smiling dreamily at all the theatregoers, while the actual plaster original is under a glass box in the Dublin Writers Musuem. However, my father kept other versions which he thought were more interesting than the original. We also had the death mask of Séamus Ennis, the piper and folklorist, and better still a cast of his hands, with their extraordinary long fingers from piping. As kids we were confused: was he a great piper because his hands were naturally long, or did they become long from playing?

Although a death mask had to be a once off, as my father argued later during a controversy over James Joyce's death mask, he kept moulds to tinker around with. It was alleged that Joyce's death mask had been inexcusably altered by having an extra piece of chin attached. Literally, *Finnegans Wake* (as in, 'Finn Again's Awake'), for technically this meant that the death mask had been 'done' twice. An echo perhaps of Joyce's endless Viconian cycle of life, as Eddie described it later in one of the very rare descriptions, or 'explanations', he gave to accompany his work (this one for the *Finnegans Wake* wall sculpture in Davy Byrne's bar, the venue for Leopold Bloom's lunchtime scene in *Ulysses*).

The death mask is an interesting paradox, for essentially the artist has no control over it. The subject has all the control, right down to the implacably shut mouth and the seedpod eyes, and yet the subject is dead and so it is nature, or mortality, which defines the piece. A further paradox is that the subject has more influence and control over his or her image when dead than when alive. Unless the finished image is distorted, as with Austin Clarke's melting head, or if it is attached to something incongruous, as with, of all people, James Joyce himself, when somebody attached a replica of his death mask to a shiny steel shovel and had it photographed: unconscious revenge perhaps on the Joyce estate, with their crippling restrictions on the use of the man's image and work.

Eddie was disappointed not to have done de Valera's death mask and claimed that he was all set to do it and was waiting in the Breffni Inn, with his bag of tools, like a doctor after the event. Charlie Haughey was among those who organised it, but others

3

were not enthusiastic. Eddie felt that Dev should have given his face to the state, and posterity, on the basis that he had been Taoiseach and President, and that his face wasn't his own but was public property.

He would have been amazing, de Valera, at the age of 93, with his long neck and his high, austere head. On our wall, we had a black and white picture of him taken from below by Colman Doyle. Dev is in his famous black cloak, regally fastened with a Celtic brooch. He looked elegant, French. He was our de Gaulle and, sure enough, in *The People of Ireland* book, he is pictured with de Gaulle, standing outdoors, like two Giacometti giants in the sun. In our house, Dev was not so much a hero as an aesthetic icon. There was little concern with his social conservatism or his vexatious twists on the Treaty. He was simply an Irish monarch, a rebel who had cheated a British execution, just like Tone, and who had then stuck around for a long time. Also, he looked good. He was a walking sculpture.

Eddie at least had a chance to 'do' de Valera's head, but this time it was sculpted by Arthur Power and cast in his workshop. He often cast other people's work. On delivering the head, he described how a sulky girl came to the door of the de Valera house and said, 'Ah, that auld thing, yeah put it in inside, we've loads of them already.' Inside, the room was full of de Valeras, like mini Napoleons or Lenins. He had already long been the subject of a cult of personality. My father claimed that the money from Dev's head went to pay for me being born, i.e. the casting fees paid for the maternity bill, which by a neat coincidence was done by his son, Éamon de Valera Jr – a real life casting, in this case.

But the other story was that it was paid for by a TV ad, which my mother did in 1961. Sitting in Bartley Dunne's, the cocktail lounge on Drury Street, she was approached by a dapper ad man who wanted to 'put her in a commercial', holding a cigarette and smiling over the slogan, *Players No 1 – For the Sophisticated Taste*. And so she appeared, puffing away, in short black hair and pink shirt. Either way, I was given de Valera's first name, and the middle name of Davis, since my mother's pregnancy coincided with our household commission to sculpt the man. Mine was a quicker gestation, since the Big Man didn't make it into the world for another four years. I have thus been sent into the world emboldened, or burdened, with the names of two of our greatest patriots.

In Easter Week 1966, my namesakes, one live and the other inanimate, met in College Green, when one pulled the cloak off the other and turned on his fountain. Yes, the Big Man, who had gone over our house, was now standing over the traffic in College Green, on a large pedestal, slim in real life but now a bulky presence, too bulky for some, although it is strange that he has small hands, just like his maker, Eddie, who was said to have unusually small hands for a monumental sculptor. Later, in a bar in Ballinasloe, a farmer held out Eddie's fingers and said to the other customers, 'Look, he has lady's hands – the sculptor who works in metal has lady's hands!' The pub was the Duck Inn which led through a back lane to Ballinasloe church where Eddie had installed altar panels and a sort of cubist Christ on top of a pole. The altar panels, of biblical scenes, were filled with so many nude women – a persistent feature of his work – that the nervous parishioners put flowers around them to cover them up. In another motif, various random animals were crammed in, wistful compensation perhaps for having so few animals back on the family farm in Mayo.

The Davis unveiling was a major affair, and the event was only one part of a week-long celebration of the Easter Rising which involved parades, pageants and other ceremonies. Each night on TV, the events of that particular day back in 1916 were re-enacted by Abbey actors, heroically firing revolvers out of windows or tending to each other's wounds inside the burning GPO, before being led off sadly but proudly to jail and, in some cases, execution.

An official book was published, called *Commemoration*, which records the week's ceremonies. Eddie's work is in it, not just Davis but also other sculptures. He did well out of 1916. Most emerging artists did. There was even a special exhibition of works at the

Mansion House. The Lord Mayor said that people may not understand it, but they should appreciate it in the new spirit of modernism and the avant garde.

This reflected the unusual confidence of the time, a combination of the old habits of commemoration with the new 1960s spirit of adventure and curiosity. Artistically, it meant that, in a curious way, nationalism and modernism went hand in hand, in this period at least. After the torpor of the 1950s, a restrictive and depressed decade, especially in Ireland, there was suddenly, and paradoxically, an exciting break with the past and 'a fulfilment of the yearning for independence'.

'It would have been feasible but not particularly original or imaginative to have the artists depict the events of 1916 in a conventional way,' said Mayor Timmons in the Mansion House, 'like the nineteenth-century historical painters, but it was evident that the exhibitors were modern in outlook and style.' This new look at the Rising 'might shock or startle at first glance, but no one could doubt the sincerity of expression or their genuine effort to do justice to the great events they depicted'.

Many of the men and women of 1916 were 'writers and visionaries, and those who contributed to this exhibition were visionaries in their own way', said Timmons in a generous and revealing linkage. (But it is also akin to saying that, as with the Easter rebels, God knows where these visionaries will lead us, but we'd better go with their imagination.) In a felicitous phrasing, which linked the three tenses in six words, Timmons said that the artists 'had peered into the past to present for the future, an image of the greatness of the Easter freedom fighters'. And perhaps of the modern imagination.

Eddie also did one of the 1916 postage stamps, and while the others were portraits of the Rising's leaders, based on iconic drawings by Seán O'Sullivan, his was a striking expressionist image of the Rising itself, with tiny figures marching near a burning GPO, overhung with a spiky red sun. Beneath the figures, white crosses are scattered, as if in instant commemoration, but they also look like erupting graves, an unfortunate resonance given the other legacy of 1916, with its contentious focus on sacrifice and violence. They even look like those little white crosses that peace protestors used to press into lawns in Northern Ireland during the 1980s.

However, in 1966, it all looked funky and modern and the stamps were very popular. 'Another siege of the GPO' was one headline about the queues of people coming in to buy them. As kids, it was an excitement we could share. Making sculpture was one thing, but making stamps was even better, and collecting them was our obsession, buying them in glassy bags from Grace's toyshop in Dún Laoghaire, or having them sent back from our cousins in Zambia, with pictures of colourful cane-cutters and happy lads working in the mines. The inscription on the stamps was the one put on all the 1916 memorials: a simple restatement of the Rising's motto and war cry – '*Éirí Amach na Cásca*' ('We will arise at Easter').

Eddie also did a memorial for his home town of Claremorris in Mayo: a group of overlapping crosses, 15 in all, rising like birds. He was very excited about it, he told *The Irish Press*, especially since they had commissioned him 'without any strings'. 'They gave me a completely free hand, which was wonderful. What I am doing will be a complete break with commemorative tradition.' Again, the interesting parallel with 1916 itself – a 'break' with tradition. 'It's made up of symbols, symbolising the men who were executed, and will be lit from the inside at night. I hope to see it up in the town square during the next couple of months.'

It was a fairly traditional proposal but unfortunately it invoked controversy and later it was simply toppled over and then removed. One newspaper assembled some local views. One chap thought it was an 'eyesore' and that they should have made 'more space for cars': 'I didn't understand it and I doubt if anybody in the town did, no matter what they tell you.' Another fellow said he'd have preferred something more 'straightforward' for the 'ordinary people' and a woman suggested that 'the fellow who blew up Nelson's Pillar should be brought down here and given the job of blasting the whole lot out of the town'.

Not everybody was ready to accept modern sculpture, in the way that the Dublin Lord Mayor and others had suggested. But it would be as well not to be smug. Such attitudes are as prevalent now, and even worse, in fact, with much of the current media giving full vent to shameless philistinism and encouraging the sort of vox-pops that prevent anything too different from appearing.

But others in the report were more positive. 'Maybe it is too arty,' said a creamery manager, 'but when you got used to it, it was impressive. I want it back.' While a local solicitor said that this was 'the 1960s and there has to be a modern outlook in everything now, including art'. Another man said that 'you can't please all the people all the time, the children of some people I know can understand what the statue represents. It's like the trunk of a tree with 15 branches, representing the signatories of the Proclamation.' As if to illustrate his point, a 14-year-old girl 'totally approved' and understood 'the message it was trying to give'. She said, 'I think it's a shame that the town should kick up a row about a man who has helped to put us on the map.' But the sculpture was not restored and, if it's any consolation, some of the locals still have bits of it on their walls.

The whole débâcle in Mayo was not helped by an unfortunate spelling error by the stonemason, who instead of *Éirí Amach na Cásca* chiselled the inscription *Éire Amach na Cásca (Ireland arise at Easter)* which, as misspellings go, is not the worst, when you think about it.

All that year, and even that very week in 1916, statues and sculptures sprung up around the land, and especially the capital. There was another Davis, this one in marble in the City Hall (originally commissioned by Oscar Wilde's father) and on St Stephen's Green there was Andrew O'Connor's graceful statue of Robert Emmet, the leader of the 1803 revolt, standing in mid oration and making his famous speech from the dock, with his arms held down at his sides and his fingers splayed with tension. 'My lamp of light is almost extinguished,' he said when he saw a lamp flickering in the hushed courtroom. He would shortly be taken to be beheaded by the British at Thomas Street, his head held up as an example.

The Emmet statue was unveiled by de Valera, one of the three editions of the same figure: the others were in Golden Gate Park in San Francisco and in Washington DC, unveiled in 1919 in the presence of US President Woodrow Wilson. This was an incredible 47 years before Dev unveiled the other Emmet in Dublin. How long the Long Fellow had been with us – the American who cheated execution!

It is important, incidentally, to get these rebellions in order: 1798 (Tone); 1803 (Emmet); 1848 (Davis); 1867 (Fenians); and 1916 (de Valera), each one feeding off the other and emulating their tradition of gesture and defiance. All of them were constantly invoked in the speeches of 1966, with much less mention of the non-violent nationalist tradition of O'Connell and Parnell. This was not only a distortion: the non-violent or parliamentary tradition was more popular, and surely as effective – if not more effective – than the militant approach, but it was also storing up violent ghosts for the future.

The most specific homage to this tradition of sacrifice was made, appropriately, at the Garden of Remembrance in Parnell Square, which was also opened in Easter week. Here the link between Christian sacrifice and the nationalist cause was made most explicit, much to the detriment surely of true Republicanism and storing up yet more problems for the future. The garden, which runs the breadth of the square, was even laid out around a large sunken pond shaped as a crucifix. Above the mosaic pond, there is a backdrop on which are inscribed words from the fable of the *Children of Lir*. This was the story of the children who rose out of the lake after 900 years, an obvious metaphor for Ireland's national struggle.

In 1972, there was the addition of a huge heroic sculpture by Oisín Kelly depicting the children rising out of the water, with their arms outstretched, to become giant swans, a stirring and powerful image. But my father dismissed it as 'fascist'. Professional rivalry no doubt – Kelly was an established sculptor – but he may have thought that the scale was just too big and too triumphalist. What it most resembles is a Soviet war memorial from Eastern Europe. It has all of Eddie's masculinity without the undercut of femininity, or an Irish sense of proportion or humility. The other reason for the charge was that the piece was cast in Italy in a foundry allegedly used by Mussolini (Davis was also cast in Italy, but that was another matter).

This accusation of 'fascist' was a popular cry of my father and his generation, imbibed, in his case, during his time in 1950s Germany. Eddie had gone to Munich in 1954, a raw country boy and ambitious art student, and immersed himself in a society struggling to recreate itself after the trauma of war. The experience was highly formative and left him with a lifelong love of Europe and bohemianism, and a corresponding distrust of authority and so-called 'bourgeois values'.

One his many boasts was about how he and some fellow students protested against the rearmament of Germany in 1955 (encouraged by the US to counter the Soviet threat). Aghast at this return to 'militarism', the students lay down in front of American tanks and then apparently stormed the sculpture department and smashed up the classical models and Roman torsos, lest there be any return to Aryan idealism. The protesters later formed radical groups which eventually gestated into the Baader-Meinhof terrorist movement of the 1970s.

The appetite for literalism and symbolism in the Garden of Remembrance was very precise, as the *Commemoration* handbook points out. 'On the floor of the central reflecting pool is a mosaic pattern of blue-green waves, bearing a design of six groups of weapons from the early Iron age, a theme derived from the custom of the Celtic people throughout Europe of placing weapons in lakes or pools of battle.' This is also what sculptors do to cool and harden their piece after casting: I remember the blasts of steam rising up over our backyard in Dún Laoghaire.

'The key used by the President to open the electronically operated gates,' it further explains, 'is a copy, enlarged three times, of the oldest known key from any Irish site. The original bronze key was found in 1936 in the earliest stratum of an excavation of the Royal Crannóg at Lagore, seat of the Kings of Deiscert Brega, near the Hill of Tara in County Meath. This would place its origin before AD 650.'

Inside the gate, overlooking the garden, there is a sort of permanent viewing platform, now popular with immigrants and East Europeans. For years, it was used almost solely by winos and druggies and the garden was usually deserted.

The same revisionist impulse could debunk all of this, but looking at *Commemoration* now, from our more recent experience of prosperity and materialism, the whole thing has a curious integrity and innocence to it: the nuns winning 1916 poetry competitions, the pageants in Croke Park, with children dressed as rebels, and the veterans lining up in country towns, square-jawed in their trilby hats and overcoats. With its emphasis on sacrifice, loyalty and community, it is a vanished time. One picture shows some women in wool overcoats 'going to their places on the platform', a caption which suggests servility but is, in reality, far from it: these steely faced women look like they wouldn't take nonsense from anyone.

And yet the endless emphasis on piety and sacrifice must have been maddening. The commemoration is simply too much, with a 'cult of personality' built around the 1916 signatories that is almost idolatrous, as if these pious men, these dreamers and poets, weren't from history at all but saints or icons out of some higher mythology. And as if all of Irish history – for which read 'Irish struggle' – ended with the *annus mirabilis* of 1916. As if, Everything Was Leading Towards That Year. And nothing happened afterwards, not even the 1919–1921 War of Independence and especially not the awkward Civil War. Nor the grim decades of post-Independence depression.

In one photo, a young well-groomed minister, Charlie Haughey, is about to turn the sod for yet another memorial, this time a tree for the martyred Thomas McDonagh. Everyone around him is immensely solemn, but Haughey, with his head down, looks like he's about to crack up laughing. In another picture, listening to yet another speech, he just looks impatient, as if he'd sooner be back at his desk, pulling in some foreign investment, or down in Grooms Hotel partying with Donogh O'Malley and a few 1960s swingers.

Around this time, an American author, Donald Connery, came to Ireland and wrote a fascinating and prophetic book entitled *The Irish* (1968) – using Eddie as one of his subjects. '1966 seemed a likely occasion for a great amount of national self-congratulation,' wrote Connery, 'but, on the contrary, the ceremonies themselves and the whole pattern of events afterwards revealed a discontent and impatience of notable proportions. Disappointment in the past and an eagerness to move on into the future were there in equal proportions.'

There was a yearning to break free – and for a bit more colour and more modernity. And yet it was coming. It was already taking place, indeed, and at the unveiling of the Davis statue, de Valera was mindful of it. 'Davis's teaching was to love our country,' he told the crowd. 'But to love our country, we must know her past. Just as we need spiritual reading to nurture the spiritual life, we must read the writings of Davis and Pearse to nurture our love for our country.'

'To love our country we must serve her, there could be no real service without love,' said Dev, in language unconsciously close to the youthful, slightly hippy mood of the day, in many ways the very modern spirit that he was ostensibly trying to quell. It was said that, towards the end, Lyndon B. Johnson grew his hair long to defy his hippy opponents. It's almost as if the aged president, who met Lyndon B. Johnson the previous year, was trying to do something similar.

Listening to him, on rows of chairs, was most of the government. In other photographs of the front row, de Valera is next to the Taoiseach, Seán Lemass, both wearing their War of Independence medals, and alongside Frank Aiken, also wearing his medal: all the men who fought the English. Jack Lynch, the

Minister for Finance, is speaking. He is not wearing a medal. Far from it, the Republican detractors would later say, when the North erupted in 1969 and Lynch was perceived to have stood idly by. But, in 1966, Lynch was still the golden boy and, within a few months, he would succeed Lemass as Taoiseach, a compromise candidate whose elevation would prevent either George Colley or the ambitious Charles Haughey from taking over. Dev disapproved of these internal struggles in Fianna Fáil, which he thought would divide and damage the party.

So, 'past, present and future' (as the Mayor Timmons might have it) we have three Fianna Fáil taoisigh together in one picture. Four, if we count Haughey who is just out of the frame, the man who would later challenge Lynch. Between speeches, de Valera sits gravely watching, purse-lipped and austere in his top hat and long coat, while Lemass holds a black umbrella to protect Dev from the rain. Above them was the bronze colossus of Davis covered from head to toe in a silken shroud, like a Christo installation or a holy statue during Lent.

From the outset, de Valera didn't mince his words. 'The site for the statue was well chosen,' he said. 'Beside the old Parliament, for which Grattan, Flood and the Volunteers won independence from the British Parliament until William Pitt, by bribery and corruption, got a majority to vote it away. Davis, the Young Irelanders and O'Connell had tried to win that free Parliament again but Davis wanted not a Parliament of the aristocracy but a Parliament for the common people, a free parliament for all Ireland. He, like Tone and Emmet, and the men of 1916, wished to unite all the people of Ireland and to abolish the memory of past dissension.'

He may also have been mindful that the spot was formerly occupied by the statue of King William II, victor at the Battle of the Boyne in 1690 and whose subsequent triumph gave power to the colonial Protestant minority at the expense of the Catholic majority. Arrogantly astride his horse, it was a provocative statue, to say the least, and Trinity students attacked it because it had 'its arse towards the college'. After which, it was repeatedly attacked by nationalists, with small night-time explosions, before being eventually removed altogether in 1929. On one famous occasion Billy was blown clean off his horse and the police sent an ambulance round, because they'd got the simple message: 'Man off his horse in College Green'.

This tradition kept up, incidentally, and lest one thinks it was all one-way traffic in 1966, with statues going up, there were some spectacular removals, such as the blowing up of Nelson's Pillar on O'Connell Street, a major explosion which left a gap on the street that would take decades to fill.

In the Millennium Year of 1981, with talk of a replacement, Eddie offered his own proposal, a giant ribbed column of pre-fabricated stainless steel, the material that he had moved on to by the 1980s, and which was not unlike the original pillar, with views out over the city. 'Bullworker Blues at the Pillar', was the terrible headline in the *Irish Independent*. 'His design resembles a giant lipstick, or, as some have unkindly said, a stainless-steel chest expander on its side.'

But the article did at least reproduce his artist's impression and intriguing description. 'Mr Delaney calls his structure *Blue City*, and said it would be equipped with lifts and spiral staircases to transport sightseers to its summit.' The circular tower would be topped by a viewing platform and 'a sculptured canopy of fluid forms'. The whole ensemble would be illuminated by blue lights at night to give the impression of a 'blue ribbon, and silhouette, moving continually'. By the 1980s, his desire to conquer the city had long moved from figurative heroes to pure form. The spot lay empty, however, until a full decade later and the installation of the Spire, a structure which was not unlike Eddie's proposal.

Back in 1966, there is no reference to Nelson's Pillar in the *Commemoration* book, or in Dev's speeches. It was as if the attack on the Pillar had taken place in a parallel world, and yet destroying it could be said to be a consequence of his incendiary talk. *The Irish Press*, barely able to contain its glee, had a front-page photo of the head in a pile of rubble, extra-whitened from the photographer's flash. In the corner was an ad for *Evo-Stik – the Impact Adhesive*, with the tagline: 'Created the quiet revolution that made it possible for everyone to be a Do It Yourselfer'. They must have been taking the piss. The bombing was apparently a freelance job, not sanctioned by the mainstream Republican movement.

In the same spirit, a song called 'Nelson's Farewell' was written by the folk band The Dubliners, a humorous homage to the removal of Nelson. The song got its first outing at a series of concerts at the Gate Theatre held to coincide with the Easter celebrations, a bawdy alternative to the more pious official commemorations. The concerts were a great success, as was a live recording released afterwards. Part of its appeal is the hilarious between-song banter of anecdotes and jokes by Luke Kelly and more especially the gravel-voiced Ronnie Drew, who could surely have done stand-up comedy if he hadn't been a singer.

Eddie's sculpture *The Great Hunger* was on the stage, a skeletal sculpture with its arms stretched upwards, similar to his famine group in St Stephen's Green. It may seem odd to have a famine sculpture in such a setting, with the band all hanging out of it on the LP's cover. But it was okay: these were prosperous times, and the famine was 'a thing of the past', just like armed rebellion, which was celebrated in other songs – although mildly. The Dubliners were never crude rebel rousers and, true to their working-class roots, they had just as many songs celebrating Irish regiments in the British army. History was a two-way street for them, and their take was ironic, as it was with 'Nelson's Farewell'.

Cleverly, the band preface the song by reciting from 'Dublin', a love/hate tribute to the seedy capital by Northern poet Louis MacNeice. The poem describes Nelson watching the old order disintegrate (the poem was written in 1930). But the band have brilliantly turned it around so that his dismay is now our triumph, in the prosperous, self-governing 1960s. Now it is Nelson himself who is collapsing, and who goes 'crashing through the quarter where once he stood so stiff and proud and rude' (Drew's rueful Dublinese spits out the words). But the song also mocks the rebels:

15

'the boys of Ireland showed them what to do'. As if to say, is this all you could do, blow up a pillar? It also mocks the ebullience of the country's new prosperity: 'But now the Irish join the race, we've got an astronaut in space. Ireland, boys, is now a world power too.' It was the sort of scepticism Dev would probably have approved of, were he ever likely to tune in and digest the sarcastic lyrics.

So it was farewell to The One-Handed Adulterer, as Joyce called Nelson. Joyce was obsessed with adulterers, perhaps because of his own fidelity. He also remarked on how the most (allegedly) Catholic capital in Europe had statues of three adulterers on its main thoroughfare (meaning Nelson, but also O'Connell and Parnell, whose major memorials punctuate the street). Both O'Connell and Parnell were titans of *constitutional* nationalism, of course, reflecting the more popular, non-militant tradition of the national struggle. Hence, the anxiety of the assertive and even triumphalist state in 1966 to put up statues of its physical-force Republicans. And over on the posh southside as well, making them part of the establishment. Putting up Davis in College Green was a cheeky variation of this, since he was a radical who had rejected, or at least 'reinvented', the tradition from whence he came.

CHAPTER 2

A Nation Once Again

As Dev told the gathering, the site for Davis in College Green was 'well-chosen'. As well as being in front of the old parliament, it was also in front of Trinity College, where the young revolutionary had stood before his fellow students in 1845 and told them, 'Gentlemen, you have a country.' You have to admire this: Dev echoing Davis and, in his own act of emulation, about to pull the cloak, not just off a new statue, but a shiny new state.

After all, they had waited long enough. The original plaque for the statue was laid in 1945, on the centenary of Davis's death, and the commission was not passed to my father until 1961, so the statue itself was a long time coming from someone who usually worked quickly. But the authorities knew they were getting something different. 'Every Irish artist worth his salt will be glad to hear that the Davis commission is going to Delaney,' an Arts Council member told the *Sunday Express*. 'He is an artist of high order. But, of course, his statue is likely to be controversial.' The reporter agreed and said the decision was 'likely to be greeted by a storm of protest – and applause. Delaney, whose sculpture has been wildly praised by many and called "incomprehensible" by others, has always poked fun at his more traditional brethren: some time ago he referred to the "bull" of much Irish art.'

Notwithstanding such opinions, or maybe because of them, Eddie was picked. 'Patriot faces another "battle"' was the headline, and (assuming they were referring to Davis, and not the sculptor), wasn't it ever thus. Poor old Davis. After all he'd been through, he was now to be a bulwark for modern art!

One of the criticisms of Davis and Tone is that they are neither traditional public statues nor pieces of outright modernism, but a halfway marriage between both. And that Eddie knew this, but persisted with his hybrid projects. However, he was also compromised by later having to negotiate with the Cabinet, who were more nervous than the Arts Council about how recognisable the 'portrait' was going to be.

For others, the hybrid element was part of the statue's appeal and reflected the mixture of these elements at a changing time, and particularly in Ireland, as the country moved awkwardly but determinedly into being a modern state. The sculpture would be modern and European, just like some of the country's new design and architecture. The national TV station, for example, was taken out of the dusty Victorian city – it had been on Henry Street – and given a fresh start in a green field site in Donnybrook. Irish design and materials would be used in a way that was both international and modern, but one that also echoed old Celtic motifs and designs.

Likewise with Eddie's sculptures. He was encouraged to break with the academic tradition, so associated with the old ruling class, and go for an aesthetic that was new and expressive, but one that would also reconnect with the country's Celtic roots and imagery. Banish Victorian banality and get back to Celtic vitality. The European background was key: its influences would save Ireland from slavish Anglophilia and flowery Edwardian pastiche. Eddie, with his European training, would be ideal.

As well as Celtic references, Eddie's sculptures often had a rural dimension, which happily reflected his own country roots but also those of the generation then coming up to Dublin to create jobs and suburbs: country boys in mohair suits, building new roads and office blocks. The long-suffering peasantry were finally taking over. For conservationists, this was fraught with risk. From 1920 on, planning Dublin was increasingly in the hands of non-Dubliners. Meanwhile, de Valera and his ilk were trying to pull energy away from the feckless, post-colonial capital and into the virtuous countryside. It was like Pol Pot without the population transfers. Indeed, people were going the other way. In the early 1960s, thousands of people like my parents were coming into the city and spreading into its suburbs.

Modern Ireland was undergoing a boom – the first Celtic Tiger – after the foundations of the Lemass era and a relatively young government wanted to make a mark on things. Eddie was from a similar background to many of the ministers and came from modest origins in the West of Ireland, getting through on scholarships and hard graft. The farmyard scenes and animals in his drawings, or on the Davis panels, were a reminder of where they had come from, the equivalent of Marc Chagall or Chaïm Soutine doing rural murals for the Paris salons or Soviet halls.

It was a time of momentous change worldwide, especially cultural change, and the government was determined to honour the country's past in a more modern and innovative way, reflecting the confidence of a state not only asserting itself in the prosperous years of the 1960s, but also claiming its cultural identity after centuries of colonialism. They commissioned projects like the Garden of Remembrance, which in its ambitious modernity now looks dated, like the outdoor set of a James Bond movie. Before this, Republican statues were usually of concrete men in belted overcoats, with little artistic energy, and reflected the often dour, pietistic nature of our political commemoration. But there was money now. This was celebratory. Davis was not going to be a grim little rebel, but a solid colossus, just as Tone was going to be a 'new type of man', stepping out like a striding rock star!

The College Green site was also where Michael Collins and de Valera himself addressed rallies in the tumultuous 1920s, and then against each other during the Civil War, with more rallies and marches into the bitter elections of the 1930s. And yet it was also where, in 1939, an all-party group of government and opposition came together to announce that we were staying out of World War Two, or the 'Emergency' as it was officially termed. Indeed, the war affected the Davis project since part of its delay was because there was an air raid shelter on the site, which needed to be removed. A shelter for the neutral country.

There was a similar long wait for the Wolfe Tone statue. So long, indeed, that in *Ulysses* reference is made to the place 'where Wolfe Tone was not'. And this was in 1904. After an explosion removed it in 1971, the same could have been said again. How interesting that Joyce, if he had minded himself, could have been around in 1971, and lived through the 1960s, TV and exploding statues. He was born in 1882, the same year as de Valera, who trundled on to 1975 – and was 47 years between unveiling different Emmets. For Joyce too, Dev was an artistic character, a stoic who turns up like a dream-like statue in *Finnegans Wake*.

As with the Tone memorial, the Davis statue was accompanied by a further group sculpture, illustrative of Irish history. For Tone, it was a famine family. For Davis, it was a fountain with life-size angels or heralds, representing the Four Provinces and blowing water out of trumpets.

With their boxy bodies and heads, the heralds are similar to the skeletal famine figures, and, as with that group, this is where the real modern art comes in, satisfying Eddie's wish to do expressive sculpture and to experiment with the form. But it also satisfied the ambition of the overall architect, Raymond McGrath, an interesting man who was the state's main architect for decades. Originally from Australia, where he was also the government architect, but by whom he felt neglected, he came to England, and then to Ireland, where at the Office of Public Works (OPW) he oversaw much of the evolving Irish state's architecture and visual aesthetic.

'In an earlier maquette,' wrote McGrath in an eloquent memo, 'two griffin-like figures were to have spouted water into the pool, but these were abandoned in favour of standing winged figures in the pool itself and these have been developed into the groups of four heralds. They are to stand in a spray of water spreading from jets at their feet and will themselves blow back streams of water into the pool. The spiky angularity of the figures may not appeal to everyone, but they are a virile conception and should prove to be a telling and dramatic feature of the memorial.'

Around the fountain is a low wall of granite blocks, inset with bronze reliefs or panels. Based on the ballads and poetry of Thomas Davis, they depict scenes from Irish history, or Irish nationalist history, and the titles are self-explanatory: *The Eviction, The Famine, The Burial, Tone's Grave, We Must Not Fail, A Nation Once Again.*

'Being afraid of damage to the waxes,' continued McGrath, 'the sculptor has proceeded with the castings at his own risk. These, I think, are works of exceptional quality.' This is a fair comment. If the uneven bulkiness of Eddie's larger figures is risky, his smaller works, such as the panels, are more assured and delicate. Eddie wrestled with scale all his life, as all sculptors do, and may only have reconciled it when he began working in stainless steel (thus his audacious proposal for the Nelson's Pillar replacement). Or indeed when he went West and built his landscape of steel trees against the panorama of the changing sky and sea.

The reliefs are typical of his work, with lots of sinewy figures with heads bowed, and are similar to altar panels he later did for Ballinasloe Church and St Marys Cathedral in Kilkenny; rural scenes of suffering and struggle, reflecting Ireland's troubled history with land and politics. *We Must Not Fail* is almost a direct replica of the 1916 stamp, with men determinedly lining up in front of a burning GPO, again with a spiky sun rising in the corner and lots of erupting crosses. The images are almost childlike in their innocence, as if they were indeed carved out by small, uncertain hands.

In the final panel, 'A Nation Once Again', we have – lift off! – modern Ireland, with TV masts, ships and aeroplanes, and two big chimneys just like the power stations being built across the land. The GPO has been seemingly rebuilt, along with a line of new and upright soldiers. Meanwhile, people are depicted working the land eagerly, with bulging biceps and ploughshares, nothing like the stricken, rack-rented labourers of the previous panels. A horse has its leg cocked, ready to go. Yes, the 1960s had finally brought the prosperity and fulfilment that independence had so long promised. *Gentlemen, you have a country.*

For Dev, of course, the prosperity was double-edged. He had finally been prevailed upon to hand over to Lemass in 1959, who immediately introduced long overdue reforms, including opening up the country to inward investment and ending Dev's naïve, if idealistic, policy of protectionism and small-scale agriculture. Years of economic growth followed and there were another seven to come before the oil crisis of 1973 began to change things. It was an exciting time, full of potential after the stagnant 1950s. However, for this ascetic icon, raised on a lifetime of piety and sacrifice, the changes were worrying. Individualism and materialism were creeping in and, in his suspicion and unease, Dev was oddly at one with the hippies who were also then coming to the fore.

The President thus concluded by talking of 'love' again, and quoted John F. Kennedy whom he, and the country, had so rapturously received on his 'homecoming' five years earlier. He warned the crowd that 'we should ask ourselves, as President Kennedy urged his fellow countrymen, not what our country can do for us, but what we can do for our country'. And in a final flourish, which was indeed almost American in its language, Dev said, 'That must be the spirit if we are to make our country the grand old nation it can be!'

After a salute from the band, which again was almost American, the President unveiled Davis of his silken sheet. The crowd applauded and 'oohed' and 'aahed'. Not everyone was impressed, of course, especially by the statue's bulky size, and the piece would create controversy for years to come. Opinion was as divided as it was on Eddie's Claremorris piece, except this was a major monument at the heart of the capital.

As the drummers and trumpeters from the Army No 1 band continued their salute, the angels starting spouting water through their trumpets, and water erupted from the jets below. The band then started into 'A Nation Once Again', accompanied by a choir of schoolchildren. This was Davis's ballad and, of course, the unofficial national anthem – not to be made official until Ireland was fully free, or so they told us. Just like the writing of Emmet's epitaph. The ceremony concluded with the official national anthem.

The unveiling is captured not just in newspaper photos but also in an intriguing newsreel, which RTÉ has since put up on the internet. There are two newsreels, in fact: one in black and white and one in colour. I prefer the black and white, which is more ghostly and captures the dramatic impact of the statue when first unveiled. By comparison, the colour clip looks dated – such is the irony of photography – with its weak or washed out colours, much like the Kodachrome photos in the *Commemoration* handbook. It is also mute, for some reason, so that we have de Valera merely gesticulating – without sound: a moving statue.

The other clip, however, has plenty of noise. It shows the scene from a number of angles, but mainly focuses on Dev's speech and on the schoolchildren, down on the street in their raincoats and hoods. They are standing beside the army band and waiting for the signal. Seeing their images, years later, we were fascinated by these children, with their mixture of nerves and eagerness, waiting in the rain which, at one stage, is falling heavily.

At first we see the statue, in its black shroud, standing dramatically over College Green, with the traffic stopped and people all around. On one side are the smooth white columns of Gandon's House of Lords portico and on the other the steep banks and Victorian offices of Dame Street. Behind is a new 1960s office block for the Royal Insurance Company. Dev does not sound nearly as confident as he appears in print, but nervous and slightly pleading, as if sensing that the mood was already going away from him. And it was. He would shortly be facing re-election for President. He had hoped to be unopposed, but Fine Gael wanted a contest, and in the end they would run him very close. In the context of the election, these film clips were controversial, for the ageing Dev had said he didn't want a full-scale election campaign. Fine Gael reluctantly agreed, but then realised that Dev was getting all this free publicity from the 1966 Commemorations, at which he dominated, and that he was usually making election-sounding speeches.

After he quotes JFK about the 'grand old nation', Dev turns to grapple for the cord that linked him to Davis. But nothing happens. An official quickly steps out to help him, and soon Dev is roping it in with two hands like an old fisherman pulling in a lobster pot. Eventually, the cord snaps and the dark shroud drops suddenly, and revealingly, from the statue and, in this moment, it really does look big and different. A colossus above the street, it looks like the effigy of some Pharaoh or Roman Emperor, wheeled out in a Cecil B. DeMille movie. It certainly punctuates the space of College Green and, in many ways, Davis looks like he had always been there, which is about the best tribute you can give any sculpture.

From one angle, the statue blots out the 'Royal' on the 'Royal Insurance', aptly since the Royal was one of those big Dublin companies that was said to operate a 'Protestants first' recruitment policy (the same was said of Sun Alliance, with which it merged). This was not so unusual at the time. Although the state's political power was in the hands of its Catholic majority, the minority Protestant community still – *still*, in the mid 1960s – controlled much of the business culture, especially in the older financial professions. Behind Davis, for example, in Foster Place, you can still see the 'Royal Bank of Ireland' on the pediment. The 'Royal' has since been removed.

The screen then dissolves. It re-opens with the children singing 'A Nation Once Again', which they do lustily, with greater energy than the adults. God bless them: their enthusiasm is unquestioning. As they sing, the camera focuses on the fountain, getting close in to the spray and froth of the water, which is wonderfully illuminated. The clip finishes with the children giving a last stirring verse of 'A Nation Once Again' which they belt out upwards, with heads nodding dreamily.

The colour clip shows the event from quite different angles. Indeed, it could be almost be a different event. The children look younger, with rosy cheeks and brown school uniforms and, in a nice coincidence, some of the girls are wearing their coats like cloaks, just like de Valera. With the singing over, the ceremony ends abruptly, and the VIPs quickly rise from their seats and fold their umbrellas. These are not ministers, but other VIPs, hard to identify. Some have top hats, but their expressions are modern: sour and purposeful, as much as to say, *it's over now, come on, let's get on with it.* It is like the crowd rising at a rugby game, the half-time ritual, the sense of the powers that be. By contrast, the camera focuses on a couple down on the street: a humble veteran standing with his wife and wearing his medals. Sensing the camera, he nods perfunctorily. He seems pleased: *that all went well.*

The newspapers gave prominent coverage to the unveiling, but especially picked up on a curious segment of the speech, where Dev had pointed across to the originally Protestant Trinity College and said, 'You too are part of the Irish nation.' At the time this was regarded as very generous and pluralist of him, but it shows, in reality, just how sectarian things must have been. As an unconscious comment on this, perhaps, Trinity students later put soap in the fountain and filled the street with bubbles, making it look like a pop-art installation: a true mid-60s 'happening'. They also put in green dye on St Patrick's Day, fulfilling my father's idea that moving water has a therapeutic effect in an urban setting. Eddie had studied in Rome, as well as in Germany, and was much taken with the soothing quality which the fountains had on the city's hassled citizens. (In the 1980s, marching gays dyed the water pink.)

The Dublin wags were quick with the wit, however, naming it 'Urination Once Again'. This was consistent with the city's often wearisome habit of giving nicknames to public sculpture, especially when it involved water – a habit that goes way back. For example, around the corner, in *Ulysses*, Bloom passes the statue of poet Tom Moore and says, 'They did well putting him over a urinal – *meeting of the waters.*' This joke is even commemorated in one of those little *Ulysses* pavement plaques, made shiny from people's shoes: the pedestrian equivalent of hands on statues.

Later the poet Anthony Cronin wrote a nice radio piece about

Davis standing over the fountain, with his hands pointing downwards, simultaneously directing the water while drawing energy from it. Others were not so respectful: a taxi rank was attached to the end of the platform and the drivers used the water to wash their cars, so my father put anti-freeze into the fountain, and strange colours started to appear on their windscreens. Well, he needed to, since in the biting winter the fountain started to freeze, with fantastic icicles hanging from the angels' trumpets and spiky stalagmites building upwards from the falling drops.

Then parts of the sculpture broke, as people climbed up on it to get a view of passing parades. And a car ran into an angel at this busy intersection of traffic. Eventually, the pump broke and it was not fixed. The whole experience was indicative not just of the poor public attitude to art, but also of a form of officialdom that really did not want such extravagance. Eddie was determined, however, and he climbed into the underground pump room, a place that used to fascinate us: a hole under a city street, like something from *Mission Impossible.* Eddie enjoyed it too and one day he surprised a passing friend by popping his head out and shouting across the traffic, 'Fancy a cup of tea?'

Controversy over the Davis and Tone memorials dragged on for years. Eddie said it was like a 'noose around his neck', but it was also the making of him and he revelled in the role of *enfant terrible*. He told the American author Donald S. Connery that putting up Davis was 'like letting a nude woman loose in the streets, or some new form of animal in the zoo', an interesting parallel given his own penchant for putting nudes into his drawings and panels, even church panels, and for creating new animals and forms. As an outsider, Connery's own description of Davis is interesting: 'The statue is bold, stark and modern, and faces a strange cluster of spindly angels blowing water out of long horns.'

There was even a debate over costs, with Fine Gael asking who had personally benefited from the Davis commission. 'How many tenders had been put out?' the opposition deputies persisted, and after one parliamentary exchange, the Taoiseach, Jack Lynch, wearily asked for 'a stop to all this mud-slinging'. There is a subtext here, for it was later alleged that Eddie was 'in' with Fianna Fáil, an unfair claim since his commissions were clearly on artistic merit and usually won through competition. In fact, back in Mayo his family were Fine Gael, but the simple fact was (and remains) that Fianna Fáil were much closer to the arts than the more conservative Fine Gael, a relationship that Charles Haughey would greatly develop.

For the more crusty establishment, there was a sense of unease. An *Irish Times* columnist thought it 'rather odd', for example, that the statue cost more money than Davis himself 'would have handled in his entire lifetime'. But why was it odd? This would suggest that Davis was around only the day before, instead of 120 years ago. You can almost see the monocle popping out at the prospect of these modern Republican statues going up in the Georgian capital. It could also be read as lip-smacking admiration that at least the mohair-suited state now had the wherewithal to fund such memorials. Indeed, the said columnist even allowed himself a snicker by quoting from the Dáil reply that 'Mr Delaney was responsible for the preparation of all necessary models ... a delightful euphemism,' he wrote approvingly (not what one would expect from *The Irish Times*).

The debate could become wearisome. On the subject of artistic merit, there were as many stalwart supporters as there were opponents, including other types of artists struggling to get a similar acceptance of change in their own disciplines.

In a letter to the *Irish Independent*, poet John F. Deane admonished a previous correspondent called 'Buns' who 'claimed to represent the "average man in the street". Maybe he is that "average man",' wrote Deane, 'whose reaction to what he slurringly calls "modern art" comes from a fundamental laziness, coupled with ignorance. He gazes for two minutes at these masterpieces and affects a pose by giggling and yelling "monstrosity", thus joining the "sophisticated" ranks of those who "won't be taken in" by the "cult". These works of art symbolise nothing to such people because they are too bigoted and lazy to take the trouble to "study and understand" them. Nothing of value is gained without a struggle.'

The last was a sentiment to which the rebels could relate. In general, Eddie was fine about the criticism, but he became fed up with the memorial's disrepair, and eventually he got a sort of revenge when he came in to fix it. As with the aftermath of Tone's bombing, it was an unusual chance to improvise and revise. Artistic licence, if you will. Basically, he did an amazing thing. He reversed the angels, so that instead of them huddled in a group, pointing inwards, they were now turned around to face outwards, with the water spraying up behind them. He also reversed their wings, so that instead of them pointing upwards, like Christian angels, they hung down, like huge bats or those gargoyle creatures on the Notre Dame. In an ironic concession to the tiresome demands for realism, in among the water jets he put some very realistic-looking fish, informing some people that they were 'the mythic Salmon of Knowledge of Irish folklore'.

They were in fact actual fish from an old pram lady on Moore Street, except instead of the noble salmon, he got some big grey mullets of a similar size. An artist who helped Eddie recalls doing some warm plaster moulds, which actual cooked the fish. They even ate it afterwards, polished off with a cold Sancerre. 'Eddie gave me valuable advice as an artist,' he said. 'He taught me how to make money.'

Neglect of the memorial continued, however, and, as the country slid into the recession of the late 1970s and 1980s, it was often behind hoardings, as if the state was reluctant to let Davis see what a mess we had made of things. In 1990, such was its dereliction that only one panel still had its metal name tag – appropriately enough, *The Burial.* Tags for the others – such as *We Must Not Fail* and *A Nation Once Again* – were missing. However, in 2006, flush with economic success and peace in the North, the memorial was unveiled again, this time by then Taoiseach Bertie Ahern, who gave a moving and powerful speech, which I shall describe later. 'Do over', as the Americans say: you are getting another chance.

In fairness, there were obvious reasons for the memorial's disrepair. It is at the centre of one of the city's busiest intersections and on a narrow strip of ground, unlike the location of O'Connell Street, where you can actually stand in from the traffic and admire them. College Green continues to be the stage for the nation's major public events, such as St Patrick's Day parades, or World Cup homecomings, or speeches by visiting dignitaries. At these events, people would climb up on the angels to get a better look. There were also night-time concerts, in front of the old spot-lit portico, with thousands of people holding up the flames of their cigarette lighters. After these events, as the crowds drifted away happily, you got a sense of what the city was like without traffic and imagined it as it was in Joyce's time – amiable and relaxed, with the streets like canyons.

Many cartoons appeared during the Davis controversy. One, which appeared in *Dublin Opinion* ('Humour Is the Safety Valve of a Nation'), showed a grumpy park attendant charging money for punters to go up a ladder and inside the voluminous statue. '6d to see the inner beauty', reads a placard.

If only they knew. For the inner beauty of Davis is actually the figure of a young Italian girl on ice skates, sculpted by his old friend and master, Giacomo Manzù. The Cabinet had urged Eddie to look again at the nineteenth-century marble statue of Davis in City Hall, but instead he was going home to look at images of Manzù's skaters. In one image, the girl is standing with legs slightly apart, keeping her balance, the way ice-skaters do, and her head is tipped upwards with one of those sullen smiles that Manzù's women have. When I saw the image myself, I thought, that's Davis.

The critic, Peter Murray, has identified another echo in the work of the German sculptor Toni Stadler, who was Eddie's teacher in Munich. The 'simplified, almost child-like features of the Davis statue', writes Murray, 'seem directly inspired by Stadler's work: a fusion of ancient, Cycladic art with a modernist concern with our volume and form.' According to *A Dictionary of Modern Sculpture* (Methuen, 1960), a subject 'appeared in Stadler's work which fascinated him for a long time – [that] of a young woman standing with arms slightly raised'. I love the magical 'appeared': it suggests that the image mysteriously materialised, which I've no doubt it did, as it did for Eddie, and as it does for any artist. Stadler did not find the image; it found him. In addition, when you see Stadler's young woman in just such a pose, you immediately see that, yes, this is Davis again, hesitantly raising his arms.

So this is the story of a sculpture sent into life, surrounded by all that traffic, and all those passing buses and parades. The angels have their heads down, while the water sprays up behind them. Now, almost every Saturday, teenage Goths put soap into the fountain so that it foams out onto the street and the Big Man is oblivious from his prime position. I often think of those kids who sang at the unveiling, coming back as adults and reflecting on that day. At one stage in the clip, a boy looks around curiously to see what else is happening, and I like to think that this is myself, if I was just a few years older.

When boyhood's fire was in my blood,
I read of ancient freemen,
For Greece and Rome who bravely stood,
Three hundred men and three men:
And then I prayed I yet might see,
Our fetters rent in twain,
And Ireland, long a province, be
A nation once again.

Thomas Davis

CHAPTER 3

Country Life

The highlight of the debate about Thomas Davis was a lively discussion on the *Late Late Show*, that crucible of change, particularly during the 1960s. Thomas Ryan, an academic painter, came on to criticise modern art and especially the sort of commemorative art that the state and society was then embracing. Ryan represented the Royal Hibernian Academy and was particularly impatient with the new trends and expressionism. He described Davis as an 'elephantine-footed Frankenstein', and said that the figure had 'Church of England clergyman's knees', a condition which comes from too much altar kneeling, and a reference which surely must have been lost on an Irish audience. It also implies fake or exaggerated devotion, adding to its spice given that the statue was intended as a homage to Irish patriotism.

By contrast, Ryan's own contribution to the 1966 commemoration was a romantic composition which, as it happens, was equally criticised. Anthony Butler (later a major advocate of Eddie's work) described it as 'melodramatic and embarrassing' and said that 'retitled "The Winter Place, Leningrad", it would be joyfully accepted in some Palace of Culture as a glowing example of Soviet realism'. The same could be said, however, of many of the 1916-related works and, in fairness, Ryan, who is now 75, is unrepentant about his 1966 attack and still regards modernism as a disastrous diversion.

When Eddie came on to the show, flash with mod jacket and polka dot tie, he pointed dramatically at Ryan and said, 'You and I have nothing in common, we have nothing to discuss and nothing to agree on.' Eddie then re-emphasised all his ideas about modern art and sculpture. It was then that he came out with the sarcastic line, 'Yes, I know the eighteenth-century sculptors were very skilled: weren't they good at chiselling people's cloaks?' To lighten the atmosphere, Sandie Shaw sang 'Puppet on a String' without wearing shoes, which also provoked some reaction.

It was clearly a memorable programme and people often still mention it. An architect, who was in the National College of Art and Design at the time, told me, 'You've no idea how conservative things were then: we went to our lectures in shirts and ties.' For the younger generation, Eddie's performance was liberating. In 1969, unsurprisingly, there would be a student revolt in the art college.

Eddie and others brought a rock 'n' roll attitude, not unlike the Beatles and the Rolling Stones who were then questioning authority on different levels. Appropriately enough, after the show Eddie went to meet the Rolling Stones at a party in deepest Wicklow. The event was the 21st birthday of Tara Browne, the younger brother of Eddie's best friend, Garech. Tara was very much part of the London scene and had a shop on the King's Road called 'Dandy Fashions'.

Garech was quite the opposite, a supporter of traditional Irish music and poetry, who founded Claddagh Records in 1959. Later, he would take to wearing an Aran jumper inside an Irish tweed suit and a belt of coloured wool, dangling behind him like a Tibetan bathrobe. He also wore his hair in a ponytail, in imitation of the legendary *cul* which the native Irish wore in defiance of the conquering English, who had forbidden such customs. He looked like one of the Gaelic earls we had in our schoolbooks. The fact that Garech was also the son of a lord meant that it was all a little incongruous, but this was the interesting contradiction, just as his name was in Irish 'An Onórach Garech de Brun'. He hadn't rejected his background outright – far from it – but combined the aristocratic and the native, so that these Yeatsian polarities could truly integrate and flower.

Garech was always leading a merry pack and usually turned up with an entourage. As kids, we enjoyed his visits. He called us the 'mouldhouses' and gave us toys and presents along with big glossy art books on Alexander Calder and Hieronymous Bosch. He enjoyed the irony of 'Stone View' as a sculptor's address, and wrote 'Pebble Gawk' and other such variations on the postcards he sent from his travels. The postcards were usually saucy but artistic – Fragonard, Gustave Klimt – or photos of old grannies force-feeding geese for *foie gras*.

The story of Eddie and Garech's friendship is, in many ways, an extraordinary one. They both came from Claremorris in County Mayo, in the west of Ireland. Garech was the son of Lord Oranmore and Browne, of Castlemacgarrett, and Eddie's family worked on the estate: mainly preparing for the hunts organised by Garech's father, big social affairs which drew in gentry from all over England and the rest of Ireland. The gatherings were like something from *Gosford Park*, with furious preparations to ensure that the guests were well looked after. One story from these gatherings has some of the visitors going into the local chemist and asking for 'pullovers'.

'Pullovers? Goodness no, sir, that'd be next door, they've lovely jumpers in McGoverns.'

Apparently the perplexed toffs required some primitive early version of condoms, which – wink, wink – were always available for the naughty quality. More than hunting was planned for these fun weekends.

The hunts required constant preparation: feeding the dogs, cleaning the guns and buying cartridges, which Eddie's father, Patrick, did with his sons. The rest of the time Patrick tended to the beehives and to his wood mill – a lucrative business supplying crates to local merchants. He would also go out shooting with the lord, or 'Dom', as he was affectionately known. It would be just the two of them, so that the Yeatsian ideal of lord and native was now a reality – all in the pursuit of game.

Patrick's favourite thing to do was to shoot two birds with one shot, as they crossed from different directions, or to take out a rake of duck by driving one shot through a flock of them as they waded in the River Robe. The land and rivers, then undrained and unpolluted, were thick with wildlife. Mayo also had a huge number of domestic fowl. The people had starved so badly during the famine that they were going to make sure they had something to eat if the crops failed again.

All of this turned up later in Eddie's work: domestic fowl, running game, famine. And hunters, endless hunters. Instead of squires in waders, however, the hunters were stripped naked and given spears. Attenuated and mythicised, they returned to being figures from the bible or the ancient past.

Patrick would hunt on his own, going out for days at a time, lying by the edge of a cold lake waiting in the darkness for that final shot; an addiction if ever there was one. He was an enigmatic figure, whom we never met – he died in 1955 – and in the only photo we had seen of him he looked like a Mexican bandit in a black stove hat and waistcoat, sitting on a wooden fence, smiling. He looked like someone from the 1850s rather than the 1950s. Eddie and he shared a bed in the long and cosy farmhouse in Farmhill, in which nine children were reared.

Castlemacgarrett was an industrious estate, which was relatively good to the town – unusual in Mayo where the land wars had been so bitter – but it was Guinness money that fuelled it. The lord's second marriage was to Oonagh Guinness, of the brewing family, and she brought considerable investment.

When the marriage failed, however, the estate went slowly downhill. Patrick and the lord got more time to go shooting. But the lord also kept his own big hunts going, feeding the incoming toffs and building up debts and unpaid bills to Patrick and to his son, PJ. When PJ eventually asked to be paid – his father had since died – the lord protested that he was broke. 'I'll take some fields instead,' said PJ. (Take them *back*, as the nationalist historians might have it.)

The lord demurred but eventually conceded four large fields in a gentleman's agreement, which was not legally confirmed for another fifty years. Still, it is a wonderful image of post-colonial revenge: helping the lord to build up a debt and then taking it back in kind.

When we buried PJ in 2008, from the little church in Crossboyne, his fields were on three sides of the church, as his brother, John, the priest officiating, reminded us. Visible through the church windows were his orphaned cattle and the huge oak trees of the original 3,000-acre estate, apparently some of the oldest trees in the country. PJ's remains were taken a short distance down the road to be buried with his parents. Across the road was the old Protestant graveyard, with the roofless ruin of a church. It was here that the Brownes had been buried.

Dom lived to the ripe old age of 100. He holds the record as the longest-serving member of the House of Lords, having held his seat from 1927 until he was evicted under the British government's reforms in 1999. Reforms that were understandable, incidentally, for it was one of the great boasts of the lord, and one for which he received back-slapping admiration from his peers, that he never once spoke in the upper chamber. Well *not* spoken, sir.

In many ways, the lord's life shows the inextricable links between Ireland and Britain, specifically through land and politics. When he celebrated his 100th birthday, with a family party at the Ritz in London, Dom received official congratulations from both the Irish president and the Queen, although he was happier with the first than the second – a colour picture of Elizabeth herself, which he thought undignified. 'Horrible,' muttered Dom, before stuffing it back in the envelope.

The working relationship between the two families was close, and furniture and old equipment from Castlemacgarret ended up in the Delaney farmhouse. These were hand-me-downs, and stuff no longer needed, but it is also a nice metaphor for the transfer of power and the natives asserting their independence. It was also why, when we visited, we found ourselves sinking into oversized armchairs, next to Louis XIV cabinets and oriental hat stands. As the Big House declined, more of the bits went down to Farmhill, including the guns. They even sold *back* to the Brownes a horse trap from their stables, with the wheel coming off it.

Eventually, the lord could no longer afford to live there, and the castle was taken over by the land Commission, which was breaking up the big estates and distributing land. By the early 1960s the house became a retirement home for nuns returning from the missions in Africa or the Far East – that hidden history of Irish society and a form of colonial or overseas activity surely as rich and colourful (and now as lost) as that of the Anglo-Irish. One imagines the nuns, somnolent with memories of Burma and the Congo, sitting where once sat the toffs with their guns on their laps, thinking about similar climes.

Eventually, Castlemacgarret became a general nursing home, and in 1980 my grandmother died there, laid out in the former drawing room where as a young girl she'd been invited each year to the staff Christmas party. (Handed a glass of brandy she didn't recognise, she threw it on the fire where it caused a whoosh of flame.) Only the shell of the original house now remains, but in *Lost Demesnes*, by Count Randal McDonnell, there are old yellow photos of its ghostly interior: the Persian carpets, the English and French furniture, the *objet d'arts*, all sold at auction in London in 1960.

Garech attended boarding school in Switzerland and in Castlepark in Dalkey, looking down on the sea, just like nearby Somerton, the school in *Ulysses*, where Stephen Dedalus talks to the children about colonialism. The pupils were given allotments, and one night, coming back from drinking in the town, the now adult Eddie and Garech climbed over the wall so that Garech could weed his patch for the first time in 20 years. 'How ghastly,' he cried. 'They've let nettles grow all over the herbs!'

Though Garech and Eddie became close, they didn't know each other while in Claremorris. Why would they? Garech was in boarding school, or cooped up in the Big House playing with his toy soldiers, while Eddie was, as he dramatically put it, roaming the fields, snaring rabbits and working with a German circus which would change his life.

The only occasion when they might have seen each other at was at the gymkhana, a lively local affair at which Eddie rode in the pony races. Dom used to sit inside his car – a rare sight in those parts – and watch proceedings while the two boys, Garech and Tara, sat in the back. There was also shooting at these events, and on one occasion, either because of confusion or an altercation, some chap turned towards Eddie and shot him in the face with a pellet gun, the marks of which were still visible over his cheek. It would be the first in a long line of scars and injuries for Eddie, as one might have expected from a hands-on sculptor pouring his own metal.

He also twisted his ankle after a fall from a horse, which thereafter gave him a slight limp and a way of standing back on his good heel. People took this to be his arrogance – well, it was, a bit – but he was also finding the best spot on which to balance, just like a sculpture: Manzù's ice-skater. The original damage was compounded by the treatment of some bonesetter from Tuam, who re-laid the bones wrongly, like an erroneous sculptor. It meant that Eddie later had to wear shoe supports, slipped into his Chelsea boots, which we imitated by buying similar supports in Connolly's shoe shop in Dún Laoghaire. We were fascinated by this bonesetter, and imagined some whiskery fellow hopping off a stagecoach with a big black bag. The fact that he was from Tuam, with its original Traveller culture, gave him a sort of gypsy mystique.

We were also impressed by how many guns seemed to be knocking around Claremorris. Reared on cowboy movies and TV shows like *Bonanza* and *High Chaparral*, it sounded to us like old-time Mayo was something close to frontier Texas. There was even a 'good' set of guns in our grandmother's house, and a more 'regular' set, kept in behind the boiler. The 'good' guns were up in the attic and included Russian single shots and bolt-action rifles.

On one occasion my father took my brother Colm out for a 'character-building' shoot, and it really was like the American frontier, with Eddie swinging around wildly when a pheasant rose behind him and being incapable of taking down a few snipe without blowing their heads off in a burst of feathers. Eddie was particularly annoyed that the game were always just behind him, as if they knew he had returned and were playing tricks, but after a while he just lit up a cigar and strolled on contentedly across the springy bog of his childhood, while Colm hid behind the heather banks, lest there be any more sudden moves.

Eddie and Garech met sporadically in Dublin in the 1950s, *en marge* of the cultural scene around the literary pubs of Grafton Street. Eddie was supposed to be studying in the National College of Art and Design, but spent quality time hanging out with Brendan Behan on the steps of the National Library next door. The friendship with Garech strengthened, however, when Eddie returned from the Continent in 1960.

By this time, Garech had set up Claddagh Records and was recording pipers and poets. The label would subsequently launch the traditional group the Chieftains. Eddie did the artwork for their sleeves: striking, original designs which were an immediate departure from conventional record covers. The artwork for the first LP showed standing disembodied figures in black lines with shimmering blood-red blobs. The figures are square shouldered and they could be disintegrating or evolving. They are just like his bronzes. Eddie had the ability as an artist to recreate his familiar figures or motifs in different media, be it bronze, fast-moving acrylic or printer's ink. He could also replicate the same figure on different scales, be it two inches of silver or five foot of bronze.

The second LP, *Chieftains Two*, was based on the *Astronauts Dream* series, a pattern of large honeycombed shapes in aquatic blues. It was a distinctive motif of Eddie's from 1969 that continued into the 1970s. He would cut out paper stencils and roll paint on to them, creating overlaid spots. In all, there were about six sleeves spaced over 17 years. The band's piper and leader, Paddy Maloney, said that wherever they went abroad they were asked about the sleeves, a nice compliment, not helped by Eddie's boast on a *Late*

Late Show (this time in the 1980s) that many people bought the LPs for the sleeves and threw away the records.

Because Garech had funds, he could afford good design, photography and sleeve notes by interesting writers and critics. He wanted to break with the cheesier end of the traditional-music market which produced LP covers featuring Bunratty Castle or a garishly coloured harpist in a field surrounded by cows. Claddagh also recorded the poet Patrick Kavanagh and composers Frederick May and Seán Ó Riada. They also did a superb recording of the actor Jack MacGowran reciting works by Samuel Beckett. However, the politician Erskine Childers asked Garech did he really want to be recording 'old women wailing songs by the hearthside, when we're trying to move on and present a new image of Ireland'. This is an interesting exchange for, as with the Davis memorial, it seemed as if the state was both trying to invoke the rustic Irish past – and leave it behind.

It is also interesting that it came from Childers who, though a Fianna Fáil minister, was himself from the landed Protestant tradition. Then he also had had a strong Republican background, with his enigmatic father, the author of *The Riddle of the Sands*, being (disgracefully) executed during the Civil War. The younger Childers, however, had moved on and was now helping the finally prosperous state to consolidate itself and attract foreign investment.

Garech retorted that this was the 'new image of Ireland': an exciting revival of our heritage and neglected folklore. However, the reality was that although the state was confident enough to celebrate our rustic past, the music of blind pipers and mystics was scorned by the new middle classes, just as it was abandoned by generations of Irish emigrants entering Britain and the US, throwing away their ethnic tunes as soon as they went down the gangplank.

Instead, such music was taken up by new elements rebelling against the conformities of society, just as 'free spirit' aristocrats flocked to the folk scene in the Britain. There, the combination of upper-class mavericks and rock music created a so-called 'popocracy' which to many epitomised the 'classless sixties', although it was a small scene, mainly located in parts of London, where there was already a bohemian tradition. However, it well described the set hanging about with the Rolling Stones, many of whom showed up for Tara's birthday. The party was given by his mother, Oonagh, who had swapped the shooting parties of Castlemacgarret for more raffish weekends at Luggala, her fairytale Gothic lodge in the Wicklow woods.

Luggala was certainly in a spectacular setting, next to a dark lake and deep inside the crater of a big valley. After a long drive over the Dublin Mountains, you would descend a long and winding road, past heavy trees and along a glittering lake. Around this were sheer cliffs, with tumbling scree, and a moss-grown forest full of game, goats and Sitka deer. The visitors' book shows an equally motley collection: Lucian Freud, Cyril Connolly and Lord Kilbracken, mixed in with traditional musicians like the piper Leo Rowsome and the singer Margaret Barry, a Traveller, who went around the country playing at fairs and football grounds. Brendan Behan was also prominent, as were other alleged Republicans, to add the whiff of sulphur, or radical chic. Again, it was the Yeatsian combination of lord and native, with the dull middle classes more or less excluded. This time the toff and the peasant were in pursuit, not of game, but of a good tune, and a good time.

Another regular visitor was Desmond Mackey, a charming rascal who had an antique shop in Dún Laoghaire called 'Curiouser and Curiouser', which, as someone said, was exactly what the customers became when they realised what they had bought. To a famous city pub he sold a camera case with the initials 'J.J.' painted upon it in gold paint, claiming it had been owned by James Joyce. The case had apparently been buried underground to age it. The same incidentally is done with sculptures. Not that the sculptures would be fake – apart perhaps from classical imitations.

Mackey was also a well-known figure on the country's racecourses, where he used to win inexplicably large bets. He was equally familiar to the more exclusive hotels where certain bills went unpaid and where he would crash weddings, without hindrance, given that the party of the bride and groom would always assume such a well-dressed man was with the other side. However, as children we greatly enjoyed his company. He was good fun, generous and always bought us sweets. He was also a good friend of Brendan Behan, and almost certainly saved his life in Ibiza when Behan foolishly attacked some men in a fishing boat, calling them fascists. They battered him underwater with their oars until Mackey intervened.

Across an inner courtyard in Luggala, Garech had converted a long shed into an 'Irish country cottage' with an open turf fire and a settle bed, where traditional musicians would play for the guests. Rowsome once played the 'Marseillaise' on the uilleann pipes in honour of the French Ambassador, causing everyone to stand respectfully except the ambassador who did not recognise the tune. On another occasion Lady Oonagh introduced a guest to the Belgian Ambassador, but the guest shook the wrong person by the hand. Quite unperturbed, Lady Oonagh made the introduction again. 'And this,' she said, 'is the *other* Belgian Ambassador.'

Tara's party was a worthy successor to these affairs and boasted a new generation of revellers. 'A Swingin' Party!' was the headline in the *Sunday Independent* and the 'night-time' correspondent sets the scene:

> Three pop groups were flown over especially for the occasion. Although Mick Jagger was there, neither he nor Brian Jones were playing. They were just friends of the host.
>
> Unlike his brother Garech, Tara is very much a mod, preferring pop music and fast sports cars to the more traditional Irish music and stately Mercedes preferred by his elder brother. At 21, Tara is now the father of two young sons, and although he admits to liking car racing, would not commit himself about entering international rallies. His mother gave him an expensive car as part of his birthday present, and of course, the party.

41

> ... A large marquee, attached to the house – simply by removing the Georgian windows – had been decorated by David Mlinaric, the top London designer. The nightclub atmosphere with the red tablecloths and gilt chairs did not somehow go with the Frug, but then opposites were the order of the day, or rather night!
>
> The Loving Spoons [sic] were the main attraction in the music field, and among the guests were David Dimbleby, Nicholas Phipps, Julian Ormsby-Gore, Siobhán McKenna, and an entourage with Sir Alfred Beit.

This would be the man whose extraordinary art collection, including Vermeers and Van Goghs, would later twice fall prey to thieves. Also at the party was John Paul Getty's son, but the night-time correspondent was unable to identify him. 'Like his father – reputed to be the richest man in the world – Paul Junior doesn't go much for publicity.'

'Also present, of course, was our own Eddie Delaney – straight from *The Late Late Show*. Sculptor Delaney had quite a few stories about the 1916 celebration which he didn't tell the viewers.'

This would be Eddie's style: conspiratorial, gossipy. What these stories were is anyone's guess, but it is interesting that he is described as 'our own', even though there were many other Irish people there. But these toffs would not be regarded as really Irish. And the actress, Siobhán McKenna, with her high-pitched Abbey performances, was presumably *so* Irish as to be stage Irish. Eddie, by contrast, was someone (apparently) connected to the real world, which is why journalists warmed to him. He gave good quotes, and off-the-record intrigues, but he was also of their background.

'As the Liverpool chatter got mixed up with the Irish racing vernacular,' continued the reporter, 'and as the AA man got all the cars safely down the Monte Carlo rally driveway, I found a taxi driver who was still waiting to be paid three hours after delivering a well-known musician who had been up to Dublin to look at Nelson. So he said anyway!'

This would be the ruins of Nelson, since the pillar had only just been bombed, and its lipstick-like stump was a major draw for locals and tourists alike. The 'place where Nelson was not' as Joyce would have it. Indeed, in a stubborn policy that Joyce would have enjoyed, the trams retained for years their destination signs for 'Nelson's Pillar', bringing people to an empty spot, like an amputee feeling for a missing limb. Just like the one-armed Nelson himself, perhaps.

The cutting goes on excitedly: 'There were Sidewinders waiting to perform and I bumped into decorator Mlinaric once more, wearing a most interesting fur coat, and he told me he was working on a new London night club, the inspiration for which was partly…' And then it cuts off abruptly.

It was also a cutting off point for Tara, for he did not make his twenty-second birthday. Later that year, he drove his Lotus Elan through red lights in London, hitting a van and killing himself. The crash was the inspiration for the Beatles song 'A Day in the Life', released the following year on the *Sergeant Pepper's Lonely Hearts Club Band* album. Tara, who had shared a flat with Brian Jones, had also been friendly with the Beatles. His death was especially tragic for his father, Dom, who had already lost both his parents in a car crash when he was young and who would himself go on to live to a ripe old 100. Obviously, as children, we were fascinated by Tara and his youthful death. By the lake in Luggala, we would go over to a little stone temple, built in memory of him and his sister, who died in Claremorris as a child.

At such moments, the whole place seemed incredibly still, as if time had frozen everything: the lake, the trees and even the hanging scree, which looked like it had been stopped while falling. It was the same inside the house, with its strange corridors and glass boxes of stuffed birds and baying foxes – 'posh animals', as we saw them – and a connection to the creatures that might be lurking on the cliffs around. 'Tara's rooms' were closed off, but we got a peek at his expensive toys. Or his children's toys, since he was so young that they were mostly his own toys quickly passed on, and thus rarely idle. These were also the rooms where some of Eddie's small silver figures were kept under lock and key. Garech's toys, if you like.

Part of the strangeness was because the house was not a family home at all but a hunting lodge, almost like an enlarged folly. Despite its elaborate turns and passageways, it was actually quite small. It had all the features of a castle, with battlements and quatrefoil windows, but built on a miniature scale – something we found satisfying as children. Seen from afar, it was a puzzle as to how the interior could accommodate so many rooms, but in fact the whole lodge was a complex design of interlocking sections, with shared bathrooms and hidden spaces. According to one article about Luggala, 'The expansion of farming in seventeenth- and eighteenth-century Ireland caused wild game to retreat into the wilderness areas which were subsequently preserved and maintained principally for sport. Lodges to provide temporary accommodation for sportsmen were often built in these areas, thus ensuring that sportsmen, by staying overnight, might take advantage of "the game's unpredictable movements".'

I do like this. I have an image of my father swinging around with the shotgun for the suddenly erupting snipe. And yet I don't know of any hunting going on at Luggala, which is curious given that it was a hunting lodge, whereas at Castlemacgarret, an industrious family home, the hunting seemed to be continuous. In the hall in Luggala, there was a huge clock from the old House of Commons on College Green, which used to 'call time' on parliamentary sessions in that bastion of Protestant self-rule. How very appropriate – just as in Farmhill, there was a hand-me-down grandfather clock calling time on Castlemacgarret.

As you descend to Luggala, you pass on one side the lake and green lawn, where the memorial is located, while on the other side the standing figure of *The Good Shepherd* suddenly appears, a startling sight under the big trees, not least because of the lead-grey colouring against the green vegetation. He is, in fact, 12-foot tall – taller even than Tone – but much flatter and narrower. The figure has a ghostly presence, with a staff in one hand and a lamb in the other, and it is one of Eddie's most arresting works: two-dimensional *and* animated (*à la* Manzù) – a hard combination to pull off. For years now, *The Good Shepherd* has watched people come and go. But I also like to think that, for Garech and Eddie, it was a reminder of their West of Ireland background and those ragged sheep on rainy mountainsides.

CHAPTER 4

Going out Live

For my parents, Tara's 21st was not the first time they'd met the media on the way to Luggala. On another occasion, they were going to a New Year's Eve party when a group of them was stopped and photographed by an evening paper. It is 1961, a more innocent time, and they are all laughing and dressed up in raincoats and scarves.

'Going to a party a little early,' wrote the reporter eagerly 'but a gay party. It was at the gate of the residence that we met. The group had travelled from the main road at Roundwood by tractor. "Come and join us," they said. We had to say "sorry". How on a night like that we would have loved to stay.' The hard-working journalists had to press on with their duties.

The photo's happy line-up includes Lady Rosemary FitzGerald, wearing a headscarf, and Mr Nicholas Phipps, a smiling square-jawed fellow with a pipe. Garech is wearing a Mackintosh. My father has his arm around my mother, who is laughing. Married the previous month, she is now two months pregnant with me. (Yes, the *other* reason they got married.) If Nabokov could a take strange pleasure from seeing a photo of his empty pram waiting in the hallway before he was born, then I can take note of my mother's happy face, expectant with her first child.

It was the night the national TV service went on air. Looking at the cuttings later, we thought that the two events were somehow connected: that because the main TV mast was in nearby Kippure, high in the mountains, people were having parties nearby, all standing out on the heath and watching sparks crackle up on the mast, as the broadcast began. It was like years later in Connemara, with us out in the storm, fixing the aerial, and our father directing us through the big bay windows. *No, the other way.* All pushing along, in the Atlantic wind. *Hurray, it's on!*

The opening ceremony was held in Dublin in the Gresham Hotel, a live broadcast from the hotel ballroom, while outside in the snow people on O'Connell Street danced to the music of the Army No 1 band, the same band who played at the Davis unveiling. As with the Davis event, the opening speech was done by de Valera. He was thus the first person to appear on Irish television, but his speech expressed great uncertainty about the new medium, and as with the hippy-like idealism he showed at the Davis unveiling, he hoped that television would bring not just 'recreation and pleasure, but instruction and knowledge'.

'But I must admit,' said the president, speaking in front of a book-lined set, just to reinforce the traditional values under threat, 'that sometimes when I think of television and radio and their immense power, I feel somewhat afraid. Like atomic energy, it can be used for incalculable good, but it can also do irreparable harm. Never before was there in the hands of men an instrument so powerful to influence the thoughts and actions of the multitude.' It is a fascinating admission, and, in terms of how the culture developed, he was right. However, it does sound rather rich coming from a man who was famous for his radio broadcasts and who milked the TV coverage of the 1966 celebrations to such great advantage.

The programmes for the opening night included poetry read by the actress Siobhán McKenna and the comedienne Maureen Potter, whom we used to go and see at the pantomime in the Gaiety Theatre and visit afterwards in the Green Room, along with Danny Cummins and Chris Curran, all them still wearing their white make-up and lime-green leggings, straight off the stage from *Jack and the Beanstalk.*

Many people in my narrative were involved in that first

broadcast, and certainly in those early years. Both Austin Clarke and Séamus Ennis, of the death masks, hosted programmes of poetry and music, and The Dubliners had their own show. There were also an impressive number of programmes on the visual arts, including features on painter Seán Keating and sculptor Seamus Murphy. And indeed on Eddie, with a film by Jim Fitzgerald for the *Spectrum* arts series. This is a strange and ambitious piece of film, which shows Eddie busily working and cuts from fiery scenes in the foundry to a group of people waiting inside the kitchen, including my mum, who is by now heavily pregnant.

De Valera would have been relieved by this pioneering focus on Irish arts and culture but, of course, the medium also brought a deluge of material from the UK and more especially the US. For example, the shows broadcast both before and after the *Spectrum* programme were American crime dramas: *Dragnet* starring Jack Webb, and the intriguing *King of Diamonds*, 'a mystery in which a beautiful woman and a kidnapped diamond merchant feature'.

Little has changed, and even then it was not much of a change from the Hollywood movies of the 1940s and 1950s that dominated the rural towns. Both Cootehill and Claremorris had busy cinemas and, around the country, the galvanised metal boxes were a familiar sight on railway platforms as they waited to be loaded on to the parcel van. The films came to the country after their run in Dublin, where there was already an astonishing number of cinemas. On the reverse side of an interview with Eddie (headlined ironically, 'I wish I'd never come to Dublin') there is a whole page of cinema ads, including cut-out heads of the stars and blurbs about the new releases.

Indeed, this is often the only way I have of dating the scrapbook cuttings – to look at the reverse side. By narrowing down the release dates of the movies, I ended up with the winter of 1966. The films are *The Great Race* at the Ambassador, *Carry on Screaming* at the Adelphi, *Sunday in New York* at the Bohemian in Phibsboro and *Morgan, a Suitable Case for Treatment* at the Academy. I was particularly interested by the latter, about an 'aggressive and self-admitted dreamer – an artist who uses his flights of fancy as refuge from external reality, where his unconventional behaviour lands him in a divorce from his wife and trouble with the police'.

Claremorris was an especially busy cinema and, given the area's propensity for guns, I wasn't at all surprised to hear that one of the most popular features was *Calamity Jane*. As the former projectionist recalled in a local journal, 'Who will ever forget Doris Day singing "The Black Hills of Dakota" as she journeyed home in the fading light?' A lovely image, indeed, and one that goes well with the area. One can just see old Patrick and the bankrupt lord, resting their rifles on a wooden fence and declaring, 'Well, glory be, that's a good day's huntin'.'

In 1996, an art show entitled *Famine* was held in the old cinema, by then a local hall. It was a group show and, for my father, a sort of homecoming. Being curious, I roamed the building and found myself on a deserted balcony: the equivalent of looking at the reverse side of the newspaper. I was not disappointed. Standing there were two big film projectors, 35-mm Phillips Projectors with carbon arc lights, still bolted to the floor. On the ground were bits of cut film and I thought, excitedly, of *Cinema Paradiso* and of the man discovering all the cut 'kisses' and bursting into tears. Could they be something similar, some bold sauciness chopped out by the local censor? I held them up to the light, but they proved to be either unspecific images of women in beehive hairdos, or, more promisingly, fellows with stove hats hiding behind a fence and presumably holding guns. Yes, an old Western: of course, it was.

There was a similar Western vibe to Cootehill and my mother grew up on a diet of Kirk Douglas, Burt Lancaster and endless heartbreaking Westerns. She and her two sisters would even write to the stars and one day a cruel trick was played on Olive when they told her that Burt Lancaster was downstairs in the shop asking for her. Olive rushed down to find some gap-toothed yokel in from Virginia baying for slacks.

But at least he *was* from Virginia. For, if Claremorris had the guns, Cootehill certainly had the names: Virginia, Latin and Mountain View. As visiting grandkids, we were always impressed by the names of the surrounding villages, which were either Western-sounding – *Take the horses yonder to Mountain View* – or dramatic, like comic book exclamations, Kill, Drung. The names went well with the way people spoke in Cootehill, which was with great emphasis, sharply and with a sideways nod of the head. *Oh, aye.* It was southern Ulster and everything seemed to have significance. *Oh, aye.* The people here appeared to have the measure of everything.

The rural cinemas were eventually replaced by TV where American popular culture continued its dominance. But it had little part in my parents' adult lives. They had a bohemian disregard for television, and especially for its English content, much of which was smutty and music hall. As kids, we were restricted in how much we could watch, and the TV set was put high up in the corner, near the art books, so you'd have a crick in your neck if you looked at it too long. I remember vividly one night the adults were sitting inside at the dinner table, all sated and cultured and pleased with themselves, while we were out front watching TV. During a lull in the conversation, the ads came on, and a banal, cheesy girl held up some sweets and said, mechanically, 'There's so much milk in a Milky Mint, you could almost hear it moo.'

'Well, *indeed*.' said my mother.

'Is there really?' said Garech sarcastically, twirling his fingers.

'Good for you, girl,' added another sophisticated voice.

Murmurs of laughter followed. Thinking about it now, there was probably some suggestive undercurrent. But the general feeling was one of amused disdain and, with the music of Ó Riada in the background, more Carr's table water crackers were laden with brie and there was a further luscious decanting of wine. And that was it: TV was for the kids. Conversation was for adults. The feeling was, and probably still is, you should be out making culture, not watching it. And culture was something vivid and tactile: it was live music, or art you could touch.

It was Garech who first introduced my parents at the *fleadh ceoil* in Swinford, one of the big outdoor music festivals that took off in the 1960s. My mum was working as a waitress in the Tandoori Rooms on Leeson Street, possibly the first ethnic restaurant in Dublin, and Garech would come in as a customer. He was unusual company and good fun. He was also something of a food connoisseur. The food was otherwise so poor in Ireland and England at the time that Garech carried a little bottle of Tabasco around in his tweed pocket to spice it up. For a man with as fastidious an upbringing as Garech's, dining with the Rothschilds in Paris at the age of 11, dry meat and vegetables were not an option. The Tandoori Rooms were the start of something positive and Garech was quite taken with Nancy, the striking waitress. 'You must meet a friend of mine,' he said in his engaging drawl, while twirling amber beads in his many ringed fingers. Garech had in mind his friend Eddie, the sculptor, just back from Germany.

Initially, there was a standoffish quality to my parents' first meeting, but soon there was a strong attraction, and the relationship moved along quickly. She was attracted by his vitality and energy, and he by her humour and looks. Nancy was known for her sly wit and mimicry, which she got from her dad, a sulphurous wisecrack back in Cootehill. Eddie invited her for dinner, which he cooked himself, a spaghetti in his studio. It was a memorable event. He strained the pasta through a tennis racket. Eddie had an ability to improvise, as the house and studio would illustrate.

It is appropriate my parents should meet at a *fleadh ceoil*, given the 1960s renaissance in traditional music. For my mother, as for a whole generation, the music was a reaction to Tom Moore's parlour melodies and the more bourgeois Irish nationalism. The *fleadh* had nothing to do with the pious ceilís of the priest-ridden establishment, but had more in common with 'the pure drop' – raw, vivid and exuberant with life and feeling. It was back to basics, just like with sculpture. Later they would buy a house in Galway, in Connemara, and embrace this more.

It was the same for Garech. The earlier image of Garech playing with his toys, while Eddie was out snaring rabbits, was only part of the story. In fact, Garech was as likely to be down in the kitchen, stomping around to Irish music with the servants. Not unusual for such an upbringing, where the parents are otherwise engaged – London, partying, hunting – but for Garech it was especially so. It has even been said that he was 'raised by pipers', an exaggeration surely, but a nice image, worthy of something out of Trollope or Daniel Corkery.

Garech was thus an exaggerated fulfilment of de Valera's hope for the landed Protestants, as expressed at the Davis unveiling. Although Dev's remarks, telling them 'they were part of the Irish nation', were regarded as somewhat patronising, they were also realistic. Much of the Anglo-Irish had cut themselves off and retreated into a privileged world of big houses, foxhunts and private clubs. They looked to London and sneered at the efforts of 'Éire' to create a meaningful independence. Dev pointed across at Trinity because, as he said, this was where they were educated – 'the young scions of nobility who are inclined to be thinking only of themselves and their class' – and he was partly right. Davis was not one of these, and neither was a whole bunch of other Protestant patriots.

Garech was completely apolitical. On one hand he was 'more Irish than the Irish themselves', and dramatically so, wearing tweeds and recording traditional music. And yet not for a moment would he be anything less than Anglo-Irish. In a paradoxical way, he showed up the more bourgeois natives, with their materialist mid-Atlantic aspiration. 'The country is theirs,' concluded de Valera about the Anglo-Irish. 'And they are of the country.' But, in Garech's case, little did he know just how much 'of the country'.

In Dublin, Garech started going to the Pipers Club in Thomas Street, as did my mother. This was like going to a beatnik speakeasy or a punk underground gig. The club was located near the Guinness brewery and on the margins of the Liberties, an old quarter of cottages, famous for traditional music. It is high up over the city and, from the top of Francis Street, you can look back and see the Wicklow Mountains, sugared with occasional snow, and the memory of other parties, and other sessions – a far cry from the rugby club dances my mum frequented when she first came to Dublin. The club is long gone, and the building a ruin, but a black marble plaque marks the spot.

The Pipers Club was part of the revival in traditional music, but the *fleadh ceoil* captured it on a grand scale. The *fleadh* drew huge crowds and were like an early version of Woodstock or Glastonbury. In his biography of Luke Kelly, Des Geraghty paints a vivid picture of their impact and development. 'The summer *fleadh*s acted like a magnet, drawing young people from across the country and into one concentrated hooley in a small rural town.' They incited 'a friendly Irish anarchy, with people dancing and singing in the streets for most of the night, reacting joyfully to an ancient and sometimes savage music that penetrated the solar plexus as well as stimulating the folk memory.'

'Organised formally for musical competitions,' he writes, 'they had a combustive effect in releasing pent-up energy and a sense of enthusiasm and pleasure, a wonderful defiance of convention, breaking down decades of Puritan constraint and respectable moralising.' It was the same with sculpture: banish slavish Anglophilia and get back to Celtic vitality. 'The music,' continues Geraghty, was now 'assuming new character and a life of its own, attracting more followers, entertaining bigger audiences and bringing new vitality into the old musical forms.'

'*Bringing new vitality into the old musical forms*': one can see how it appealed to Eddie, for this is what he was doing with sculpture. Not to mention 'reacting joyfully to ancient and sometimes savage forms'.

Indeed, it would retrospectively inspire, or fulfil – if that is the phrase – one of his more unusual works, *Land of Music*, which was a 'large theatre door of beaten copper panels depicting various early Irish scenes of piping and dancing of the primitive herdsman and his companion'. The panels show exquisite full-bodied nudes exclaiming to each other, inclined on the ground or draped over animals and carts. They have a clear eroticism, similar to the charged naturalism of Rousseau or the languid exoticism of Gauguin, and are not unlike Eddie's church panels, except here, clearly, the atmosphere is more appropriate.

In one panel, a woman lies stretched out on the ground while a man sits obediently beside her, either entranced or worn out. In another, two naked figures stand before a grazing animal, with the man stretching his arms as if to declare, *all this can be yours*, or *what a delightful thing the natural world is*. Though the figures are small, the woman's generous proportions are captured in detail, not an easy thing to achieve with beaten copper where the light-catching curves must be patiently tapped out with a pointy-headed hammer.

According to one review in the *Irish Tatler and Sketch*, the panels 'reminded one of that early and pagan joy such as Yeats depicted in his poem "The Wanderings of Usheen" – though in spirit it is more Virgilian than Yeatsian. But the whole effect is decorative and lyrical – and would suit very well the purpose for which it has been designed.' Which was what, one wonders: to woo women? Or to celebrate the woman who will fulfil your fantasies? 'In detail, the figures may be rather inadequate for classical taste, but, nevertheless they represent music and happiness more effectively since those things are of themselves more nebulous that more realistic figures.'

How true, indeed. Far-seeing critic! The nebulous figures I see are my parents, emerging from the metal, just as I see them emerge from the famous poem about the *fleadh*s, 'The Siege of Mullingar, 1963', by their friend, John Montague.

> *At the Fleadh Cheoil in Mullingar*
> *There were two sounds, the breaking*
> *Of glass, and the background pulse*
> *Of music. Young girls roamed*
> *The streets with eager faces,*
> *Shoving for men. Bottles in*

Hand, they rowed out a song:
Puritan Ireland's dead and gone
A myth of O'Connor and Ó Faoláin

The repressed 1950s were over and the official Ireland condemned by writers Frank O'Connor and Seán Ó Faoláin as having sold out on the freedom struggle and settled into a myopia of censorship and clerical control was now over, and the liberated 1960s had begun.

My parents developed their relationship at further events, including other *fleadh*s. I have no photos of these, but I did see a news clipping of the Swinford *fleadh* for Amharclann na hÉireann. This was the Irish newsreel package which preceded Hollywood movies in cinemas, much like Movietone or Pathé except it was Irish and very much focused on the post-Lemass prosperity, with lots of shots of parades, new office blocks and foreign dignitaries arriving into seemingly endless sunshine at Dublin airport.

I watched the clip eagerly and went with the camera down a main street full of fiddlers and pipers. I am like a lost child, looking for my parents, except now I am a grown man, older than they were then, aware of all the drama that is to come. But the camera moves quickly and they are nowhere to be seen. Either they are indoors watching the musicians or subsumed into the crowd, or each other. Anyway, it was too late. 'The stopper was off the bottle,' writes Geraghty. 'Young blood was having its course and no one was going to stop it.'

It is a fine description by Geraghty, who as an inner-city boy appreciated the sense of liberation from the tenements. It is also good at describing what happens when art is taken out of its personal incubator and put on public show, like sculptures put into galleries: 'The musicians who had been keeping their talents for small intimate gatherings of the converted suddenly found themselves with a mass audience.'

In tandem with the *fleadh*s, there was the folk revival, again important for the likes of Des Geraghty, since it took the workers' songs and put them up on a major stage. Hearing such music in

England, the young Luke Kelly returned to Ireland and hooked up with Ronnie Drew, who had been equally inspired by Ciaran MacMathuna's radio programmes. They soon formed The Dubliners and began holding ballad sessions in O'Donoghue's Pub and the International Bar on Wicklow Street, where the unofficial party was held for the Wolfe Tone unveiling.

The simplicity of their name reflected their obvious Dublin working-class accents and demeanour, which at that time seemed especially democratic and even subversive. These were the accents you usually only heard at the pantomime in the Gaiety shouting *Go away out of that* or *Get up the yard, ye bowsey!* And, of course, it was the persona of Brendan Behan, which is why today in inner city locals you will see affectionate portraits of Behan and Luke Kelly. It was also the stoic black humour of Joyce, which the band echoed on their *Finnegan's Wake* LP, with their banter about drinking, navvies and Monto, the infamous red-light area of Edwardian Dublin.

The Dubliners also had beards – all of them – which was something you rarely saw in Irish life, apart from on painters and poets. You also never saw it on an Irish politician, which is curious given all those bearded Fenians and Parnellites. After the fall of Parnell, and the burial of O'Donovan Rossa, the rebels became strictly clean-shaven.

The band's informality was a counterblast to Dev's official piety, and they were very popular, eventually appearing on *The Ed Sullivan Show* in the US and in 1967 on *Top of the Pops* singing their chart hit 'Seven Drunken Nights', despite the fact that the song was banned from broadcasting in Ireland.

Also appearing on *The Ed Sullivan Show* and even more successful were The Clancy Brothers, who tapped into a large Irish American audience and the folk boom already created by the likes of Pete Seeger, Odetta and Joan Baez. With their Aran jumpers and cheeky demeanour, the band was quite obviously packaged, but their origins were authentic and Bob Dylan, among others, would continuously pay tribute to their influence. Bobby, the youngest

Clancy, became good friends with my parents, and came to their wedding. He had a sweet voice and, with his sister Peggy, recorded an album of wonderful Irish songs. He was an impulsive sort of fellow and apparently, at one *fleadh*, he threw me up in the air and caught me again, repeatedly, until my mother finally had to cry, 'For God's sake, leave the child down!'

The turning point for The Dubliners was playing in the Hibernian Hotel on Dawson Street, a posh hotel much frequented by the 'stranded gentry'. Also there was the emerging Rat Pack of young businessmen, mohair suits and Fianna Fáil ministers like Haughey and Donogh O'Malley, themselves rebelling against the old values by strangely fulfilling those aspirations with the economic boom of the 1960s – itself a paradox. But here, everyone sang along, in the spirit of the time.

And Garech, the diminutive lord, was in the middle of it all. He was affectionately known as the 'Lord of the *Fleadhs*', although a doorman at the Pipers Club was later to declare, in that wonderful Joycean Dublinese, 'Ah, Garech Browne, sure he was only here for the flamboyance!' However, he was certainly in the thick of it, and far from being the effete aristocrat wilting from the affray, he even airily explained away (in a *Hibernia* interview) the many fights that erupted at the *fleadhs*, making the valid point that if you have 50,000 congregated in one place, with poor policing, you are bound to have a 'little argy-bargy'.

However, this 'youthful exuberance was not always appreciated by parish priests and bishops', according to Geraghty, and 'some alarm was sounded at their liberal, lively and Rabelaisian character'. Nor were the secular authorities entirely happy with this free embrace of an older Irish culture. Although the authorities encouraged an engagement with the country's traditions, they didn't expect this to be taken seriously. As they built up the apparatus of a bourgeois state, they didn't want its modernity threatened by a reconnection with the country's unconventional pagan roots. It was the same with nationalism. They may have praised the past actions of violent Republicans, but they didn't expect people to actually go out and emulate them by blowing up Nelson's Pillar.

It was the same with the folk revival, which reflected the rising political consciousness of young people in the 1960s. Many nationalist songs were tired and clichéd, but others were seen as inspirational with, as Geraghty says, 'a lot of genuine and legitimate feeling about the past'. They served to 'record historic events and bridge the gap between past and present in a unique way'. This revival became awkward, of course, with the onset of serious violence in the North, but in the mid-1960s the songs were part of a radical political expression that was both Irish and universal. For others, it was simply their energy and audacity, and so at night we'd hear the adults downstairs singing 'The Jolly Ploughboy', followed by the mock-heroic 'Oh, the Captains and the Kings', extolling the virtues of empire.

The fact that a 'ballad' was worth commemorating has been remarked upon in relation to the Davis statue. In a fascinating book entitled *1916 in 1966, Commemorating the Easter Rising*, Roisín Higgins writes about the memorial to Davis and the impetus to have his ballad 'turned into bronze', so to speak. It is as if Davis is himself an artist or sculptor, trying to *imagine* another Ireland into being – against all odds, and despite famine and emigration. And now his ballad is commemorated as reality: 'A Nation Once Again'.

Higgins contrasted the official memory incorporated in public monuments 'with those memories of the vanquished which attach themselves to fugitive and endangered cultural forms such as the street ballad'. Ireland's national identity 'existed in unstable images and the fractured, fluid power of allegory and the oral tradition. The Young Irelanders [in the 1840s] sought to harness the street ballad to their aim of creating an Irish nationality.' The process, she writes, 'takes another step further in the Davis memorial in which the ballad is solidified. Rather than being a form that is open and oppositional, it is incorporated into an official public monument, denoting a shift in Irish nationalism from nationhood to statehood. Through this process, the ballad is in some ways divested of its power – which rested in its informal status and encoded meaning – by being formalised.'

It is as if to say the bulk of our struggle is complete, and the ballad can now be decommissioned and solidified in bronze. This was not the case, however, and with the folk boom, the ballads and songs were back out in the open, contributing to the Civil Rights movement and confrontation in Northern Ireland.

There is a further paradox, which I will talk about later, which has to do with Davis's own philosophy, which seems to call for Ireland to return to its roots while simultaneously embracing the future. For decades, this paradox was reflected in the split personality of the Irish state, a point made crucially apparent when the then Taoiseach Bertie Ahern came to 're-unveil' the Davis memorial in 2006 and, in a heartfelt tribute to the Celtic Tiger, made a speech that was truly all things to all men.

As in the writing of Davis, argues Higgins, 'An appeal to nationhood was used to obscure the structural inequalities in Irish society.' However, this was not something to concern Eddie or Garech or the government. They were out to bring art to the people, and teach them how to live it to the full. Luke Kelly may have been applauded for his Communism, but no one ever expected his ideals to be implemented. Lose all those hunts and corporate commissions? God forbid. Each unto their own, was the motto, and whatever you do, do it with feeling.

Meanwhile my parents got engaged. The party was held in Hartigan's Pub just off St Stephen's Green. The pub is unchanged to this day and is still frequented by medical students. They would marry only a few hundred yards away in the University Church, and the reception was held in Powers Hotel on Kildare Street. This would be an interesting walk for both of them. My mum would pass the big door of Loreto Hall, where she'd been resident before her beatnik flats around Baggotonia. My father, meanwhile, would pass the spot which many years earlier had changed his life. This was a memorial to German suffering after World War Two.

Garech attended the reception with his Tabasco bottle and a

Chinese girl in costume called Li Fung (or 'Li Fang' as she was mistakenly described). *Fleadh* friends such as Bobby Clancy and Séamus Ennis also came. Ennis brought his pipes but at the end of the night he looked down at them sadly and said, 'There you are now and no one asked me to play you.'

For two country people, my parents could not have been more metropolitan. However, they didn't stay in Dublin but moved to Dún Laoghaire, the harbour town five miles south of the city, where Eddie had a studio and where my mum had already moved in the previous year.

The following year, they had their first child, and if I was raised with bronze, my arrival was greeted with silver, in the shape of a little Regency spoon from Mackey with the inscription 'May your platter always be filled – DM' and a Georgian hip flask from Garech, with my name inscribed.

The gift from Mackey was especially thoughtful, given his roguish reputation. Indeed, decades later, when I was stuck for funds and had both items valued, I discovered that while the spoon is indeed genuine, the flask was, alas, not Georgian as in the 1780s but Georgian in the sense of King George V from the 1930s. 'It's worth about €100,' said the dealer disdainfully. And so it is all the better for not being sold: a present received twice over. Or like the memory of childhood, given away in one's head and then retrieved for renewed contemplation. Just like a memoir.

CHAPTER 5

Stone View

Our house in Dún Laoghaire was down a cul de sac, off the main street of the town. It comprised two terraced cottages knocked into one – a rambling stretch of alcoves and bedrooms, a bit like the Beatles' house in *Help*. At the top of the lane was a pub, and on the other side a newsagent.

It was here that Wolfe Tone was constructed and then hoisted over the rooftop. There is a picture of him inside the workshop, with his head to the ceiling. He looks like he's moving, just as in the Green, and heading towards the door, with his shoulder forward: *this room is too small for me now; I'm getting out of here.* In the background, framed by the workshop door, my mum is sitting in the yard in the sun, and lying back on a wicker settee, with a book and a cooling juice. Thomas Davis was also made here but not cast. He was put into plaster and sent to Italy, after which he was polished up to go on the town.

Eddie had been renting the house and then bought it and created a workshop out the back. He had a canny ability with property and money, exceptionally so for an artist. Eddie seemed always to have a roll of notes in his pocket and a raw deal-maker's instinct. He made a living almost all his life directly from sculpture, without having to do other things such as teach or cast other people's work, although he did cast some in the early days, more as a favour or out of curiosity. It was always a pleasant surprise to see other people's work lying around the yard.

My mother brought money too, and with a donation from her

father they bought the adjoining cottage, which they then turned into a big studio room, with a sort of stage area and French windows looking out on the yard. This was where Colm and I slept. A side lane led in from the street, but it also led towards a bigger building behind us, which housed a pool hall and a cosmetics warehouse. Typical of a port town, Dún Laoghaire had all these buildings tightly constructed on top of each other. It was like an industrial version of Luggala, with its concealed lanes and unexpected levels. No wonder Eddie felt entitled to construct a foundry, with blazing furnace and ovens, an amazing arrangement that would later be challenged in court, only to be given a reprieve from an artistically indulgent judge.

There was thus No 1 and No 1A. The first cottage was the main house, with kitchen and living room and an extension out the back comprising bathroom and parents' bedroom. On the roof of the extension was an asphalt roof, where you could look over the rooftops and gardens of the cottages below, and down towards the steeples of Dún Laoghaire. People could sunbathe on the roof, and it was always popular with Garech and his companions, cat-like creatures who uncoiled in the summer air while the lord's son finger-beaded his way through the latest news and gossip.

If people knocked on one door, Eddie would answer the other one. This was handy for avoiding curious callers, but also for evading tax inspectors and gas meter men. 'But I knocked on your door,' they would protest later.

'Oh, that was the wrong door.'

Or he was out the back, in the workshop, where he couldn't hear anything. He told Donald Connery that 'curious callers' were the reason he couldn't work in the city.

Inside the house, the rooms were filled with sculpture: climbing figures and pipers and indeterminate animals. Although I described it earlier as reminiscent of Picasso's *Guernica*, there was also tremendous spotlit softness. Think of Rodin's *Gates of Hell*, and on that scale, with wriggling little figures wrestling and moving, like a child's world of *marla* come to life. For, despite its title, Rodin's

Gates are really a depiction of the cycles of life, with the scenes depicted and then re-enacted on a larger scale. It was the same with Eddie's *Land of Music*, whose beaten panels of nudes and animals were echoed by the sculptures around the house and yard.

The house was all very 1960s, with lots of wood shelving, exposed brickwork and cement walls with criss-cross motifs scored on them when wet, as if Matisse himself had just dropped by. And one sensed he might, as so many other artists did. There were drawings on the wall, theirs and others, and Colman Doyle's photo portrait of Dev gazing with blind regard at the nudes beneath him. In this case, it was the reverse to the drinker's tale of ruin: fast woman and slow horses. For here were horses all turning a corner, like in the wild west – the corporates loved these – while, on lower shelves, pensive nudes played the harp, or reclined, with heads propped up on resting arms.

The interior walls were faced with roughly cut red brick, which added to the cosiness and provided lots of edges to perch things on: figures, masks, half-made jewellery. Spotlights brought their shapes to life, so that small figures could throw large shapes against the wall and gigantic shadows crept across the ceiling, like the hump-backed monster going up the stairs in the classic German expressionist film *Nosferatu* – an appropriate image given that there was a strong German atmosphere to it all, and especially of post-war German expressionism. Except that this was not of the 1920s, but the post-war expressionism of another kind.

There were no death masks yet. These were done in the 1970s. But, in a sense, there was a death mask, for there was a bronze face of an unfortunate man called Uri, a depressed sculptor whom Eddie had studied with in Munich and who one day smashed up all his sculpture in a rage, and then apparently committed suicide by jumping into the oven, or furnace. It was an extraordinary story, which stayed with us, as did the startled-looking mask. Eddie rescued it from the studio floor and it has been with him ever since, hanging over the fireplace in Dún Laoghaire, and then over the big chimneybreast in Connemara. It always faced where he sat: a mask of death, or life, rescued from the rubble and tragedy, and hanging over a constant, bubbling fire: *the work outliveth the fire, the work outliveth the man.*

We used to wonder later if Uri was one of those students who attacked the classical models in 1955, protesting against the re-armament of Germany, only to end up smashing his own. What an amazing act of directness, incidentally, actually to physically attack a previous tradition's art. Can you imagine the Cubists attacking the old masters with scalpels and knives? Well, perhaps in their heads, you can.

As if to recompense, we also had a standing nude, cast from the leftover shell casings of bombs dropped on Germany. This was not the usual willowy nude of Eddie's, but a tall and proud figure almost two foot high, with slender calves and full hips and shoulders, like an Olympic swimmer. Here's revenge on the fire bombers – a triumphant *mädchen.* Her head is poised proudly and her arms are behind her back, the torso of a particularly rich green hue, such is the quality of the metal leached from the spent shells of the Americans and British. In the sculptural or Arcadian imagination, everything could be reborn through a nude woman – or man.

This German atmosphere filtered through the house. We wore Bavarian folk smocks of an indigo blue, with white stitching along the shoulders. To this day, they look fresh and new. The Germans made products that lasted. If you looked at the back of a drill in the workshop, it invariably said 'Made in West Germany' whereas the foundry tools were all 'Made in England': wrought iron, 'drop-forged', borne out of the industrial north and built to endure. The tools had become worn and were themselves sculptural, as Eddie knew when he hung them lovingly on hooks along the wall. (Today some of them sit on my windowsill, facing Mountjoy Prison.)

In the 1950s, however, Germany was a place of poverty – or at least temporary poverty since it was also a place where people were very smart and progressive. 'What are you doing?' protested my father when he saw us cutting the yucky fat off our meat. 'Sure, in Germany, they throw away the lean, and only eat the fat. It's called *speck.'* We would sigh and go back to our rinds. Later, when we got cheeky, we used to retort, 'No wonder they were hungry.'

And then there was the story about some lovely meat that Eddie used to eat every week in the student cafés. 'This is very tasty,' he told his German companion, chewing away. 'What is it?' His companion pointed out the window at some people dragging a dead horse down the street.

'Ah,' said Eddie. In fairness, it didn't change his opinion. Nor did his childhood – and sculptural – love of horses prevent him from eating them.

Around the kitchen table, we sat to eat and be raised. For it was not just where Tone and Davis were raised, but where we grew up as well. Colm was born a year after me, in 1963, then Cathy, two years later. Gary and Hugh came much later, in the 1970s – the World Cup years of 1970 and 1974 respectively.

My mother was a fine cook, interested in Indian and Italian food, and we had a lot of Italian meals, like spaghetti bolognese, lasagne or homemade pizza. We also had family specials such as tarragon chicken, with a creamy-oily yellow sauce over baked potatoes. Like Garech, with his emergency bottle of Tabasco, we were little food snobs and couldn't eat in other people's houses, where we were invariably offered the national diet of gravy and mashed vegetables, where everything was over-cooked, especially the meat.

'Tarragon chicken?' said an uncle, mockingly, when I stayed with my cousins. 'He wants *'Tar Isteach Chicken.'* And to the merriment of his ketchup-faced kids, he foisted on us more Calvita cheese and marrowfat peas.

We also had big curries, which were a special treat given all the sideline extras such as chutney, salted peanuts, poppadoms, yoghurt and sliced banana. This wasn't so much a dinner as a party!

Not that we didn't also have our share of regular food, such as the cold-cut 'meat teas', a speciality of the *fleadh*s, and, of course, the full Irish fry, with crispy rashers, sausages and toast. Still today, whenever I get a whiff of those old back rashers, with their yellowed crispy rinds, I think of childhood. Best of all was the fried bread, with the toast soaking up all the grease, something that, in our much more regulated age, people would be reluctant to give kids today.

Among the kitchenware was the cutlery my mum used at boarding school, with her maiden initials still on them. In our granny's house in Cootehill, we used cutlery with the initials of her siblings, now returned from the boarding schools all battered and scratched. I can't remember the cutlery in Claremorris, but I hope it didn't include any of the lord's silverware.

Quite a bit of old tableware went into the sculpture. You could sometimes recognise a bent spoon as a leaning woman's back and, in the big *Fisherman* lobby sculpture in Ballsbridge, a whole colander was visibly melted into the torso. But the opposite also took place: Eddie making household stuff, such as stencilled orange tablemats, which echoed his *Astronaut Dream* series. There seemed to be nothing that could not either be painted or sculpted. He even did bronze candleholders for the Tandoori Rooms where my mum had worked. Everything had aesthetic value, and we were taught to appreciate art and life, and how closely they were interwoven.

Much later, when another child, Hughie, was born in 1974, Eddie took spare rods of metal and welded the frame of a new cot. It looked like a giant lobster pot, which amused us – we had been using such pots in the west – but for my mother this was the last straw. She wanted some form of bourgeois stability and normality, but Eddie was determined to stay with his bohemianism, and eventually go west – permanently. For my mother, the house in Stone View was simply not suitable or big enough for this many growing kids.

As Donald S. Connery wrote in his book, *The Irish*, after he came to visit: 'I could see that it was something of a problem living in the midst of enormous chunks of metal, enough finished pieces of sculpture to fill a small museum, and little bronzes hanging from the clothes line with the baby's nappies.'

But, in the early years, it was all part of the magic, with horses on the floor and masks on the walls. The routine was for my father to work most of the day, and often into the night, especially when casting. We would come home from school and he would still be in the workshop, grinding metal, boiling wax or washing down the yard, while inside the kitchen we'd be eating our cereal and preparing for bed. After a while, he would go around to Walter's pub for a nightcap.

In the daytime, he'd go up to the Bamboo Café on George's Street, where he'd meet other artists, while my mum took us to the People's Park or down the seafront where she was usually stuck into a book. She had brought most of her library into the marriage: the Penguin classics and novels and modern poetry. It made for an eclectic collection, next to the tomes on European art and the pamphlets on Irish history. However, I don't remember Eddie ever really reading, apart from art books and manuals, which he looked at more than read, and the daily newspaper, which he read from cover to cover. He must have done all his serious reading early on.

We were, of course, encouraged to read widely ourselves. Our parents seemed to combine hippy values with Victorian self-improvement. (There may, indeed, be little difference, as de Valera illustrated.) As well as having the TV rationed, we were not allowed chewing gum, hard-boiled sweets or toffee, because of the damage it could do to our teeth. But secretly we bought these up on the main street. As for the famous *speck*, let the Germans have it, if it's so great.

Around the table, my parents would engage in passionate discussions about art, or gossip. This was my abiding memory of those early years, my parents facing each other and excitedly trading news and opinions. The visual arts scene, and the broader arts world, provided a ready-made social life and the mantelpiece filled up with white card invites to galleries in the city. There was Charlie Brady, the painter, who looked like Colombo, the TV detective, with his crumpled white Mac and a New York accent that seemed to get stronger the longer he was out of the US, especially when he spoke about the 'old days' in the Cedar Tavern, with Jackson Pollock and de Kooning. It was as if he was trying to recreate some of this ambience down in the Bamboo Café.

In his house on Royal Terrace West, he showed us how to paint, applying soft layers and building up a luminous background. Brady had a trademark style of painting a single object – a jug, or spool of thread, or an upended leather wallet. He was proud of his work and of his career since he'd come to Ireland. One day he took out his Oireachtas gold medal, with which he was clearly very pleased. 'Your father lost his,' he said dismissively, as if to say, that's typical.

Eddie and Brady had a good relationship, with lots of banter and back slapping. But it was tested later when Charlie began making sculptures: small bronze versions of the subjects he'd been painting. One was a wallet. 'Hey, Charlie,' Eddie goaded him at the opening, 'there must be money in that wallet?' But later they exhibited together in a two-man show in the North – a sculptor and a painter – an unusual type of pairing, certainly for Eddie who usually exhibited alone or in a larger group. And, in the early days, you'd see Charlie on a purchaser's list for one of Eddie's shows, next to the pin-striped lawyers and corporate collectors.

Visual artists help each other out and have a much better camaraderie than other artists have, and certainly more than writers who have little interest in each other's work and mostly live in self-absorbed bubbles. By contrast, painters and sculptors were interested in the style and direction of their peers and frequently bought each other's work to put it in their houses. They socialised together and went out to studios and openings. There was also the solidarity – or healthy division – of the various 'movements' and associations, especially in the 1960s and 1970s.

We also did painting classes in Sandycove with Eddie McGuire, who painted in a haunted realist fashion, like early Freud. His speciality was seated portraits, including many of the people in this narrative: Seamus Heaney, Garech with uilleann pipes on the floor or, more notoriously, Charlie Haughey on a horse. His other specialty was game, or dead birds, and inside his studio, with its easel and skylights and smell of the nearby sea, there were always a few dead birds lying around: woodcock, grouse, pheasant – all the birds that were hunted in Claremorris and stuffed in Luggala. Sometimes the birds appeared in the portraits, eerily peeping out of some background shrubbery.

McGuire's entire studio was later donated to the Irish Museum of Modern Art, with the hope that it might one day be reassembled and displayed as a working artist's studio, just like the Francis Bacon Studio in the Hugh Lane, with its strange morbid attraction, like a deserted peepshow. Perhaps the same could be done with Eddie's foundry, rather than leaving it lying idle, surrounded by ferns and the sound of the sea. But what is a studio without the artist – or the dead birds?

Next to McGuire in Sandycove, and near to the Martello tower from the opening scene in *Ulysses*, were Imogen and Ian Stuart. They were both sculptors and had met in Germany in the 1950s when Ian went there, just as Eddie did. Ian was the son of Francis Stuart and a grandson of Maud Gonne, who was wooed by Yeats. Imogen worked in wood and made church sculptures and Ian worked in steel, creating 'hard edge' abstractions. By Galway Harbour there was a big set of oil storage drums, painted in different colours, and each time we passed it my father would say, 'There's Ian Stuart's sculpture.' It wasn't of course, but it could have been.

On the way to Galway, we also passed an actual sculpture by Imogen Stuart, in the midlands town of Tyrrellspass. It is on the town's green, and shows three children going to school. We used to think it was a memorial to some kids who had drowned in a nearby river. In fact, it is another 1916 memorial, and Imogen's experience in devising it was interesting. At first, the committee wanted the usual gunman or Celtic cross. But Imogen won them round by presenting a very good model and a sense of *fait accompli*. They couldn't resist the simple image of 'a new dawn for Ireland' and three kids crossing the town's green.

Imogen used her own daughters as models. Such a fate is common for artists' children. Robert Ballagh put his daughter Rachel on the back of one of our banknotes. The Stuarts had two daughters, Ashie and Pussy, who later babysat us in Stone View, hip 1960s chicks who were in touch with 'the scene' in Dalkey and Dún Laoghaire, including Murray's Record Centre around the corner.

Finally, in Sandycove, there was Michael Farrell, who painted in distinctive pop-art style and did political paintings about the North. Long-haired and handsome, he was a live wire and had a clather of kids. He had a big terraced house near Bullock Harbour, and my abiding memory of it is sitting in a big white room on air-filled plastic seats of see-through primary colours: very pop, very Batman. But Farrell was an artist for whom the bohemian life took its toll on marriage and home life, and he ended up estranged from much of his family.

In our own kitchen, we sat on big wooden chairs, built by a man called Al O'Dea in Tuam, a furniture maker who was ahead of his time, who produced Scandinavian-type structures of dark sturdy wood. He was a former band leader and visiting his studio was always a treat, with the smell of carved wood and sawdust mixed in among the musical instruments.

Eddie would trade him sculpture for furniture. A lot of stuff in our house was acquired like this, through barter and exchange. But Al in particular had his eye on St Patrick. This was a two-foot-high sculpture of the national saint in the shape of a cone, or better still as a bell, directly inspired by Manzù's famous bishops. It seems that Al was promised the piece but the deal fell through, something that often happened.

'You be good little fellows,' Al told us, 'and the next time you visit, hide Patrick in the boot of the car and then when your father comes in, you come in behind him with Patrick wrapped in an old sheet.'

'That sounds like a great trick,' we said, and this we did. Eddie had only settled into the armchair and was telling some long tale about his car journey – tinkers, Ballinrobe, a loose horse – when we suddenly unrolled St Patrick out on to the floor.

'Ah!' exclaimed Al with satisfaction, as the national saint lay at his feet. But Eddie was furious. He couldn't believe the sculpture was on Al's floor. He relented somewhat when Al gave him yet more furniture. He also gave us sawdust to smoke mackerel with, the dust of his hardwoods being better for the flavour of the fish. Eddie was equally impressed that we'd actually carried off such a plan: smuggled a sculpture into the car and brought it across the country.

Besides, it was not unlike Eddie's own raids on the family farm in Farmhill, when we called in on the way to Galway. While Granny sat in the big living room, next to the stove, Eddie would stand in the far corner, half listening to her, while encouraging us to explore his childhood milieu and pick up things 'which weren't being used' – old farm irons, bottles, baskets. This was his family home and, presumably, it was okay to help yourself. 'Yes, yes,' he told us. 'Just put the stuff in the car. Oh, and lads – don't take the guns, obviously.'

'Okay,' we nodded, although not taking at least one gun was something of a disappointment. Otherwise, it extended to apples from the orchard and honey from the hives – most of which Granny would have given us anyway. But Eddie also had his eye on the bits of rusty tractor parts – presumably for scrap – that were strewn around the hay barn and animal sheds facing the house. We had to be careful as Uncle PJ was wandering in and out, checking on his cattle.

'Sorry, you were saying …' Eddie would prompt his mother, as he muttered instructions to his sons. 'Lordy was around again, was he?' 'Lordy' was our granny's name for Lord Oranmore and Brown: half-affectionate, half-derisive.

Eddie and his mother had a curious relationship. They looked alike, sitting in opposite corners of the room and talking loudly at each other, as if they were on a stage (with Lordy's props). As we left, she would come to the car, with great conspiracy, and pass in a large 7UP bottle. This was *poitín* and, for years, we wouldn't drink from a 7UP bottle lest it turn out to be this potent moonshine. She could have handed it over in the house, but to do so through a car window was all part of the intrigue. Unfortunately, we'd taken the intrigue a step further, and there was now a danger that if granny leaned in too close she'd see all the other stuff. PJ, meanwhile, stared on at the over-laden car, with just a glimmer of suspicion.

Unwanted furniture was also given to us, or taken – milking stools, cabinets – and so the goods which had descended from Castlemacgarret were now in turn making their across Ireland to Stone View, and across again to Carraroe, usually tied to the roof of a Renault 12 hatchback. This was the family car, a succession of them, two in red and one in white: all traded in with a car dealer in Ballinasloe, invariably with the sweetener of a drawing or – if the bills mounted – a small bronze.

Meanwhile, Stone View was also being furnished from local auction rooms, or from the rogue Mackey. From him, we got wooden dressers and Irish Victoriana, such as delph jugs with colleens painted on them – genuine stuff: he was also a serious collector. Best of all was a wrought-iron hat stand with the figure of a bare-chested Hibernia on its ivy-strewn headpiece and the slogan *Érin go Brágh.*

'Erin go Bra-less,' quipped Garech as he came through the door. The 'right' door, by the way: a secret knock had been developed for 1A.

Invariably, Eddie would try to improve the furniture, or fix it, with wire fastenings or lop-sided castors. In general, anything metal had better be on its best behaviour or there was a danger that it would follow PJ's farmyard implements into the voracious furnace.

In the early years, the physical atmosphere of the house was well captured in an *Irish Times* photo essay entitled, appropriately, 'Living with Sculpture'.

There is no date, but it is about 1964 – one of Eddie's 'breakthrough' years. I know, because I managed to get into one of the (unpublished) pictures in the shoot and I look about 2 years old. There are six photos, the crispness of their shadows enhanced by the old black and white photography.

In one photo, two small figures are in alcoves, and another is on the wall, as if climbing, and drenched in the light of a spotlight. I've no idea where these figures are now. In the foreground are the two horns of a heavy life-size figure, entitled *Two Wives*. It is now one part of *Adam and Eve*, a pair of figures standing in FitzGerald Park in Cork, like upright meat carcasses cast in bronze, with truncated limbs and necks for heads. Eddie had an interesting if somewhat confusing habit of renaming sculptures. But it is worth recording, if one can, where these sculptures have ended up, after their curious journeys.

Another photo shows a sideboard, or shelf of work. At the back are some of Eddie's *Bronze Groups*, two-legged figures that seem to grow into flat bodies with many attenuated heads. They are also known as *Family Groups*, with the heads imitating each other but which seem to be struggling to be separate, which one critic described as an 'apt if unintended depiction of the strains of family'. They are made with regular long candles, the columns or shrunken heads taking their shape by melting slowly. Candle-makers use the wick to build up wax upon, but in this case they are used to drip wax off, shedding layers but retaining their length.

The pieces were later bought by the collector Maurice Fridberg and eventually donated to the Municipal Art Gallery on Parnell Square. Or 'The Hugh Lane', as it is more commonly known, since it was set up with the munificence of that major collector of another era. Lane was famously drowned with the *Lusitania* in 1915, but a contest over his will meant that Ireland, rather unfairly, had to share his valuable collection with the National Gallery in London.

His gallery is housed in the former residence of Lord Charlemont (1728–1799), himself an extraordinary collector who had amassed a major collection of books, antiquities and artworks, so here we have three generations of quite different Dublin collectors, spanning three centuries.

In a gallery catalogue called *Images and Insights* (1989), the Fridberg donations are well described: '*Bronze Groups*, with their elongated architectonic forms, are characteristic of Delaney's abstract figurative style of this period. Here the individual multi-headed figures stand alone and isolated, yet at the same time are related to each other by virtue of their human male/female attributes.' Again, this is as useful a description of family life – or human life – as any I have heard.

Also on the shelf is a woman piping, and blowing the pipe upwards, as if setting the notes free. *The Piper* was also donated to the Hugh Lane and, for years, it was on the cover of a gallery leaflet, calling the people to come and look at art. She looked well inside Charlemont house, on a white box, just yards from Degas's horses and Rodin's *Age of Bronze*, with the paintings of Renoir and Manet in the background. Visible through her arms is Courbet's big and strange canvas, *The Diligence in the Snow*, which we used to love as kids, mainly because it seemed to be so poorly painted, with far too much snow and tiny cartoon-style passengers.

It is appropriate that Eddie's sculptures are close to Rodin, the man who began the whole tradition of modern sculpture, and who broke the idea of representation into concepts of form and space – indeed with this very sculpture. In the Rodin museum in Paris it has pride of place, and I do like their description: 'The Age of Bronze illustrates the third age of humanity when men shaped bronze to make tools and weapons. It is also a poetic allusion to Jean-Jacques Rousseau: innocent man, untainted by civilisation, awakened painfully and must learn to survive in this new society.'

How true that is: Eddie embarking on his career, or a new state emerging into independence. Just like Davis, up on his pedestal. *Gentlemen, you have a country.*

Although Eddie would respect Rodin's breakthrough, he would still regard him as traditional. There is a theatrical, even vulgar quality to much of Rodin's work, and a slickness to the finish which makes it obvious it is not unique, but produced in glossy editions by assistants. It may well be this that makes him so popular, for the Museé Rodin packs them in – and packs the sculpture into rooms. Yet on the beautiful back lawn, with its topiarised trees, there is not a single piece of art. The French may be *avant garde*, but they also know how to preserve a precious lawn.

Also in the background, at The Hugh Lane, is *Walking Horse* by Edgar Degas. This was more Eddie's thing: a 'fervid realism which reduces all the elements to form and movement, with a muscular body suspended on narrow legs and a surface that is rough and ready'. Eddie loved horses and loved sculpting them, just as he liked riding them as a child.

Again, however, there are many editions of Degas's works, but in this case it was beyond the artist's control. Amazingly, although acclaimed as a painter, his work was only discovered (and cast) after his death. In fact, Degas had secretly and industriously sculpted all his life, an extraordinary idea – imagine being a 'secret sculptor' – and a condition that Eddie himself almost aspired to in later years, out in the remote West, when he was constructing his steel sculptures by the ocean in almost splendid isolation.

Degas's withdrawal was partly because of the reaction to the only piece he ever publicly exhibited, the famous *Little Dancer, Aged 14 Years*, a figure that my father was obsessed with. The figure was controversial because of its everyday 'real' additions: a tutu of actual gauze, real stockings and shoes, and a wig of human hair, tied with a green ribbon. All of these are attached to a figure of brown uncast wax. However, the real controversy was the figure's posture, standing with arms behind her back, as a dancer would, but defiantly, with the face slightly sour and stubborn. It was a realism that was 'ugly and provocative and a challenge to the traditional concept of elegance'. Davis, Tone: the assertions were similar.

It's as if the emotions have been shut down within, not unlike Manzù's ice skater, which inspired Davis. The subject has retreated from our world as onlookers and into its own world. Modern sculpture doesn't reflect our world but creates one of its own. It seemed that Eddie spent his life trying to find a way to retreat with them, climb into the metaphorical furnace like Uri. On balance, it was a communion with sculpture that I think he fully achieved in his twilight years.

Eddie's interest in the Degas figure extended to gymnasts, dancers and even dolls. He used to examine closely the cindy doll with the bendy leg. Again, this was a major theme of his work: *Standing Girl, Resting Dancer, Leaning Woman.* In the late 1970s, inspired by the Women's Peace marches in the North, he did a whole series of women marching, slender anonymous figures, with variations such as *Women Gathering* or *Women Marching in a Storm.* The solitary figure also endured and, inspired by the 1972 Olympics and the Russian gymnast Olga Korbut, he did a life-size figure for Trinity residence hall in Dartry, an outdoor sculpture of a girl spinning over high bars. It is about twelve feet off the ground. However, during a hasty renovation of the site, the *Gymnast* went missing, and the Trinity authorities had to go in search of her.

Eddie was always taken by a striking pose. In a book called *My Wallet of Photographs*, a collection of photos of Aran islanders taken by J. M. Synge in 1905, he would look closely at a picture of a man walking slowly up a beach with his wife and child. The man is wearing breeches, a dark waistcoat and a Spanish hat, and looks slim and handsome like Clint Eastwood in a spaghetti western, with his head down and his arms behind his back. He could be a matador described by Hemingway. He is also wearing pampooties, the soft shoes made of animal hide, which enabled even the heaviest islanders to walk across sharp rocks nimbly, like a ballet dancer. It was as with sculpture – great weight carried nimbly: brute force rendered gently.

Also in the *Irish Times* photo essay is the bust of a girl done in soft stone or chalk, a very early work done before Eddie embraced bronze, but which he still kept. He retained such work – marble carvings, oil paintings of harbours – as neglected children, just as he kept some of his favourite works, the so called 'family jewels', until the very end, or close to the end. On the wall, hanging from an edge, is Uri's death mask, a big, moon-eyed face seeking understanding. The doomed German sculptor has unwittingly made it into the Irish newspapers.

Other photos show Eddie at work. In one shot, he is welding an arm on to a hanging figure of Christ. Except Christ is not on the cross but taken down to be repaired, with his knees apart and his head hanging wearily to the side – an amazing image. There was always a Jesus or two around the house; Christ in various stages of life or crucifixion. This was not necessarily because we were religious, but because he was such a common figure to portray: the original sculpted man.

Eddie is wearing black goggles as he welds and holds the torch up to the statue's shoulder, which in the photo produces a white explosion at the point of contact, like the spark you see in those 'God creating man' images – except here it's the reverse. While one hand holds the torch, the other applies the thin soldering rod, which is melted onto the surface, dipped into white powder to help it dissolve into a solid scar. As one of his assistants said, Eddie loved welding and could weld all day. There was a whole ritual, of running the gas with a little knob, and then the oxygen, lighting it with a white taper, and then condensing the flame, before rejecting it twice, with loud cracks, and then starting again.

In other pictures, Eddie is using not goggles but a welding mask, with a glass eye slit, which he holds up with his free hand. It looks like one of those masks used by workers in a nuclear power plant or riot police, except in this case it is being held up temporarily, like Eddie has assumed some role in a Japanese Noh play.

In Munich, he made extra money welding tramlines. 'I was paid ten marks a metre,' he told one interviewer, 'so I could knock out forty pounds between the last tram at night, at 2.30 a.m., and the first tram in the morning, at 5.30 a.m. You had to be a professional welder and that, believe it or not, is a degree that I have.'

Eddie was constantly photographed welding, and much later, in a full colour ad, he sits proudly with the welder in his hand, like a rock star with an upended guitar or his own father with a rifle cocked. He was proud of the ad, and no wonder. It was for Bayer Chemicals, a German multinational, and was emblazoned with the slogan 'Edward Delaney changed the face of Irish sculpture.' Nor is the blurb lacking in hyperbole: the sculptor's 'massive masterpieces, which enliven the streets and squares of Dublin, are monuments to his vision and technical expertise', just like Frederick

Bayer, the company's founder, who shared this 'gift of vision and enterprise, and helped create the first modern dyestuffs, and establish the chemical industry as we know it today. Bayer's productivity ranges from agriculture to the moon … the plastics around us, and the shapes and colours now possible in architecture, building, engineering.' Sure, is this not sculpture itself?

As a corporate endorsement, the ad did no harm to Eddie's ability to pick up commissions. It also emphasised the intense physicality of sculpture, and Eddie oozes machismo, tanned from a Connemara summer and filling out his purple T-shirt and a baggy indigo blue shirt. It is 1978 and his hair is curly. Beside him are the oxy-acetylene bottles for welding, delivered to Stone View in noisy lorries which racked them at the back, like the kegs on beer lorries. Sometimes when the pub up the lane was being restocked at the same time, there would be a competitive clanking of barrels: both of them fuel for Eddie's artistic visions.

The *Irish Times* photo essay also shows Eddie 'constructing an armature, on which he will build a figure'. The armature is an iron framework, like the skeleton underneath, or the steel fixing inside poured concrete. Another more dramatic photo shows him stirring molten metal in a pot, the black and white photography softening the subject so that it looks like a harmless activity, with a cosy glow through the smoke. In fact, it probably wasn't harmless at all but no protection is being worn, not even on the face, as Eddie nonchalantly, almost wistfully, stirs the mix. He is wearing just the standard donkey jacket that coalmen wore at that time with the black plastic shoulders.

Finally, there is a photo of the backyard where a number of works are visible. They are seen through the French doors of the 'lounge', as the caption quaintly put it, 'with a bronze of *St Michael* dominant'. This is a life-size standing figure, semi abstract and of heavy bronze, with ribbed skin and a large protruding limb like an elephant's trunk. It is now known as *Swords of Steel* and stands in a garden in Northern Ireland. The confusing habit of renaming pieces is here further confused by the mention of another metal.

The piece is bronze, *very* bronze, and it would take a few men just to shift it a few yards, as would all of his larger works. In the absence of such men, Eddie moved stuff around with improvised pipe runners and scaffolding, in a system he had gradually worked out.

On the ground, a marble figure crouches away from view, as if avoiding the camera. Another figure looks like he's clinging to a tree trunk, or struggling with his burden of stone, and trying to emerge himself – as opposed to being emerged by the sculptor who has left him to finish the job himself. These are also photographed from the other side, looking back at the big windows, along with *Swords of Steel* and the *Land of Music* theatre panel. Eddie's produce is thus represented in four forms: bronze, copper, marble – and flesh, for looking out the window is myself, nosily checking out the photographer. Here, there is no shyness, unlike the marble man, who from this perspective is still covering his head, his haunches gathered in tightly.

CHAPTER 6

Getting into the Picture

My own first appearance in the media was in connection with the making of jewellery, which my parents had turned into a sideline cottage industry.

'Wanted: jewellery with new look' was the *Sunday Press* headline with the sub head: 'And now a designer with new ideas'. There was a large photo with the caption: 'The family assemble in the studio to see the work in progress.' At this stage, the 'family' consists of just the three of us, and I am in my mother's arms while my father tends to a sculpture. I have a rather fat head and both father and son are wearing Aran jumpers. It is a posed shot, and the 'work in progress' is actually a bit of pretend work as Eddie rubs a filing iron against the already well-finished *Two Wives*. In the background is the *Land of Music*. The bacchanalia of the *fleadh* has led to a new creation and a domestic atmosphere of happy labour.

'Sculptor Edward Delaney is an artist of many interests,' writes the reporter, Kathleen Hickey. 'How often do you see a perfectly made tweed suit of imitation jewellery? He and wife Nancy talked about this when I called on them.'

Hickey's account gives an idea of the atmosphere in the house-cum-workshop, and especially of its constant activity. 'Nancy helps with the making of these pieces, suggesting colours and ideas and working on the finishing of the jewellery. "We hope," she said, "to arrange an exhibition of jewellery in Dublin in the near future. Eddie started making these pieces in the first place as a way of filling in time while working on large bronze casts. The casts take about four days. This means sitting up for two nights in a row to watch the ovens, and the jewellery gives him something small to work on. Concentrating on this helps to keep him awake." '

The nocturnal commitment sounds like someone on the prow of a battleship. On the subject of jewellery, there was, of course, a chance for another broadside, as there was on many topics.

'Edward, who designed and made copper buttons for a famous fashion house in Munich, thinks that we in this country do not appreciate originality of thought on the question of these accessories. "If you look around the shops you'll see hardly any good modern jewellery," he commented. "In every country in Europe at present there is a growing demand for original silver and copper jewellery. Here they want to wear all this pseudo-Egyptian stuff – Cleopatra's profile on medallions! Of course there is some good Irish jewellery but on the other hand there is too much of this Celtic Twilight stuff. These Celtic motifs can become as meaningless as the rest." '

This is an interesting criticism. Although Eddie drew from Celtic mythology, it was usually obliquely and in a modernist way. It was rarely imitative. However, it is ironic that he uses the phrase 'Celtic Twilight' so negatively given that it was the title for one of his largest works, the steel structure next to Mount Street Bridge. Unless, of course, in the context of a modern office block, he was being deeply ironic, which I don't think he was.

The jewellery is described as 'discs of irregular shaped pieces of enamelled copper and silver, linked together by small silver links', while 'the brooches are made in all kinds of unusual shapes and are sometimes constructed out of several pieces mounted together and brilliantly coloured. The enamel is laid on like paint and the result is like a miniature action painting.'

In the *Spectrum* documentary, Eddie is filmed making these. In fact, the enamel is like powdered paint and is sprinkled onto the copper, so that under an intense flame it comes up as gorgeous welts of colour. The powder was kept in small screw-top bottles, which, in our innocence, we were tempted to mix in with our toyshop watercolours. Eddie also did plaques and panels, which looked like little Jack Yeats paintings with their swirling colours and flecks of yellow and blue.

As well as the enamel pieces, the report describes the making of bracelets and bangles out of beaten copper. Eddie loved making jewellery and later he did a whole series of work in cast silver, including knuckle-duster rings shaped out of a nude woman or, in some cases, two nudes entwined. These were much sought after and unlikely to have gone astray, as I well know, having tried to procure one in 2007 for use as an engagement ring.

Garech was especially fond of these rings and introduced them to people like John Boorman and Bianca Jagger. Alas, he fell asleep one time at a foreign film festival – hopefully, not at a Boorman film – and when he woke up his ring was gone. I consoled him by telling him that apparently in Colombia they can cut your hand off if it's hanging out of a car window with a big shiny ring upon it. Garech assured me he had no plans to go to Colombia.

My mother has an especially personal gift, which is one of these rings depicting herself as a young odalisque. It is particularly shiny, from constant polishing. What a wonderful thing: sculpture you can wear, and a naked portrait of yourself on your own finger. She also has a necklace in which the pendant is a cluster of tiny honeycombed circles: Eddie's trademark motif from the 1970s, like a miniaturised version of the *Finnegans Wake* wall panel in Davy Byrne's. She also has a tiny silver maquette for the 1916 memorial in Claremorris, a bunch of overlapping crosses, but this is rather too large to wear, so instead it was mounted on a small base of hewn white marble and put out on display – unlike the finished work in Mayo.

After appearing in the jewellery cutting, I now made more appearances in the newspapers, next to sculpture.

In one picture, my father is holding me so that I can reach out and touch the *Great Hunger* at the Living Art Exhibition in 1964, the same sculpture that Luke Kelly has his hand upon on the cover of *Finnegan's Wake.* Thankfully, in the photo I am no longer a fat-headed child but a blonde young boy like the chap in *The Tin Drum.*

We even made it to the front of *The Irish Times.* It is October 1966, and Colm and I are in the Hugh Lane Gallery again; this time we are upstairs at a temporary exhibition and sitting underneath *Snámhaí* (or *The Bather*), a life-size copper figure of a woman leaning over, washing her hair with her hands. Her hair is dark copper wiring. It is Varnishing Day for the Oireachtas art exhibition and Colm and I are bunched together in our small Aran sweaters and sensible shoes. The image is now on the cover of this book. I am looking towards the photographer and making a point with finger raised.

A variation of the moment appeared in the *Irish Press* with the headline 'It's Daddy's!' In this one, I am pointing more excitedly towards the sculpture and have my mouth open.

The Bather was later owned by Karl Mullen, the surgeon and former rugby international who played for Ireland and captained the British and Irish Lions. He also delivered my wife, Fiona, and I like to think of him retrieving the infant from a touchline turnover, a metaphor that her rugby-loving family would greatly appreciate. Mullen later opened a gallery at Tulfarris Lodge in Wicklow and held exhibitions which combined artists both past and living.

The Bather was regularly in the yard, and in her permanent posture of bathing she seemed connected to the constant washing going on. Her skin was all pimpled, as if beaded with sweat, which we imagined to be caused by heat from the workshop: sweat made permanent. It was an image that we knew was contradictory but yet enjoyed, as kids do: like the paradox of great weight rendered lightly.

At another exhibition we are pictured playing with Matchbox cars on a segmented sculpture, another person's work: I'm not sure whose. We have our German smocks on, with the white stitching. The cars we got from Graces' Toyshop in Dún Laoghaire, a fascinating treasure trove, with glass cabinets filled with little trucks and painted soldiers in gestures of battle. We also bought stamps there for our collection, which we supplemented with raids on the plastic bags of used stamps that our granny kept in Cavan to send to the Overseas Missions.

Later the Graces' son, Tom, played rugby for Ireland and for the Lions – just like Karl Mullen. He scored a famous try at Murrayfield and we painted the event with watercolours, his figure elongated as he stretches over the line to score. The Graces were delighted and promised a reward. Excitedly, we expected some special toys: lovely dye-cast cars maybe, with open roofs and ejector seats. Even better, we got the autographs of the entire Lions squad which had recently toured Australia. We used to collect such autographs, waiting outside the dressing rooms in Lansdowne Road, but here we didn't need to, since they were all on one sheet. Unfortunately, we cut up the list to paste the names into our autograph books, thereby diminishing their value. Still, it was a nice gesture.

So two pieces of family art are connected through the decades and through Irish rugby internationals for the Lions.

Also in the backyard there was an old woman seated with her hand raised. She was inspired by the begging women Eddie constantly saw in Germany in the 1950s, and as a sculpture she would go on some amazing journeys. Her name was *Anna*, and we were regularly photographed sitting beside her or up on her bony knees, cradled by the woman's concave body and outstretched arm.

She was a complete contrast to *The Bather* or the big-hipped nude made out of bomb casings. She was life-size, or near enough when old age gets to you and the body begins to shrink. Her gender was also indeterminate. There are no clothes, just a breast-less body which poverty has turned into that of an old man. One leg is crossed with a foot propped up on the knee of another leg, while a splayed hand rests wearily on the other thigh. Her feet are long, like thin little flippers, and she has a shrinking, emaciated head with tight hair.

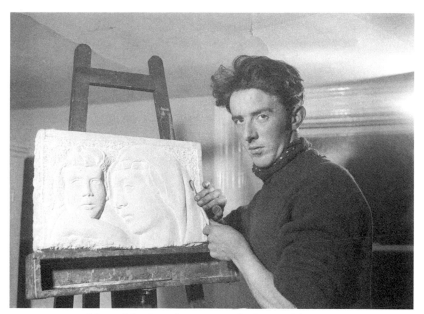

Man of destiny: the young artist in Munich, 1957
Photograph © Lensmen Photo Agency

A new decade: examining *Cuchulain and Hound*, Building Centre,
Baggot Street, Dublin 1960
Photograph © Lensmen Photo Agency

Eddie in front of *Land of Music*, his Yeats-inspired copper panel
to love and music.
Photograph © G.A. Duncan

A 1960s moment: poet Patrick Kavanagh in front of *Cathedral* on
RTÉ TV programme, *Spectrum*, 1964

Photograph © RTÉ Stills Library

A monotype drawing
of the author by his
father, 1962

Heading for casting in Milan: Thomas Davis in the back garden
in Dún Laoghaire
Photograph © Office of Public Works

DUBLIN OPINION

Humour is the Safety Valve of a Nation

Dublin Opinion cartoon on the Davis statue

A crayon drawing of the author by his father, at a children's birthday party, wearing a paper crown.

The sculptor fixing the Davis fountain
Photograph © *The Irish Times*

Ready to march: Wolfe Tone in the workshop, Dún Laoghaire

Eddie absorbed in welding
Photograph © John Walker

Chieftains 4
album cover

I vaguely knew she was inspired by German suffering, but it was only when I came across a scrapbook cutting that I got the full story. The accompanying photo shows Eddie sitting beside *Anna* and tenderly holding her hand, a spirit of empathy which is reflected in the article. 'Memory of a war-time city' is the headline, with the sub-head 'Statue is a symbol of Munich mystery'.

At first, I thought the photo was taken in Germany itself, given Eddie's baggy, 1950s-style suit, white open-necked shirt and what look like large brothel creepers: Eddie Cochran as a sculptor. In fact, it is in Dublin, 1960, at his third one-man show, and the exhibition that put him on the map. Here is the article:

> A few years ago a young Irish wandering-student sat looking out of the window of his lodgings in the great city of Munich.
>
> It was in the dread lean years at the end of war, and across the street from him was an office where bereft, war-stricken, poverty-stricken people queued up looking for various forms of material relief.
>
> There was a bench by the side of the street where a few old women sat, tired from long journeys in search of aid, worn and twisted, also, from old age. Every time they raised a hand in a gesture it seemed as if they were imploring the skies for assistance.
>
> And looking at them the young Irishman made a statue so that he would never forget them and so that other people might see in bronze his symbol of the mystery of agony and life surviving in spite of agony. You can see that extraordinary piece of bronze if you go to Edward Delaney's exhibition at the Building Centre in Baggot Street.
>
> With insight and wisdom, the young sculptor has called his Munich memory: 'Anna Livia'. For he realises, as James Joyce did, that every great river is an old woman and every river on which towns and villages

85

live and grow and die holds in itself, as old age does,
the mystery of simultaneous life and decay.

Alas, the cutting is unsigned, which is a pity, for it is a singular piece
of writing. Nor is the newspaper identifiable – it could be a
provincial title. But it invokes other images, like the eating of dead
horses or the famous image of a white statue over Dresden,
beholding the destruction below – another woman with her arm
outstretched. This is always a poignant sight, incidentally:
sculptures outliving the human destruction around them, like
Daniel O'Connell, wise and magisterial, looking down grimly over
the wreckage of 1916 and of the subsequent Civil War. *So this is
what your revolution has brought us.*

At the 1960 exhibition, *Anna* is at one end of a long room, with
other works and drawings around the walls. Another photo shows
her from behind, with her head looking down to her side, as if she's
checking her change: counting the day's takings, as it were. This is
a key asset of sculpture if properly executed – the ability of the
figure to be seen from all angles and to offer different aspects. And
Anna photographed well from any angle.

This was not always the case with Eddie's work, a point made
by the critic Bruce Arnold, in an *Irish Independent* review entitled
'One Way View of Delaney'. Arnold's point was that Eddie was
often drawing from a different European sculptural tradition. For
example, also visible in this Building Centre show is a nude figure,
against the wall, with her hands behind her back; mainly because
her back is problematic and she is intended to be seen from the
front. I know this because when I visited the figure's current
owners, Sean and Rosemarie Mulcahy, I found her standing just
like this in a staircase window, her front lit by the garden daylight.
We were trying to decide on her inclusion in the 2004
retrospective.

The Mulcahys have a beautiful house, filled with art and fine
furniture. But I was surprised to see also a framed photo of Michael
Collins and Richard Mulcahy, in the uniform of the Free State.

Mulcahy had been head of the army during the Civil War and had presided over the execution of Republicans. 'How come there's a picture of Richard Mulcahy?' I asked.

'Because he was my father,' said Sean and, after a pause, we resumed our discussion about the art.

'Right,' I said, and we decided to put the nude into the retrospective.

Meeting the collectors was always an interesting experience.

For example, at the other end of the Building Centre exhibition is a large *Dancing Figure*, now owned by a family in Dublin who have only Eddie's work in their house. And his work is all over their house, with dancers and horses on shelves and tables. It was such a close relationship that Eddie gave them a present of an unusual sculpture, fashioned from the spillages of metal on his studio floor: branches of bubbled bronze shaped into trees and further figures. The elderly parents told me wearily that their children had already divided up the sculpture for their future inheritance.

At the centre of the room, meanwhile, is *Sea Creature*, a large abstract bronze which stands like a headless seal or a twisted root vegetable. In Colman Doyle's *People of Ireland*, the piece is pictured next to Eddie. It is another of those hammed-up 'working sculptor' shots with Eddie leaning back in his torn overalls and an upended hat. By his side, *Sea Creature* seems to be imitating him – or is it the other way round? – as it coyly folds back a single flipper, or arm.

Also visible at the Building Centre show is *Cuchulain and Hound*, a mid-sized figure crouching forward with a spear, while an animal leaps up beside him. Later it was bought by Dr Kearney in Cork and sold as part of his extensive collection at Adams in December 2007. A catalogue photo showed the piece inside the family home in Cork, and in a report about the sale on the TV news, Kearney's daughter, Mary, described growing up with such art and how 'you'd come in the door and throw your coat over an Eddie Delaney'. Hearing this confirmed how much these sculptures had become a part of other people's childhood. Just as meeting the collectors confirmed how much they'd become a part of someone else's day.

At the Adams auction, *Cuchulain and Hound* was sold to a collector in London, where hopefully it will go on to become part of someone else's childhood. (The identity of buyers at auction is supposed to be confidential but they often make contact later, seeking information.) At the 1960 exhibition, *Anna* presides over them all, and sits in the room like a tired gallery attendant. A wide-angled photograph of the show, taken from the far end of the room, won a prize for Richard Deegan at the 'One in a Hundred' photo exhibition held by the Photographic Society in Dublin. It is entitled *At an Exhibition*.

Anna's next outing was to Ardmore Studios in Wicklow to appear in a movie called *Dementia 13*, directed by Francis Ford Coppola and produced by Roger Corman. The film was Coppola's first film as a director and so has become something of a feature on the B-movie circuit. The film was originally called *The Haunted and the Hunted*, which, I think, is a better title. It could even describe his work.

Coppola had become a protégé of Roger Corman, a stalwart of American exploitation cinema, and came with Corman to Ireland for the making of *The Young Racers*. After securing money from an English producer he met in Dublin, and another investment from Corman, he made *Dementia 13* with a crew of nine and a script he had written in three nights. (Just about the timeframe for the casting of a sculpture.) The film clearly intended to cash in on *Les Diaboliques* and *Psycho* and was shot over three weeks at Ardmore and County Wicklow. It stars Patrick Magee and William Campbell, for whom Samuel Beckett wrote *Krapp's Last Tape*.

As one critic put it, the 'confused drama is standard psycho-thriller nonsense', but there are 'glimpses of Coppola's later talent, especially in the claustrophobic atmosphere and a couple of dream sequences'. The plot involves an axe murderer running amok during a family reunion in an isolated castle. One of them is a sculptor, busy in his studio, with his 'creations', which are basically Eddie's sculptures on loan. *Anna* is particularly prominent. She even appears on the movie's poster, with its garish lettering, as well as in the film's main publicity still, which is an image of the sculptor sinisterly embracing his girlfriend, while *Anna* looms in the foreground. She appears to be looking away: *I don't want to see what you guys are up to.*

In one scene, we see the absorbed sculptor chipping away at his work – pretend chipping, obviously – while his bored girlfriend declares grumpily, 'I wish you'd spend as much time on me as you spend on your sculptures.' To which my mum – and ourselves – might have said, 'Amen to that.'

There is also a major endorsement for Aer Lingus, since the national airline had supported the production. This involved visitors being met at Dublin airport while the airline's logo was repeatedly and ostentatiously shown – along with Tannoy announcements about 'Aer Lingus flights'. It is an outrageous early example of product placement and gave Ireland the sort of energetic 1960s glamour that the then government would have wanted.

Eddie was waiting for a big cheque for his own 'product placement', but instead Francis Ford Coppola just gave him a ten bob note and said, 'Here, buy yourself a drink.' Eddie was furious. Years later, whenever Coppola's subsequent classics came on the TV, Eddie would mutter something about how 'that fecker still owes me money'.

Anna is also the star of Jim Fitzgerald's *Spectrum* documentary, made around the same time. Indeed, the film is so similar to *Dementia 13* in some of its imagery and atmosphere – the darkened skies and haunted shapes – that one almost suspects Corman and Coppola had seen it and got the idea for the use of sculpture.

After each of these appearances, *Anna* returned to Stone View, where she continued to be photographed. In the *Farmers Journal* Eddie is shown repairing her feet, leaning in close so that her head is gazing at the back of his head. She looks suddenly older, like an aged lady in a nursing home. *Thank you for looking after me.*

In one family photo, Colm and I are sitting up on her, in our small dungarees and tartan shirts, like something out of the TV series *The Waltons*. And then we have the whole family around her, with my mum looking fairly glum. She looks like she'd willingly trade places with the bronze old woman. It is 1969 and she is pregnant again, a situation that made her want to leave Stone View altogether and persuade Eddie to get a new house somewhere else. The pregnancy would be her fourth and would give us another brother, Gary, or Garech, as he was properly christened, after the pony-tailed man himself.

Anna was then brought to Connemara, sitting right up front in the Renault 12 and startling fellow motorists at traffic lights. These were lively car rides, in which Eddie transported sculpture – and furniture – across Ireland, including bouncing rods of steel, which created sparks on the road. Rather than focus on finding a new house in Dublin, he was building up a base in the West, where a large extension was now planned for the original farmhouse. But my mother had no intention of making this her new permanent home, or ours, and the marriage endured further strain.

In Galway, *Anna* was put on a rock facing the bay and sat imploring the ocean like the old woman in Synge's *Riders of the Sea*. And then she was finally sold and went down the coastline, to the small village of Costelloe, and into the back garden of Jack Toohey, a former businessman who had himself moved permanently to Connemara, having made his fortune in Dublin in the rag trade. Jack was originally from Limerick and of Lithuanian Jewish background. The family name was Tooch, but it had been changed to the more Irish-sounding Toohey. (This was not the only collector of Eddie's work to have a truncated Jewish surname. Among his collectors in New York were Roger Deitz and Norman Arnoff, originally Deitzman and Arnofski, until their forbears, or an obliging Ellis Island clerk, thought that the shorter version would do better in Anglo-Saxon America.)

Jack Toohey was an old friend of Eddie's and had built up an impressive art collection, much of it housed in Costelloe Lodge, which, with its mown lawns and stables, was an unusual feature in this Connemara landscape of rocks and cottages. It also adjoins the spot where the Casla River and upper Connemara connects to the sea, and hence it is rich fishing ground. Like the Ellis Island clerk, the English surveyors dealt in euphonics and changed 'Casla' to the more recognisable 'Costelloe'. The house's original owners were detached colonials who had a life almost completely separate from the local community and held parties just like at Castlemacgarrett, except the Brownes were, by contrast, almost native. Other toffs came in from 'the rest of the UK' for fishing parties and long weekends. Lemons were shipped in and endless supplies of ice. But the colonials faded away, as they do, and the house was bought by Bruce Ismay, who owned the White Star shipping line and, most notoriously, the *Titanic*. Apparently, he never recovered from the shock and used to pace the garden thinking about it, the very garden in which *Anna* would eventually sit.

When Jack died, his widow Agnes donated *Anna*, and other sculptures, to the Irish Museum of Modern Art (IMMA) in Dublin, situated in the Royal Hospital in Kilmainham. This was the old soldiers' hospital modelled on Les Invalides in Paris. The idea was to erect *Anna* outside in Jack's memory. And so a sculpture inspired by German suffering would become the subject of Jewish philanthropy. And, by a further irony, she would go into a hospital for British soldiers. But whereas they were all in the ground, she would be visible and sitting up, like a defiant nude cast from Allied shells. And she would sit by Joyce's Liffey, a winding river, just like the winding story of one sculpture, which begins in Munich in the 1950s, takes in Francis Ford Coppola and the *Titanic*, and ends in a field near Dublin City. As that anonymous journalist wrote, 'Every great river is an old woman … which holds in itself, as old age does, the mystery of simultaneous life and decay.'

CHAPTER 7

Making the Mould

It is worth describing the casting process, as best I can remember it.

Basically, the oven was a small space, in a corner of the workshop, which was built up each time and destroyed, for it was not just the moulds that were temporary, but the actual ovens. It had a long stove chimney, and for each cast the walls were carefully assembled again with small bricks and plaster, just like the makeshift ovens you'd see in those illustrations of the ancient Greeks or Egyptians, and whom Eddie claimed to be emulating. The moulds, of hard but brittle white plaster, were then lined up inside and the oven closed over. Sometimes, if it was a big project, the oven was like a small room or stable, and Eddie would stand there building up the wall like Vincent Price in *The Pit and the Pendulum*, the horror story by Edgar Allen Poe, whom coincidentally he loved and was endlessly quoting. What also comes to mind is another Vincent Price movie, *House of Wax* (and another Roger Corman film) in which a deranged sculptor turns people into wax statues. We alerted Eddie to this in later years and when he saw it he was delighted.

Once sealed, the ovens are set alight with a gas supply and filled with coke, a sort of oxidised coal, which is slow burning and thus used for railway engines. It takes a long time to reach the required temperature and as long again to bring it down. In the meantime, the moulds are left there, cooking away. Eddie would get up during the night to feed more coke into the oven, shovelling it in through side vents. He would check in on us lying in our beds and then on his moulds. And on ours too, if we had sculptures included. For much of the night, we lay there, thinking about our little statues cooking away and the moulds taking shape.

Catherine Ann Heaney told me she would go to sleep at night with the noise of her father typing away at his poetry. And, as a child, Séamus Ennis went to sleep to the sound of his father's pipes and remembers desperately trying to stay awake to hear the end of the *Munster Buttermilk*. But, for us, it was the humming of the ovens and the screech of shovelled coal.

After a day or two, the wax inside the moulds would melt away and the moulds were removed and brought out into the workshop. Meanwhile, the furnace would be switched on. This was like a giant vat with thick cement-clad sides and a slide-on lid. Into it went crucibles filled with scrap and metal ingots. These were the pots or urns in which the metal was melted. This would require the heat being increased dramatically, during which the furnace would shudder furiously, until it reached 700°C. As the metal began to liquefy, Eddie would slide off the lid and help the melt along by stoking it with a long pole. The crucible was then removed with long tongs and allowed to stand for a moment, although not for too long as molten metal hardens quickly.

A number of procedures now occur which I don't have the precise details of, such as the addition of powders and elements to the bubbling mix. This is where the famous personal nature of the process comes in. Much depends, for example, on what percentages of metal – copper, manganese or tin – is in the crucible. Silicon is added to clean the mix and remove gases. The key thing is to move quickly, stirring the surface until it glows a bright red and getting rid of bits of dross and slag. What remains is the flux, the pure molten metal that will go into the waiting moulds and fill up the air spaces inside to create sculptures. These are all words that have gone into the language: dross, slag, crucible.

As Eddie often said, the basic process was unchanged from ancient times, and it certainly looked that way. With the long tongs, for example, a man took either side of the crucible and poured out the metal, just like in our history schoolbooks or a scene from one those biblical epics by Cecil B. DeMille, with leather-sandaled soldiers in the castle dungeon, casting more swords for battle. One pot could fill two or three small moulds, beginning with those for the most intricate sculptures, since the metal is at its most fluid at the start and needs to get around the mould and its cavities at an even pace. 'Turbulence' has to be avoided and the trapped air bubbles which put holes in the bronze.

The 'Dance of the Pour', as it was called, was a fast and nimble exercise for which Eddie needed an assistant. It could be his brother Tim, called out from his plastics business, or the sculptor John Behan, for whom a place was often kept at the dinner table. But some unexpected people have become assistants in the pour, often having to leave the dinner table – as in dinner party table – if they'd stayed beyond midnight, and rolling up their sleeves for a bout in the burning workshop. I don't think Garech was ever prevailed upon – I don't think Garech ever did a tap of physical labour – but some of the more macho journalists enjoyed getting stuck in and recounted the tales afterwards in print, and in pubs.

Needless to say, all of the above was done in great heat, during which Eddie would lose pounds of weight in perspiration. It was the 'Dance of the Pour' in more ways than one. Like his wax figures, he too was melting away, and if his bronze pieces came out all bulked up, he himself emerged thinner from the process, a transformation that pleased him. No wonder journalists commented on his 'lean and rakish' appearance.

Once the metal is allowed to cool, the moulds are broken open and hunks of plaster pulled off. This was an extraordinary act of destruction that amazed us. As kids, you love to go wrecking things, so to see it done so wantonly by our father was impressive. Plaster is hacked off, until eventually a raw figure starts to emerge. It was like the stone carver 'freeing the figure', except in this case the figure is already made. It was then scraped down, but the metal is still extremely hot and would be put under water to erupt in spumes of steam. By now Eddie was very happy and broke into poetry again: *Water, water everywhere and not a drop to drink.*

The steam would clear and further cleaning was done. This is a process known as 'devestment', as opposed to 'investment', which is the building up of the mould around the original wax figure. Runners and risers are also removed. Runners are applied as wax rods to the figure to help the metal flow around the space and risers, meanwhile, allow the air to escape as the metal runs in. A runner connecting the legs, for example, would let the metal flow directly between two knees rather than have to go back through the trunk, as blood would do in a human body. These rods are cut off with an electric saw, and the loud whine of the blade was a sign that the serious work had begun. The wheel blade made a noise like a racing car, peaking and moaning as it dragged on the metal, and spilled out a delightful fizzle of sparks. The smell of cut metal was strong.

After this, the long and patient task of 'chasing' the metal begins, with holes being welded shut or bronze being gouged back out of intended fissures. Hammers and chisels are used here, and for the larger sculptures, which have been cast in sections, chasing was needed to remove the weld lines and smooth the joins. It is a sensitive process, which requires much filing and brazing, or in some cases roughing up, especially if the texture needs to be punched back into the metal. In effect, the sculptor is seeking to recreate the wax model, with all its delicacy and energy. It is like with writing, where the objective of all the re-working and revision is often nothing less than retrieving the freshness of the original creation. Or as Yeats put it, if a line which could take us hours 'does not seem a moment's thought', then 'our stitching and unstitching has been naught'.

The whole process would be done pleasantly to music in the workshop, where the radio was almost permanently on. It was the same with our own sculptures, although obviously we were kept away from dangerous tools. Over subsequent days, the polishing continued and the patina prepared. This is the chemical colouring that enhances the sculpture's surface, using durable, darker colours for outdoor sculptures, so they can blend with the natural elements. Direct patinas are usually stippled on and then scorched with a flame to bond the colour. Finally, in an unintended echo of the original, a thin protective coat of wax is rubbed over the whole figure.

After the cast, there was the cleaning up and collecting of bricks for future moulds. There was also the picking up of metal spillages, those branches of bronze, with their wrinkled surfaces, which were either reused or shaped into little sculptures. Some years ago a small piece of Eddie's came up for auction: a girl sitting on a bench under a tree – the girl was very slender with knees together and the tree was a burst of frozen bronze. I thought it was exquisite but I lost out at auction: these were the impecunious days when I tried to flog Garech's 'Georgian' hip flask. The girl then appeared in the window of a fine art shop in Clare Street, looking across at the office of Samuel Beckett's father. This is known as a 'turnaround', where a dealer buys a lot at auction only to sell it again quickly. However, after making enquiries, I missed out again on the sitting figure. Third time lucky perhaps.

Eddie made much of the casting process and spoke about it repeatedly, as do many in the art world, and it is a core feature of modern sculpture. On the floor of his studio in Carraroe, I found a copy of *Sculpture* magazine and was intrigued to see that some American artists had regarded the foundry itself as an art form. They would video a casting and metal pour – 'a spectacular, sizzling one-night-only performance' – and show the film at art events. 'It's perfectly choreographed,' they said. 'It's like you move pragmatically to the timing of the furnace.' They were also keen to pay homage to the great American tradition of industrial casting and held commemorative 'pours' at the sites of now disused iron works.

Sculpture magazine was published by the International Sculpture Centre in Washington, and for years it arrived in Galway, a long-term gift subscription from the collector Roger Dietz in New York.

It must have sustained Eddie through all those years making sculpture out on the deserted west coast, with just the trawlers and seagulls visible through the window. The magazine connected him to a global brotherhood with its articles on trends and exhibitions, and practical advice on commissions and legalities. In the issue mentioned above, for example, there was an article on the rusting tendencies of Cor-Ten Steel, a material that in the 1970s transformed sculpture, especially in the US. The self-protecting rust was usually welcomed by the artist, but not by the commissioning officials.

The ritual of the foundry was a process that bewitched many. Seamus Murphy was one of those whose work Eddie cast and, in a book about him, his daughter Orla described coming to workshops such as my father's. 'Foundries have almost mythological magic,' she wrote. 'The great heavy implements, the noise of the smelting, the vibration of the furnace and its terrifying exhilarating heat-becoming-light as the door is opened. The whole complex chemistry of *cire perdue* (lost wax) and the processes by which different colours are created fascinated Murphy, and when he no longer had to send his work to Fiorini & Kearney and other great foundries because casting was being done in Ireland, he enjoyed many visits.'

Murphy, who worked mainly in stone, was Eddie's forbear in Irish sculpture and it was a compliment for him to cast his work. The only item in the big red scrapbook that is not a cutting is a telegram from Murphy after the Tone unveiling. When Murphy died in 1975, Eddie was quoted in the *Irish Press*, lamenting the loss of 'one of the last stonecutters and an outstanding crafts man. He did not get involved in theory. He was very simple in his work. You could not have learned from a better man. He will be a great loss to Cork, as the people there supported him.'

The last line was a dig at Eddie's host towns of Dún Laoghaire and Galway, neither of which he felt supported him. In Cork, however, there was a sculpture park and art museums and practitioners such as Murphy and Jerome Connor. In later years, there was even the Sculpture Factory, a dedicated space with special industrial-type studios, and galleries such as the Crawford. There were also many private collectors in Cork, with names such as Kearney, Hennessy and Gerry Goldberg, the former Lord Mayor, who also collected Matisse and Picasso. This tradition continues with the recent building on the university campus of the excellent Glucksman Gallery, through the generosity of benefactor Loretta Brennan Glucksman.

According to Peter Murray, Eddie was 'responsible for an output of sculpture in the 1960s and 1970s which was simply remarkable given that he did so much of the casting work himself'. But this was why he did so: it enabled him to have total control over the process and all its aspects.

Murray was writing in the *Irish Arts Review* on the occasion of the 2004 retrospective in Dublin. (It could never be said, incidentally, that Dublin has not been kind to Eddie.) The RHA show was the subject of a number of essays that describe my father's work better than I ever could, and from which I intend to quote during the course of this book. This is not false modesty. I could never have the sufficient critical distance or broader context that they have and I am too bound up with the origin (and fate) of the actual works.

Here, for example, is Aidan Dunne in *The Irish Times*:

> Delaney's expenditure of energy throughout the 1960s was prodigious. Yet there was nothing modish or ephemeral about what he was doing. The works he created then combine the age-old mystique of the medieval master-craftsman with the sensibility of a European modernist. Add to the mix a concern with Irish national identity and a romanticised Celtic imagery and you have something of the distinctive flavour of his rugged, ancient-modern figures. His feat in casting the three-quarter ton figure of Wolfe Tone out in the open at his own studio in Dún Laoghaire

was positively heroic and recalls a key episode in Andrei Tarkovsky's film about the icon painter, Andrei Rublev. The episode is an allegory about the artistic process. The cathedral needs a new bell but the master bell-caster has died. His teenage son claims to have inherited his secret and supervises the huge project. Failure means death. Only when the bell has tolled does he break down and confess to Rublev that his father had died before he could pass on the secret of his passing.

This is interesting. Yet I don't know all the secrets by now. It is frustrating, perhaps, but obviously I'd left it too long to be a father to get advice from him on rearing a newborn son. But then maybe I didn't want to know. I had to find out myself. But I was still in search of an engagement ring and on that subject there was a suggestion.

When my father went into a nursing home and reluctantly left his house and studio – still full of his work – he sowed the rumour that somewhere in or around the house were 30 silver rings that he had made and buried. Paranoid about thieves, he would hide things so well that he couldn't find them himself. The implication was that the rings were there to be found, if one had the energy to look for them. But I wasn't going to get into this charade: you could be searching for ever. Somebody (who clearly hadn't visited the house) suggested that a metal detector be used, not realising that to do such would be to risk being torn apart by a shower of metal, coming out of everywhere: the floor, the grass and possibly even the trees and sky. Sometimes a 'found object' is best left unfound.

The secrets that were passed on, however, were the techniques for making sculpture. Not casting them, but creating the originals in wax. Our sticky brown figures were inspired by his, but the subjects were our own: footballers, dancers, a cat – in no particular order. The wax was scooped out of a bubbling pot, a soft material that hardened slowly and cracked pleasurably when splashed on the skin. The cauldron was added to with the burnt candles of dinner parties, and we would finish our figures inside the house by the fireplace, with knives reddened by the open grate.

A delicious sizzle would sound as the hot knife smoothed the figure, along with the distinctive sweet smell of the burning wax. Things could be added: twigs as limbs or material for clothing. To give it bulk, a figure could be wrapped in hessian, as if it was medical dressing, and often it was medical dressing, or bandages to see it through. The original armature, meanwhile (if there was one), looked like a series of splints or artificial limbs. Sometimes a further mould might be taken of the figure for future editions, created with a covering of gelatine rubber and known as the 'mother mould'.

This mould is different, obviously, to the casting mould, which is destroyed. Instead, it becomes the one for future editions. However, in Eddie's case these were few. Usually for him, the figure was a once off and there were no duplicates. Almost all of his work is unique. The only exceptions were some of the *Marching Women* series and a few horses, although even these he varied by changing the legs a bit. In retrospect, his dedication to a sculpture's 'uniqueness' was impressive, given how many artists retain their moulds carefully so as to knock out future editions. One of Eddie's problems with the Yeats memorial in St Stephen's Green, for example, is that the sculpture is one of three and so is not specifically inspired by Yeats. The piece may even have been made before Henry Moore got the commission. (Although there is another debate here, as to whether this is such a bad thing.)

In the yard were the heaps of scrap for melting down. The sources were interesting – spent bullets, railings, doorknobs. Many victorious powers used the ordnance of defeated enemies for their celebratory war memorials. The panels on the Wellington war memorial in the Phoenix Park are cast from captured Prussian cannons. Tone was possibly cast with stolen metal. This was the rumour afterwards. Eddie would be relying on scrap dealers, after all, who often had dodgy channels for their stuff. Sometimes there would be legless cherubs or ornate bits of Victorian kitsch. One was a mock classical figure of a man throwing a disc, like something you would see in a garden centre. Awaiting meltdown, the naked disc thrower was perched on top of a wall. 'Ah, but this is lovely!' cried Mrs Mulligan, a neighbour. A dentist's wife, she was relieved that Eddie could make something so conventional. My father was tickled by this backhanded compliment and gave the frozen disc-thrower a reprieve, leaving him to fade away in the grass.

However, often the scrap *was* worth saving and had a sculptural quality, whether intended or not. Much of it came from his brother Tim. Tim was actually in plastics and had a company called Irish Plastic Developments – great 1960s name – but he could also lay his hands on metal units, baths and fabricators. Eddie would go through crates of the stuff and suddenly come upon some pop-art oddity. 'Woah, hold on to that,' he'd tell Gary. 'That can go on the wall.'

One was a tray for making ice pops, an aluminium square of dropped tubes like tentacles. Another was an old van radiator of compressed lead, like the layers of a Flake chocolate bar. Eddie boxed it in a polished steel frame and mounted it on a base of black stone. It looked great, like a honey box, except in metal. Another was a big brass clock piece, with a section cut away to reveal its inner workings, like the Pomodoro sculpture in Trinity College.

Meanwhile I was particularly proud of the frame of an old radio I had found on the shoreline, which had turned a gorgeous rusted orange, and which I still have to this day, with its strange buttonhole eyes and punched-out squares like a cookie cutter. All of these discoveries were heartening, of course. If almost everything has some aesthetic value, then we are all much closer to the concept of sculpture than we imagine. Not only the objects humanised by wear and tear – old farm irons, a worn out gate – especially if taken out of context, but also those twisted into new and 'alternative' shapes.

Eddie would, however, face the dilemma common to many artists: if it's good enough as it is, why make it into something different and possibly destroy its original effect? This was even more the case in Galway, where we would bring in driftwood from the beach or old animal bones from the fields, washed by the rain and bleached by the wind and sun. Or weather-beaten stones, twisted like pieces of lunar lava. Striking in themselves, these shouldn't and couldn't be 'improved' upon. Thus, a luminous sea urchin, shorn of its spikes, didn't need to be turned into a parlour lampshade, with a cockleshell base. An ancient bog oak, pulled from the peat, was magnificent as it was and didn't need to be carved and polished, like you'd see in the craftwork galleries of country towns.

In an *Irish Press* article, Eddie explained how the West had changed his aesthetic. 'Not far away from where I live I used to pass a wrecked car lying in the bog. The patina of the car had changed to gold. It looked beautiful and powerful. I eventually brought it home but the effect was lost when I placed it among the stones. It looked better in the bog.'

Sometimes a 'found object' is best left unfound.

In the same article, he also discusses why he didn't want to make bronze work in Connemara. 'A bronze sculpture doesn't look anything down there, because of being surrounded by the age-old sculptures of rocks and stone walls.'

This was what the west would do. But this discovery would coincide with other things in his life. It was 1980 and his marriage had broken up, and he was now living in Galway with a new partner and family. The *Irish Press* interview was done to accompany an exhibition called *Blue City*, which was of large-scale work done entirely in stainless steel. Bronze was fine in an urban environment, but in the barren west, it was simply overwhelmed by the landscape, and its abandonment by Eddie must have come as something of a relief.

It is ironic that someone so in love with the casting process should just abandon it, but this was in tandem with what was happening elsewhere. In the US, sculptors had shown the effect of large pre-fabricated iron and steel sculptures in overpowering landscapes – the desert or flat plains or downtown plazas. Eddie had always had an interest in this sort of work, especially that done by David Smith and now by Richard Serra. Reading the American sculpture magazines encouraged him in this direction, as well as an easy access to pre-fabricated steel. Soon he was over in Rossaveal Harbour looking at the sheet-iron sides of trawlers and ships. The magazines also highlighted ceramic shell casting, which was a fast alternative to the lost-wax method and tended to demystify the rituals of the ancient *cire perdue*.

Art was increasingly moving towards concept and theory (disastrously so, in some cases) and away from an emphasis on process and physicality. Some even questioned whether an artist should get involved at all in the casting of their work and suggested that they just submit a model or plan. For Eddie, such an abdication would seem to defeat the whole purpose of being a sculptor, but he was anxious himself to move away from the polished, 'craftsman-like' aspect of the profession.

Besides, bronze had become too much like something you'd put on a pedestal, or on the boardroom table, and Eddie didn't want to feel like he was just pre-programmed to keep knocking them out. 'I could have made a lot of money making twelve Robert Emmets,' he said in the same *Irish Press* article, 'or dozens of horses, but I wasn't interested in that.'

It is curious that Eddie should pick Emmet as an example, since he didn't sculpt him. Was this to show just how interchangeable these sculpted patriots were? The derisive 'twelve' is also interesting. A production-line output would have been demoralising enough, but can you imagine the effect of producing multiple war heroes?

Eddie would resist this commercial tendency in a radical fashion, as the *Irish Press* journalist discovered. 'I stood in the gallery totally amazed at the new and exciting direction his sculpture had taken. It was completely unlike anything he had previously done. Almost three dozen stainless-steel works were either freestanding or hanging on the walls. They were largely non-representational, although they owed their inspiration to natural phenomena such as forests, clouds, stars and the sun.'

'Certainly these new sculptures couldn't lose their identity on any site,' she added. 'For one thing they are big, some of them reach 18 to 30 feet: soaring shapes which are basically steel columns topped by elaborate arrangements of fronds, circular shapes and cascading rods.' The series was related to *Blue City*, the same name he gave his proposal to replace Nelson's Pillar, the giant 'bull-worker', so to speak.

The *Irish Press* writer was Blaithín Ó Ciobháin, who also presented a TV art show for kids called *Let's Draw with Blaithín*. (The show has been described as 'the world's first televised fine arts master class' and ran for 14 years.) This is appropriate for, in a sense, what Eddie was trying to do with *Blue City* and, indeed, throughout his whole life: to restore the magic of making art as a child. His objective was to retain the child-like wonder of creativity, much as Blaithín explored, and not to get stuck in a rut like other artists. By playing with us, and teaching us, he was re-igniting this adventure and momentarily getting his childhood back (just as I am doing, by re-enacting the memory of it all in print).

Eddie treated his pieces like toys, placing them all out in a line, or putting them up in a tree, and then lying down on the ground and looking up at them to get their perspective. For what were sculptures (or paintings), after all, but oversized toys. This also goes for the collectors, gazing at their pieces in the garden or talking about collecting 'the full set'. When I met Gordon Lambert, whose bequest formed the original core of the IMMA collection, he was sitting in front of a small bronze dancer. Frail and elderly, he was like a young girl before a doll. He had already told me in a phone message, his voice strained by a stroke, that he had nothing left of Eddie's work except a dancer 'whom I love dearly and from whom I shall never be parted'. Think of sculptures as toys for adults and you will be a happy man all your life.

It was more practical to learn how to draw. Here the secrets were more easily passed on: how to sketch quickly and how to build up shadow. How, by drawing quickly, you lost your inhibitions and became loose and free, but also focused. The key was to approach the paper with confidence and exploration: see where the pen took you. You might start with a vanishing point and then get the perspective. Perspective was important. The sky was not up high as a blue line, as other kids at school drew, but everywhere – it was the air, essentially, and came around your head. The sun wasn't spiky but round. The eyes on a face were not fully defined, but open and unfinished, as was the mouth, with the lips as light markings.

Nothing was wrong, everything was process and 'mistakes' were as valid as the 'correct version'. This was extraordinarily liberating. You master what is ostensibly the correct procedure and then depart from it: this was even more empowering. You were in control of the process, and yet – an apparent paradox – the process was controlling you. All artists aspire to create as a child does, but Eddie particularly did. He loved children's art. Opening a children's art show in Portlaoise, he was full of praise but criticised the organisers for encouraging the kids to copy from Christmas cards, rather than their own imagination.

He did his own drawings on a big architect's set of drawers, with a large worktop. On this he would have his tools: Stanley knives, rollers, masking tape. Again, he would often work quickly, and he needed to, because clients were on the phone, urgently looking for commissioned work. Inside in the house, we would take phone messages. 'Eamon, me ould flower, how are you? Would you get your dad?'

'Hold on. He's out in the workshop.'

It was Paddy Maloney of the Chieftains. Taking phone calls from Paddy was always a treat, with his friendly salutations. 'He's like one of the little people – a lovely, lively leprechaun, with an enormous musical talent, and a sense of humour to match.' So wrote Peter Sellers and Spike Milligan on the sleeve of one of the Chieftains' records, and now Paddy was anxious to get the artwork to go with that quote.

'Oh, I'd better get cracking,' Eddie would say and he'd spring into action, like a musician himself.

His Chieftains covers were like action paintings, done with brightly coloured acrylic paint, which dripped like honey from a stick or knife. This was another reason to move quickly and yet what was surprising was again how precisely the images resembled those he did in pen and ink, or bronze or silver. *Chieftains 4* had standing figures in turquoise and black against a blue background, but *Chieftains 7* featured the band itself, sitting as fragmented purple silhouettes and playing against a blue and green background, just as if the music was shaking the paint and their bodies. I have some of the early drafts, done on square boards the size of an LP. In one case, he just took an LP by guitar player José Feliciano (*10 to 23*) and dipped the white sleeve in paint, with the disc still inside it. Another discarded draft has just the background but no figures: the place where the Chieftains 'were not'.

Our own paints were not acrylic, obviously, but watercolours, discs of hard powder like coloured mints in which we dabbed our wet brushes to release the colour gradually, and then tubes of stronger paint, which we diluted in glasses of water. We all worked around the table or down on the parquet floor, a cluster of us hunched over and surrounded by paints, crayons and pencils, both plain and coloured. Best of all were the markers, with which you could effectively draw and paint at the same time.

You draw something to comprehend it, whether it is a vision in your head or what is in front of you every day. Each night in the farmhouse the young Eddie sketched his parents when they feel asleep in front of the fire. He drew his father when he fell asleep for the last time in 1955, laid out on his deathbed: Patrick, the hunter, finally hunted himself. It is a fearless thing, to look at your father's corpse and try to capture it. I found it strange enough to look at my uncle, PJ. This was Eddie's way of digesting the event and achieving self-control in the face of grief. And in this very process, new truths will arise and clarify for the first time.

Could it be the same with the portrait of a newborn son? For, by contrast, Eddie did a drawing of me, at about 6 months old, in which I look as if I've just woken up. In the same way that he sketched his father leaving the world, he had drawn his son come into it – just the framework of my own narrative. Yet it didn't seem to bother Eddie that his father was dead before any of his children were born. The drawing is a mono print, so it is actually done as a negative, against glass, and drawn in reverse – a very difficult thing to do. The signature is wrong, with the D upside down. Eddie was dyslexic anyway and a poor speller, something not unusual among his generation and especially those of a modest background. Dyslexia is also not uncommon among visual artists.

My father also did another picture of me, which some collectors found when I was researching for the RHA retrospective. This time I am a few years old and at a children's party, an event I well remember with rice-crispie cakes, lemonade and paper hats. The drawing is done with crayons, and again I am looking alert and even glowing – it's a kid's party after all – with a green jumper and a blue paper crown on my head: pretender to the throne. The collectors kindly said they would give it to me when I had a child of my own.

Both portraits are very good likenesses, especially the first which is an almost photographic reproduction. People are often reassured when a modern artist art can do conventional realism, or that they have been trained and have clearly apparent 'natural talent'. They see an early traditional portrait by Picasso, are relieved and can go back reassured to his more difficult 'modern work'. Well, here's the proof. Eddie could be a traditional artist before being a modern one, just as he could be a regular father before being an artistic one.

CHAPTER 8

'The Man of Hard Materials'

It is clear from the scrapbooks that my father had a great rapport with journalists, and got a lot of publicity as a result. One reason is that he took them in on 'the performance': the modelling, the casting and the whole smoky ritual. It was an old and still primitive business, in contrast to the increasing delicacy of society and of their own profession, although their prose often rose to the occasion, as they sought to emulate the ritual with their own finely hewn descriptions.

Modern art was still covered as a news event, and this was part of Eddie's appeal: he defended contemporary art for the layman, away from the more specialised art magazines, which anyway barely existed then – even in the UK – and certainly nothing like today. Art was still just 'art' and there was a broader desire to understand, perhaps symptomatic of the curiosity and experimentation of the time. Although Eddie would never try to 'explain' contemporary visual art, and especially his own, he would happily talk about it and give it context.

A good example is Vinnie Doyle in the *Irish Independent*. Doyle would later become editor of the *Independent*, and remain editor there for nearly 30 years, but back then he was a young reporter, and his interview is a nice mixture of gritty American-style reporting and straight-talking Dub. 'The man of hard materials' was the headline.

> For the second time within an hour, Edward Delaney,
> Ireland's most promising young sculptor left his

backyard studio and returned with a half-dozen. Planking the parcel on the table he explained: 'Foresight. The backyard runs into a pub.'

Looking at Eddie Delaney drinking stout 'by the neck' you find him a man without dross. So direct, yet never disconcerting, a man who has been through the fires. Rather tall, gaunt and rakishly unkempt, he is, in one being a dreamer, a worker and an adventurer. Hacking away at a piece of stone he is always fully exposed, always ready to receive the first blow and the critics' jabs have been numerous. His career has been short but turbulent.

Squatting on an angel, the 30-year-old sculptor talked to me about his critics' favourite bandwagon – the price tag on his work. 'Of course my work is dear. I have got to do my own casting and I have one of the few places in Ireland where sculptors can cast. It costs me exactly a £100 a foot to cast work in bronze, and on top of that there is the cost of the bronze, plaster and other equipment. Anywhere else they charge from £150 to £180 a foot. Believe me, it is very hard work. How would you like to work for 10 hours a day in conditions like this?'

He pointed to the clay, coke and sand underfoot and to the smoke gushing from his furnace, frequently making us cough. After five hours in his studio I'm prepared to take his word for it. He emptied some bronze scrap into the furnace and went on about the money.

'You know,' he said, 'it is quite easy to be a success as a sculptor, providing the right sort of people like you. For instance, if you are a young and unconventional sculptor and three rich people get together and buy a pile of your stuff for say £15,000. Well no matter what you do in the future they must keep buying your work or else the value of the previous pieces they bought will slump.'

Another interview from a year earlier gives an account of Eddie's life before he married or went abroad. It was for the *Sunday Review*, a short-lived Sunday title for *The Irish Times.* The series was called 'Purely Personal' by Marion Fitzgerald, and in it Eddie is given full scope to go into detail about his artistic development, his background and his views on art.

'Red paint will not do to depict blood' is the curious headline.

When I first knew Edward Delaney he was known to all and sundry as 'The Colonel'. I didn't even know what his right name was for quite a while. We were all students at the College of Art together, and when the classes were over in the evening a crowd of us used to go and drink coffee and talk about art and life and what-have-you. The Colonel was always full of talk, of sculpture and painting, of the poetry he was writing and of the play he was working on.

I don't suppose we took him very seriously. For one thing, he was full of such enthusiasm for whatever he was talking about at a particular moment that his words could never keep up with what he wanted to say – and neither could we. Now, of all the people in that group, he is the only one who could be described as well known, not only in Ireland, but outside it as well.

Delaney lives out in Dún Laoghaire, where he has rebuilt, from two cottages, a home and a workshop. Everywhere there are bronzes: bronzes in the big spacious living room, with the inlaid wood floor – 'it was from an old house. I picked it up for £5 and laid it down myself' – bronzes in the yard outside, bronzes leaning against the walls.

Fitzgerald then broaches the big question.

> Unaccustomed as many people are to modern sculpture in this country, unattracted as many people might feel themselves to his work, I asked him to tell me something of his feelings about it.
>
> 'Well, I couldn't explain it at all,' he said. 'I don't think an artist could ever explain a piece of sculpture. An artist makes a statement: I make a statement in bronze. If anyone doesn't understand a statement made by an artist, I don't think it can be explained to them. I don't think people should expect to see an academic representation of the human body in a sculpture of an angel, for instance.
>
> 'I believe a spiritual figure should be an abstract form of harmony. Just as I don't believe in putting red paint on a figure of Christ and saying it's blood. Surely the figure of Christ should have a spiritual quality? I believe that spiritual quality should come from the way an artist shapes the material, moulds the forms. And sculpture, like every other art form, is always looking for a new way of expressing itself. There is no point in going back to the past and, say, trying to paint a fourteenth-century Madonna today. This was fine in the fourteenth century but not now.
>
> 'If you go to a non-Christian country and bring a European representation of a saint, a spiritual figure, you are immediately narrowing its terms of reference. But if you do a figure which tries to create an abstract symbol of spirituality, its appeal is much wider, more universal: it's not tied to a race, or a country, or even a creed.'
>
> He is primarily interested, he says, in sculpture which can be exhibited out of doors. 'I would love to see more sculpture in the public parks. I would love to

111

see cities like Dublin borrowing bronzes and sculptures and putting them up in the summer. I'd much prefer, for instance, to have my work in a garden in Dublin than in my garden.'

And this is what he got, a few years later: when both Davis and Tone went up in the Dublin 'gardens' of College Green and St Stephen's Green. And, of course, with his own sculpture park in Galway 20 years later.

My father did many Christs, including a giant figure, which he told the *Sunday Review* about, for the Drogheda hospital of the Medical Missionaries of Mary. The sculpture, about nine feet high, was entitled *Resurrection* and included 'about 90 square feet of reliefs inside the dome of the mortuary chapel, depicting the life of Jesus'. It was a big break early on for Eddie, and required many site visits. On one such trip, my mother gave birth inside the hospital to a second son, Colm.

Eddie valued his relationship with the church, which was one of his biggest patrons, as it has been for many artists, right down through the centuries. Indeed, his very first public display of a painting was in his local church at Crossboyne, where we went in 2007 to bury his brother, PJ, surrounded by the 2,000-year-old trees of Lord Oranmore's estate, and from where Eddie himself planned to be buried.

He subsequently did altar work for the church in Ballinasloe, and for St Marys Cathedral in Kilkenny, during which he developed a close relationship with Bishop Birch, a progressive prelate who held masses for Travellers. Both he and Eddie, the two boys, would consult over brandies in the bishop's quarter. Kilkenny was quite an Anglo-Irish town, with an emphasis on crafts and heritage. 'The Protestants think they're great with their Arts festival,' Birch told him. 'We'll show them.' Eddie loved this.

He also enjoyed the relationship because it was a meeting of like-minded opposites.

He liked to compare it to the relationship between Pope John and the Marxist Manzù, which became close during the making of the doors for St Peter's in Rome. The friendship is described in a book entitled *The Artist and the Pope* which Eddie picked as one of his favourite books for a radio series called *Speaking Volumes*. The others were *David Smith* by David Smith, with photographs and text by the American sculptor; *Selected Poems* by Austin Clarke; a coffee-table book called *Bronzes* by Jennifer Montague; and *Brendan Behan's Island: An Irish Sketchbook* by Behan, with drawings by Paul Hogarth, including one of our house and beach in Galway.

Also in Galway, but not among the list, is a hardback *History of Kilkenny College* by Bishop Birch, a gift from the progressive prelate before he died.

The panels in Kilkenny were essentially 'sculpted paintings', or two-dimensional sculptures, just like the doors of St Peter's. Eddie later told RTÉ Radio that he even helped Manzù put an actual chicken into a panel, dipping the dead bird in wax and casting it as it was: a chicken to match the Moore Street 'salmon'. No doubt Manzù also had some casting 'tricks' to pass on.

Eddie was very proud of the relationship with Manzù, and even said that he (unwittingly) introduced Manzù to his wife, the famous Susana of his drawings and sculptures, when he was asked to find the maestro a model. He describes going to see Manzù some years later and a woman answering the door, surrounded by a horde of children. I've no doubt people said the same about him. When I was in Rome, with my fiancée, I was very excited to see wax models of Susana. However, Eddie's story couldn't be true, since Manzù met Susana in 1953, years before Eddie met either of them. Nor could I find any chickens on the doors when Fiona and I did some charcoal rubbings, much to the bemusement of the strolling pilgrims.

According to Roisín Kennedy, in the catalogue essay for the RHA retrospective in 2004:

> Manzù was an important figure in Delaney's develop-
> ment as an artist because of his complex relationship to

Catholicism and his singular approach to his work. The experience of Fascism had led Manzù to become a Marxist during the Second World War but his later work continued to show a concern with religious subjects.

[Eddie's] choice of a Christian subject related to much wider aesthetic and psychological concerns. The elongated figure of Christ is echoed in the subsequent development of the attenuated anthropomorphic forms of his later work. *The Good Shepherd*, another ostensibly Christian subject, is presented in Delaney's work as a timeless Arcadian figure and bears no overt connection to any specific religious context. It is a vehicle for Delaney to experiment with the isolated human form. He plays on its stance – the arms folded behind the back, the relationship of the crook to the figure, the position of the shepherd's hat – all allow subtle and often amusing variations on a theme.

Ideas about art and spirituality are given more explicit expression in 1964 in an interview Eddie did in, of all places, the *Farmers Journal*. 'Out and About with the Farm Home Editor' is the tag line, 'An Artist and his work'.

The interview is interwoven with the passionate view of the writer himself, and is such a direct appeal for the artistic in the everyday that I excitedly assumed that it must be the poet Patrick Kavanagh, who wrote for the *Journal* at the time. But in fact, Kavanagh had just retired from the paper and the writer is Larry Sheedy, who was inspired by Kavanagh's style and views. Either way, it is clearly based on a substantial and passionate discussion with Eddie himself. It is worth quoting in full:

Everybody who knows Percy Ffrench is aware that 'there's a bog below in Belmullet in the County of

Mayo', but it's not quite from there that Eddie Delaney comes. Mayo, all right, but a tidy farm in a place called Crossboyne where his mother and two brothers are still in the farming profession. Eddie might now be out spreading bagstuff on the grass were it not for those little tricks of fate, those little pathways which seem to be bye-roads but which lead to great destinies. Not that Eddie Delaney would regard art as a greater destiny than tilling the soil.

For Eddie, in spite of his renown, has lost none of that simplicity, wisdom and purity of mind of the small tiller of the soil, and his heart is more in the land than many a man who has the mud on his boots. That is why he is such a safe guide for us ordinary folk in matters of art.

Now there are those in the modern world – and I will not arbitrate between them – who believe that money is everything and the problem of modern Ireland is purely an economic one. Eddie Delaney is not one of them. He believes that a man is a man. That he hopes and fears and feels like a man. That he has an infinite hunger for the things of the spirit. That if his body is fed and his mind allowed to starve he will be restless, unhappy and a prey to any kind of nonsense that any kind of prophet wants to put into his head.

Parallel with the economic solution, there must be a cultural solution. Art is only part of that but it is the part that concerns Eddie Delaney. When you admire a well-made stack, the straight line of a furrow, the curve of a neat hedge or the shapely head of a fine animal, you are satisfying something of your appetite for beauty, your need for the spiritual and that other hunger in you:

The hunger not of the belly kind
That's banished with bacon and beans

115

But the gnawing hunger of lonely men
For a home and all that it means

All that it means. There's the question. What does the home mean? Not just a place to eat and sleep, but a place where there is much love and a little beauty. A little beauty in the choice of furniture and fittings and in the harmony of colour. When daily life on the farm was a tranquil harmonious thing, where men could practise and appreciate the arts and crafts, something of this rhythm was carried indoors to good taste in the house.

In these days of rush and mechanisation and chaos, there is both a greater deficiency and a greater need for beauty in the home. The home should be not merely a shelter but an oasis in the desert.

There are those who confuse beauty with costliness. But a milking stool beside the kitchen fire is more beautiful than a Louis Quinze chair which belongs in Versailles. More than money it is a matter of proportion, of things in their place, colour appropriate to the surroundings and the good manners that prevent one object from lording it over another. A highly painted enamel article may be beautiful in a new office: it is usually outrageous taste in a mellow living room.

A cement wall is tolerable at the entrance to a factory, but under a thatched roof it is ridiculous. A mauve-painted door might not be so bad in a modern urban flat, but if you paint your farmhouse kitchen mauve it will drive you to drink or to Lanosshire, and that without you knowing it.

Apart from the beauty in the surroundings, Mr Delaney believes it is vitally important to develop not only a passive interest but even local talent. Fifty years ago people would have laughed at the idea of the modern rural drama festival. Fifty years hence we shall have our village art festivals. It is a question of confidence in local endeavour and local capacity. Having spent eight years living in various continental countries, he speaks from experience and not from theory. And he believes that one of the first things to be eliminated is the massive, commercial, impersonal ballroom – 'the lowest form of entertainment', he says.

One last question I asked Eddie Delaney: 'What about the scandal of modern art?' And he answered that the scandal is in us and not in the artists. We are scandalised when an artist makes a man who doesn't look like a man. Why should it? You dye a sheep yellow and call it beautiful though it's unlike any sheep on the face of the earth. You turn a sod at a ploughing match that bears little relation to the reality of spring's work. You deck out an animal for the show to make it look unlike any animal ever looked in its natural condition.

It is an expression of man's creative freedom to visualise shapes and forms that are different from reality and to express certain feelings or characteristics through line or colour.

What's wrong with a man standing on his head anyway? Aren't we all?

It is a fine article in the *Farmers Journal* and looks even better in its printed version, laid out in the *Journal*'s Berliner format, with varying typefaces and small photos of sculptures such as a horse, a woman's head and Eddie welding and 'making a creel joint'. I like to think of farmers coming in from the fields at dusk and reading it by the fireside, inspired and reassured that art is something physical, spiritual and part of their everyday lives.

A similar point is made in an interview with Liam Robinson for the *Daily Express*.

> 'Why should a sculptured man look like a man?' he [Eddie] said. 'It is an ideal and you can't put a rope around the neck of an ideal. People accept the convention that a two-ton operatic prima donna can die of TB on a stage in front of their eyes. Why can't they stretch their imagination when it comes to sculpture?'

On the occasion of the RHA retrospective, John Bowman did one of his radio archive programmes, based on interviews with Eddie over the years. It is an interesting collage, but a bit like Brendan Behan, with the boasting and well-rounded anecdotes. It is certainly fascinating to hear how quickly my father speaks and how his accent changes over the years, from high-pitched West of Ireland to the more modulated, assured tones of later and what one might call the 'Haughey gravitas'.

In terms of critics, an early and passionate advocate was Anthony Butler of the *Irish Press*. Butler was an interesting man, who had a bold and imaginative style. In a piece entitled 'Artist is a worker' he makes his case. It is a review of the big show that Eddie had in 1966 in the David Hendriks Gallery in Dublin.

> The automatic success of Edward Delaney in art competitions and his established position as sculptor laureate of officialdom might suggest that he is slick, competent and safe in his work.

On the contrary, Butler continues, identifying in the work a continuous tension and struggle.

This is a fascinating parallel between the man and his 'rebellious' material, and with the spirit of the times. It runs through much of the coverage. Later, Terrence Connelly describes Eddie 'taming the mutinous metal', when he was sculpting Tone, just as if he was securing the mercurial rebel.

Butler continues: 'This gives his artifices depth and understanding beyond that possible to those handled by the foundry man. The great shapes he creates – airy and light or massive and stubborn – gain some of their life from the struggle between man and metal. They grow from the material itself and do not deny its essence.'

Eddie was held up as example beyond art, as an emblem of a larger national drama.

> He is to be saluted for his example in doing here in Ireland what so many would feel impossible to achieve. He is in this way a symbol of effort, work and imagination and his example is worthy of serious consideration by industrialists, businessmen or anyone else who doubts our national capacity.
>
> The forms he moulds have multiple references to natural structures, to topography, geology and life. It is these layers, interacting and influencing each other, that enrich his visual semantics. This is particularly relevant to his Irish qualities. He himself admits that he conceives most of his work in terms of an outdoor setting. One can easily visualise his sculptures on an Atlantic headland with the wind whistling through their complex spaces and the rain cupping on their raw textures and they would be as natural as the limestone cliffs of Aran. Indeed, they seem to demand exposure to the elements.

This is a suggestion that was truly prophetic. For 20 years later, that is exactly what became of many of these sculptures, facing the sea with the Atlantic wind whistling through them.

'*Cuchulain* is no inert and tragic image,' continues Butler about one piece:

> As if against Fate itself, the metal resists the form imposed on it and strains against shape with deep,

muscular energy, exuding the ultimate spirit of the undefeated. *Vision 65* is a geography of statement. Abrasive and unwilling to the eye, its harsh texture suddenly gapes into a private interior where small holes bleed light.

Although much more massive and solid, *Astronaut's Dream 2* has spiritual power. It holds a bronze grotto scooped as from a meteorite, which radiates the quiet promise of miracle. A particularly fine piece of work, *Éirí Amach na Cásca*, is a crescendo of cross-shaped forms that tell of Crucifixion and Resurrection to soar finally in spires of faith to triumphant resolution.

In a series called Art Forum in *The Irish Times*, the critic John FitzMaurice Mills sounded a note of caution: this mutinous quality of the sculpted metal also suggested danger.

Bronze is at one and the same time the liberator and the mentor for the sculptor. It is a material which can echo the fluent plasticity of modelled clay, combining at the same time infinite nuances of final surface treatment. In history the material has been employed by almost every civilisation, each giving an individual appearance. The Romans with their often-minute castings, the greats of the Renaissance, the superb Benin bronzes from Africa.

Today the sculptor can see in the freedom of the cast an expression not possible from chisel and mallet in wood or stone. But all freedom brings with it the need for care to control such an outburst. The very character of bronze is that it can give not only texture and plastic form, but also such varieties of finish and 'skin'.

Edward Delaney, with the small standing figure

entitled *Fisherwoman*, demonstrates much of the free treatment possible with bronze today. In this and other pieces he has sought a final surface treatment that is a long way from the smooth satin surface of the Chinese master casts. There is little attempt to bring out the rich metallic possibilities of bronze material sheen, or feel. The surface is deliberately treated rough almost in argument with the basic material. An argument which is won by the diversity and imagination in the figure construction itself.

Delaney's work is alive and vibrant, and calls for a setting that can respond to his emotional and idyllic conception.

This is prophetic too. Did all these writers foresee the west? But so too is the line about 'all freedom bringing with it the need for care to control such an outburst'. One thinks about what Dev said about the power of television, or what indeed his critics said about him and the effects of his nationalist rhetoric.

CHAPTER 9

'This is Real Living Art'

Where did it all begin for Eddie?

It is clear from interviews that there were a number of turning points in my father's career, to which he constantly refers. One was the unveiling of a German sculpture in Dublin. Another is bluffing his way into NCAD, and then finding a book in the National Library next door. But before all that, there was the arrival of the circus into a townland near his home when he was a child. Again it was a German influence – the circus was the famous Herkenberg troupe – and nothing before (or since, it seems) could quite match the effect of its spectacle.

As a dreamy child, Eddie had already been at work on his art, partly indulged and even inspired by the wanderings of his loafer father. 'I was supposed to be doing my homework, but my father would sit around the fire with all the dogs; they would all be lying down and you couldn't get near the fire, and he would refuse to put any of the dogs away, he didn't care whether I did my homework or not. I never did my homework, I drew fantastic pictures.'

This was in an interview by James Ryan, done for a thesis about the home lives of visual artists. It was done in Galway in 1984 with Eddie by now more rueful and reflective. Ryan later became a novelist (*Home from England*, *South of the Border*), and his thesis is written in an academic style. It is, however, a fascinating perspective, despite or even because of Eddie's occasional contradictions.

Eddie even held up his own father as an example of a sort of unfulfilled artistic temperament. 'He had an independence of spirit which Delaney described with admiration, as he recounted various episodes, which suggested that his father was wholly absorbed by his interest in the environment and wild life of his native Mayo. "My father wasn't really interested in education at all; he himself, one would consider a drop-out, he didn't socialise very much and he had a very free thing on education, because he was visually an artist to a degree."'

As Ryan writes, 'Delaney presents his father as content in his isolation and implicitly attributes this contentment to the distance he cultivated from society, suggesting that the liberty this distance afforded him was employed to forge, on his own terms, an individual relationship with the world.'

Just like the state itself, maybe, and the way de Valera wanted it, but it could also reflect Eddie himself. Now that I am writing about my own father, it is interesting to hear him describe his own. He is perhaps being a little unfair on my grandfather. In fact, Patrick could work hard, tending to the beehives and wood mill of the lord, and accompanying him on energetic shoots, although he as often went out hunting himself for long periods.

It certainly sounds like something from Thomas Hardy: shooting, fishing and working on Lordy's estate. Patrick was also a nifty fiddler and played at the fireside. Eddie paints a bleak picture of the local school, however, and tells Ryan about the rote learning system and how he was forced to write with his right hand, having been born a *ciotóg*, or left-handed. (Did such 'correction' contribute to his two-handed ability to make sculpture?) Out of defiance, he carved 'fantastic pictures, and animals on desks'.

And then some other fantastic animals arrived into town, along with the circus. It is a fairy-lit Fellini-like image almost too good to be true: for him as an experience, for me as material. An entire circus troupe spent the winter months in Brook Hill, a nearby Anglo-Irish estate, with elephants and tigers. Eddie began working with them, painting posters, and 'spent so much time with the poster painter that before the circus left to go on tour, he had become his unofficial assistant'. Presumably, Eddie now realised he didn't have to stay on in Mayo.

It was an experience he would talk about all his life and what impressed James Ryan was how vividly he recalled it.

Delaney relived the excitement and wonder he experienced as he described the sensation of looking at a field, adjoining the house of the circus troupe, which was covered with hundreds of colourful posters left out to dry. Prior to this, and in the absence of opportunities at school to develop his painting, his development was almost entirely self-directed. He very much cherished the sense of possibility and excitement he experienced in his isolation, as he gave full expression to his imagination. Subsequently, in order to master the technique of his medium, he had to consider consciously many aspects of the artistic process and as a consequence the process lost the delight it previously held for him.

His contact with the poster painter, which led him 'directly into art', marked the first of many steps on a path of conscious exploration of the process of artistic expression. In his quest for isolation today [living by the sea in Connemara] Delaney would seem to be seeking to retrace these steps, in the hope of recapturing both the childhood delight that he derived from giving expression to his perceptions in forms wholly of his own imaginings and the liberty that accommodated this sensation. 'I used to draw strange figures and the amount of delight I used to get out of painting those pictures. I wouldn't get as much today out of sculpture because I know too much about it.'

Eventually, the young Eddie sent his pictures off to the Royal Hibernian Academy in Dublin, although there's no evidence he ever got a reply. He then arrived in the capital, walked into the National College of Art and Design and simply started attending lectures.

According to Aidan Dunne, 'He infiltrated himself into the NCAD, bypassing formal enrolment and just turned up at classes, becoming part of the fabric, a strategy that took him right through to graduation and won him the support of some, though not all, staff members.' Peter Murray adds that, 'Eventually, at the prize-giving day in the Aula Maxima, one of the professors objected to Delaney's stone carvings being awarded first prize and his unorthodox college days in Dublin were over.' The teachers, including Maurice McGonigal and Seán Keating, 'either assumed he was enrolled as a student or, more likely, recognising his talents, had turned a blind eye'.

Another of his teachers was Professor Herkner, a further German influence. Many German academics were prominent in Irish cultural institutions at this time. Whatever his official status, Eddie was not a model student and came and went of his own accord. He was working by day in a hardware store in Rathmines. McGonigal, in particular, persevered with him and later helped him secure support for his European travels. What struck them all was his utter determination. If he were blocked from doing something, he would simply find a way around it.

He even, for example, became president of the art students' union. When we heard this as children, we thought it was a wind-up, but here in the scrapbook is a newspaper photo of Eddie in an artist's smock, with palette in hand, painting around the head of a live, laughing girl who has put her head through a burst canvas.

The headline is ' "Living Art That's Ours," say students', presumably a pop at the annual Living Art exhibition, which catered for modernist work but which, in the students' eyes, would also be seen as rather precious.

'This is real Living Art,' cracked Eamonn Delaney [sic], president of the Students Council, as he put the

125

finishing touches to a poster for Dublin's annual Arts Ball. Because through each poster advertising the ball, a pretty girl sticks her head. This one is Peggy Flanagan. The theme of the ballroom decoration is Puck Fair, Ireland's biggest, noisiest festival, which goes on for three days and nights in Killorglin town, Co Kerry. 'We are collecting ideas for a vast mural that will catch the fun of the Kerry festival,' says Eamonn.

Eddie later claimed he was 'expelled' from the college, but he could hardly be expelled if he had never been enrolled. However, it sounded better, especially given his pithy explanation: 'inspiration didn't automatically come to me between nine and five'. It was a memorable line, which he used later in a *Time* magazine interview. As kids we used to use it gleefully when he scolded us to do our homework: 'inspiration doesn't come to us between six and nine!' He was furious. Just because he played truant from school himself didn't mean his children could: far from it. And while others may have treated art college as a finishing school, Eddie took his vocation seriously.

But the NCAD was completely traditional and limited in what it offered. Eddie's real education was in either the National Library next door or the National Museum directly across the way, which had a treasure trove of Celtic crosses and antiquities – the golden age of Irish sculpture and jewellery making. It is a tribute to the public library system that Eddie could educate himself in this way. For example, John Behan, who was originally from Sheriff Street, similarly informed himself through the public library in Marino.

One day in the National Library Eddie found a book that hit him with the force of a revelation. It was about bronze sculpture in the West African country of Benin and the process of lost-wax casting. I do like this, I must say. It wasn't a sculpture he found, or a sculptor, but a book. And in the National Library too, where Stephen Dedalus debated modernism – and the dubious notion of paternity – with the traditionalist librarian Mr Eglinton.

Aidan Dunne explains Eddie's discovery: 'lost-wax is a venerable, highly skilled and indeed secretive method of casting. Its appeal lies in the fact that it is an exceptionally faithful method of casting from an original wax model, allowing fine detail. Such is its mystique that when British troops looted lost-wax cast sculptures from Benin at the end of the nineteenth century, European scholars simply refused to believe that African artists could have mastered the technique, and came up with crackpot theories about kidnapped Renaissance sculptors being transported to the bight of Benin.'

Eddie was excited by this and by the cast figures, which were much more expressive than the Victorian realism on offer at the NCAD. He heard that such casting was being revived in Germany and Italy, where again the work was more expressive and inspired by medieval sources. There was an existing Irish sculptural tradition, but Eddie had little interest in it (except for the ancient Celts, of course). The most illustrious Irish sculptor was the outstanding Foley, but he was a conventional realist and Victorian: literally so, for he was Victoria's favourite sculptor and famously did a statue of her, which used to sit right outside the National Library. It was taken away in 1948, another sculpture politically removed, although this time without explosives. A sarcastic cartoon appeared in *Dublin Opinion* with Victoria being hoisted away and telling de Valera, 'Begob, Éamon, there's great changes around here.' Meaning, there's no change at all, you're just getting rid of statues. Victoria ended up being buried under ground in Cork and then transported to Australia, just like the Fenians she exiled. Today, she sits outside the Australian parliament in Melbourne.

There now came another turning point when Eddie went along to St Stephen's Green for the unveiling of a memorial to German suffering after World War Two. Yes, another bronze sculpture, on another corner of the Green – a decade before his own. The piece was done by the German sculptor Joseph Wackerle and comprises three pensive women, grouped upon on a rock, with rushing water. Appropriately, it depicts the 'three fates spinning and measuring the thread of man's destiny'. At the event, Eddie met some German officials, and possibly the sculptor, but either way he had blagged a scholarship to Germany, the embassy officials being only too happy to cultivate goodwill after the war.

There can't, after all, have been many cities in Europe putting up such memorials. There is, by contrast, none for Allied suffering. Dublin must be one of the very few European capitals that doesn't have a memorial to the Allied, or Soviet, struggle against Germany, yet does have one to German suffering, albeit just *after* the war. Interestingly, a similar memorial was donated by the Italian government, an eight-foot-high marble *Pietà* located off Marlborough Street. It is in gratitude for 'relief during 1945–46'. Italy changed sides, but for most of the war it was an Axis power.

The Wackerle fountain is described as a gift in gratitude for Irish help after 'the war of 1939–45', as if '*the* war' was something that was brought on the Germans, as opposed to them bringing it on everyone else. But the memorial is consistent with the good relationship between Germany and Ireland. 'My enemy's enemy is my friend,' was another motto of Irish nationalism and whoever was fighting England was worthy of respect. For Wolfe Tone, it was the French, and more latterly it was the Germans. In the *Commemoration* handbook there are photos of the former crew of the U-19 U-boat, walking the strand in Kerry in 1966 where they landed Roger Casement in 1916. Just as Tone tried to land with the French. Another photo shows the surviving crew of the German arms ship the *Aud* enjoying similar hospitality. In the 1916 Proclamation specific tribute is given to 'our gallant allies in Europe'. This was at a time when tens of thousands of Irishmen were fighting on the Western Front.

In reality, most Irish people, as opposed to most Irish nationalists, were firmly for the Allies in both wars. But there was always a bit of sneaking regard for the Germans. Apparently, back in Mayo, Patrick Delaney was a regular listener to Lord Haw-Haw, the radio propagandist used by the Nazis, but this was as much for the mischief. Also, Lord Haw-Haw, or William Joyce, originally came from nearby Galway. We used to imagine Patrick, in front of the fire, his shotgun across his knees, having a good chuckle at the wireless crackling away in the corner. Meanwhile, Patrick's ostensible employer, Lord Oranmore, was close to the appeasement movement in England before the war, or at least among those seeking an accommodation with the Nazis. Ireland was non-judgemental about German war records. Professor Herkner, Eddie's teacher, went to fight for the Wehrmacht but then returned to Ireland after the war, to resume his teaching position. Meanwhile, in London, Lord Haw-Haw tried to evade the British hangman by claiming his Irish nationality, but he was hung regardless as a traitor.

The *Three Fates* fountain is a key connection for Eddie and he often mentions it. However, he never refers to Wackerle's work and any possible influence it may have had. This is surprising, for Wackerle's memorial is also inspired by German suffering, just like *Anna*. It is also a fountain with figures inside it, just like the later famine group, only a few hundred yards away. It is curious also that critics have made no connection between this and Eddie's work.

Wackerle seems to be dismissed as an unremarkable German sculptor, but he was anything but. In fact, he was quite an important German sculptor, and a simple internet search reveals why. His best-known work is the Neptune fountain in Munich, inaugurated in 1937. This makes it also surprising Eddie didn't mention him since he would have passed this fountain every week. Wackerle also did a series of commissions for prominent buildings, such as the Zeiss Optics Company in Jena as well as the large bell figures on an early high-rise building in Leipzig. He taught at the art academy in Munich from 1924 to the end of the war when, as a sympathetic website put it, 'all of his public duties and positions were suddenly terminated'.

But not without good reason. Wackerle is best known for a style known as tectonic sculpture, in which movement and baroque forms are combined. 'Like Albiker, he accomplished this with his *Men Leading Horses* on the Reich Sports field,' describes the website, 'a work of art which, in its closed, powerful form, ranks them among the very best works in the monumental sculpture of the time.' Basically, it was fascist art: militaristic and unmistakably Aryan. Or, as the website put it, full of 'primal power'. Wackerle also did the monumental figures for the Olympic Complex in Berlin, at which in 1936 visiting teams were forced to give the Nazi salute.

Wackerle went on to become a favourite of the Nazi regime and especially of Hitler. From 1936 on, 'the admired and successful sculptor' was a member of Reich Cultural Council, followed by membership in the Presidential Council of the Reich Cultural Chamber. On the occasion of his sixtieth birthday in 1940, the Führer nominated him for the award of the Goethe Medal for Art and Science. Hitler even visited Wackerle's atelier, 'a fact which brought the sculptor severe criticism after the war'. Well, no kidding. He was effectively put on a blacklist and employed no more. He died in 1959 in Partenkirchen in Bavaria, where 'for 200 years his ancestors had lived as woodcutters and farmers'. This is as long as the Delaneys were in Crossboyne, also, curiously, as woodcutters and farmers. Wackerle's last years in Bavaria would have coincided with the time Eddie was living there himself.

The fate of Wackerle is, of course, a sad one but he was a keen supporter of the Nazi government and helped to celebrate its fascist aesthetic. Let us contrast his elevation, for example, to the fate of another German sculptor, whose work is actually not dissimilar to the *Three Fates*, and who was probably also an inspiration for Eddie. This is Ernst Barlach, an expressionist sculptor who mixed cubist structure with the German medieval tradition. Barlach's characteristic style was a cube, from which a figure or figures are shaped. Or, as one fine description has it, 'subject to a single vitalising movement which sweeps over each sculpture and integrates it'.

Barlach was also blacklisted, but this was *before* the war. The ironic thing is that one of Barlach's main subjects was also German suffering and his memorials to the First World War are profoundly moving, precisely because they don't glorify militarism. For this reason, however, they aroused suspicion, and in 1936, even though the Vienna Secession had just elected him an honorary member, the Nazis ordered his works to be withdrawn from the jubilee exhibition of the Berlin Academy. In 1938, his war memorial at Kiel was destroyed and another one in Gustrow was sawn up and melted down. As a result of the campaign against 'degenerate art', 380 of his works were banned from public collections and confiscated. He died the same year, without ever having a chance to see his name and work redeemed.

Meanwhile, if it is true that Wackerle was blacklisted in Germany after the war, how come he came to do a sculpture in Dublin in the mid 1950s, donated by the German government? And was he entitled to do a memorial to German suffering? Perhaps he was the ideal person to do so, having contributed to a regime that had brought so much of it about.

During his years in Munich Eddie did, indeed, see much suffering, as Germany struggled to emerge from the trauma of the war, and especially the war's end, when incendiary bombing by the Allies destroyed the cities and killed thousands of civilians in a single night. Their aim was to set the cities alight, an incredible prospect, like a flaming furnace. The extent of this pain has only recently been acknowledged, as has the subsequent treatment of Germans in surrounding countries. Just because one group of people has suffered doesn't mean that others haven't, as we know well from Irish history.

However, despite this backdrop, they were halcyon years for Eddie and his fellow students. Germany was starting again from scratch, and there was no law, as such, or very little, as they drove around in old Volkswagens in a wasteland of ruined buildings, jazz clubs and bombsites. It was bohemian self-rule. And this was not the slightly jaded bohemianism of Paris or even New York, but something more radical, as the culture of the Weimar was rediscovered along with Bauhaus and Dada and everything that preceded the Nazi period. There was poverty too, but for students it was part of the experience, like eating horsemeat and, one on occasion, shooting ducks in Englisher Garden.

The stories that struck us as kids were about people who disappeared, like Uri in the foundry or some fellow who got lost while they were skiing high up in the mountains. He fell down a gorge and his body couldn't be found. Like a sculpture, he was frozen in the ice and waiting to be brought back to life. *Finn Again's Awake.* In the wardrobe, next to the tennis rackets my parents used in Clarinda Park, were a pair of old wooden skis my father had brought back with him. Were these the dead man's skis?

There was another story of how Eddie was on a tram one snowy night when it was stopped near the airport because of a crash. 'It's footballers from your country,' a man told him. England and Ireland would be the same to many Germans. In fact, it was the Munich air disaster of 1958. Apparently, one of the Manchester United footballers, Kenny Morgan, had been found in the ruins by complete accident after the search for survivors had been abandoned for the night. Just like the fellow in the snow.

A lot of American troops were still around and among them one night he met Elvis Presley. He told the story years later to the *Galway Advertiser.* 'A friend of mine told me he'd get me 200 Camel cigarette packets out of the Army PX store. He had to smuggle them past the camp gates and he said he'd meet me in this very tatty bar in the city. Another night he arrived with this guy he introduced as Elvis Presley. Now, I'd never heard of Elvis Presley. He could have said, "This is Joe Murphy" for all the difference it would have made to me! Somebody else in the bar, who knew who he was, told him his record was on the jukebox. So Elvis said, "Let's play it." But unfortunately the feckin' record was stuck and wouldn't come down into the turntable, so it was a while before I actually got to hear him sing. I told that story to a girl in a bar in Ireland years later and she refused to serve me. She said I was a liar!'

He also met Louis Armstrong, who was in town to help a charity that looked after the children of black American GIs. Eddie made a sculpture that was presented to Armstrong at a special dinner. 'When the sculpture was finished they asked me to make the kids black, so I tinted the bronze,' said Eddie, adding proudly, 'Louis Armstrong must have been the first person to get one of my bronze sculptures.'

The tutors at the college included Heinrich Kirchner and Toni Stadler, who had been a student of Aristide Maillol in Paris and was inspired by early Greek and Etruscan sculpture. The linkage is important because Maillol was a key figure in modern sculpture, possibly more important even than Rodin. His main feature is strong and robust nudes that carry off their solidity and mass with a serenity and grace. It is the old paradox again: great weight rendered lightly. Compared to the stormy and tormented work of Rodin, Maillol brought new qualities of harmony and balance and looked back to the classics, from which, as one critic put it, he fashioned an art that would 'speak to modern times from an ancient source'.

Eddie's contemporaries in Munich included the German artist Maria Munz-Natterer, who had a similar interest in grouping figures into 'families', and Meera Mukherjee, an Indian sculptor, who was equally fascinated with lost-wax casting and connected it to the metal folk art of her native India. She depicted the ordinary figures of rural life as well as archetypal figures such as archers, dancers and boatswains. Like Eddie, she too had returned from Munich in 1960 and had a major one-man show, and descriptions of her work mirror his: 'The opposing pulls of mass and movement, strength and vulnerability give an intense character to her figures, enhanced by the textural play of the surface.' Her art 'moves easily from the physical to the spiritual,' wrote one critic, 'from nuanced detail to symbolic abstraction, and has a quality of simultaneously inhabiting both the everyday life and fantasy, just as the two co-exist in a child's imagination.'

We didn't hear about these artists when growing up. Instead we heard about other students who were Eddie's mates, fellows such as Waki Zöllner, who later became a major environmental artist and built artificial islands out in the sea, an early example of ecological art. One project, *Atoll*, looked like a large space capsule, but another, *Floatel 2000*, was a self-supporting island with room for nearly 2,000 people to live. It sounded like something out of James Bond, and Blofeld's oilrig community in *You Only Live Twice*, being manned by men in red boiler suits.

In recent years, however, Zöllner has been involved in a bitter dispute with the German government over their campaign against the Church of Scientology, of which he is a member. Apparently, certain artists had their commissions dropped when it was revealed they were Scientologists, just like Wackerle after the war because of his Nazi links, or Barlach before it because he was not Nazi enough. The German authorities claim they are protecting the country from another dangerous cult, but their attitude seems harsh. In Germany, the law is absolute and even the state's secular liberalism has a compulsory quality.

Another student friend of Eddie's was an English chap called Peter Dineley, who later created a successful props business in London providing weapons for movies, mainly German militaria, it must be said. He even had a small role in a movie called *It Happened Here*, about an imaginary Nazi conquest of Britain.

When we got older we used to look up these people when we were abroad. My brother, Gary, worked with Dinely's company in London, supplying props for TV dramas, while in Munich the rest of us stayed with another friend of Eddie's, George Lotter, a former radical who was now a bearded, burly TV cameraman. Lotter had lost none of his old attitude and would walk us through the Munich streets, deriding American consumer culture. 'Look at this plastic society,' he'd shout, to the bemusement of café sitters. 'It's dreadful. They have ruined everything!' When he visited us in Connemara, he used to kiss the sods of turf.

Eddie also had a girlfriend in Munich, or a sort of girlfriend, a dreamy Swedish girl called Christina Rundquist-Andersson, who looked like Ingrid Bergman and appeared in moody black and white photos with Eddie, smoking and gazing out a big studio window.

Eddie brought her to Ireland but apparently lost her over an Easter weekend when he went west to visit his family. He used to deny she was his girlfriend. 'I was only carrying her purse,' he told us. It is quite possible that Eddie actually had no proper girlfriend until he met my mother.

Christina was certainly a fine artist, and one thing that has passed down to me is a sketchbook full of her drawings of animals in a zoo, presumably in Munich. There are pencil and ink sketches of lions, buffalo, monkeys and elephants, with a concentration on the lions and lionesses, because of their musculature and lean bodies. Eddie used to bring us into the Natural History Museum in Dublin to do the same, except Christina's animals here are alive. The images remind me of how my father used to draw and teach us to do the same: his hand hovering over the paper, and going back and forth before settling on a spot to begin. There would be a few jagged strikes, before a smooth confident line took off, sketching the outline and turns of a subject.

In the red scrapbook, Christina turns up with Eddie at the Living Art show in 1963. They are looking at the *Two Wives* sculpture and holding catalogues. 'Guessing can be fun at new art exhibit' is the headline. Eddie is now married with two kids. Christina was also in that year's Living Art, so she had clearly stayed on in Ireland for a while. Either way, she fascinated us. And we thought: she could even have been our mother. We loved our mother, of course, but we were intrigued by this mysterious Swedish woman. As young kids, these contradictions didn't trouble us, and we didn't distinguish (or want to) between different timelines.

For example, we also heard that Hitler did the same entrance exam to the Munich academy that Eddie did – and failed. In our minds, we imagined them doing the exam at the same time, and Eddie looking over to see some guy with a small moustache struggling over his sketches. It was a costly failure given the vengeful havoc that Hitler later wreaked. Meanwhile, what an extraordinary story it is that Hitler's brother – or half brother –

came to Dublin and worked in the Shelbourne Hotel in the 1930s. (*'Here, Hitler, would ye get them bins out.'*) The Führer's brother then relocated to Liverpool where, in an irony almost too ridiculous to believe, his house was destroyed in one of the very last German air raids on England.

Hitler certainly got his revenge on the arts world, elevating the Teutonic heroes of Josef Wackerle and damning the likes of Ernst Barlach and Oskar Kokoschka. With the end of the war came change: Eddie and his fellow students rejected the classical models, even lay down on the street to protest against the rearmament of Germany in 1955.

Years later, he reminisced about this to the *Connacht Tribune*. 'We wanted to break the code of art,' he said, 'break with the German tradition, those propagandistic fascist figures.' So he and a few others went into the art studio, chucked all the clay statues out the window and brought an ass up into the room in place of the model. While they went to the pub, the other students returned to find their work gone and the classroom flooded. The ass had been tied to the sink, 'a small, cross ass', which decided to roll on the floor and pull the sink off the wall. The water seeped down from one studio to the next, destroying paintings below too. 'They weren't too happy with us,' he adds, 'and I got a bad name for myself with the Embassy.'

Truly, the West of Ireland had arrived in Munich.

In their articles for the RHA retrospective, both Aidan Dunne and Peter Murray wrote about the German influence on Eddie's work.

'Delaney's achievement,' writes Peter Murray, 'lay in his ability to unite the instinctive, unpretentious approach of his rural background, where memories of the Great Famine were still alive in the memories of people, with the stricken anxiety evident in post-war German culture.' His [later] 'establishment of a sculpture park in Connemara in 1980 was to be the culmination of this attempt to link together the redemptive abstraction of Central Europe, where academic figuration had been tainted through association with totalitarian government, and the wished-for primal innocence of the West of Ireland.'

In *The Irish Times*, Aidan Dunne agrees and connects Eddie to the broad post-war tradition of European figurative sculpture, such as Giacometti, Germaine Richier, Marino Marini and Giacomo Manzù. 'These artists shared a commitment to figuration, to modelling and casting, and to bronze. In the disillusioned aftermath of a cataclysmic war, some of them looked to existentialist humanism, depicting the troubled, isolated human presence afflicted with all the doubts and anxieties of the mid century. Paradoxically perhaps, an underlying sense of doubt and fragility comes through the intractable, material substance of Delaney's figures, human, animal and mythical. The most robust forms have an awkwardness, a tenderness about them.'

'Strikingly,' writes Dunne, 'this quality is evident in his public, monumental work, although as Judith Hill has pointed out, it is not something typical of such a heroic form. Actually, it gives the monuments an appealing, human character. That character, a compound toughness and fragility, touches virtually everything in the RHA show: single human figures, close family groupings, mythical heroes and animals, notably horses, a favourite subject. All have a hard-won, tragic dignity about them and a sense of being frayed by mortality and uncertainty.'

I think of the old German woman, and her face, globular-eyed, saying, 'Why me? Why should I suffer?'

'The poverty of Germany made a profound impression on him,' writes Murray, 'providing stark images that would reappear in his later work in Ireland.'

If this is true, then images such as the *Famine Group* are as much about Germany as they are about Ireland. It is said, after all, that the German infatuation with 'unspoilt Ireland' is as much about an old Germany as it is about Ireland. Maybe the opposite is true and Eddie's depictions of Germany are as much about the Ireland he left behind. Such was the case with Heinrich Böll's *Irish Journal* in the late 1950s. As one critic put it, 'For traumatised post-war

Germans, the undeveloped Ireland of the 1950s served as a sentimental backdrop, a scenic surface on to which could be projected romantic notions of nature, landscape and homeland (*heimat*): the very notions that were ruthlessly co-opted by the Third Reich, but could now be explored again in a protected isolation of Achill Island – a kind of Nürburgring for the battered German soul.'

Böll's book was originally published in 1957, but an English version didn't appear until 1967, by which time, as we know, official Ireland wanted to project a very different image. Conor Cruise O'Brien, then a diplomat, criticised its portrait. 'Böll idealises everything that is most wishy-washy in Ireland and naturally laments any sign of progress.' It was like Erskine Childers asking Garech not to be recording old women wailing by the hearthside when 'we're trying to move on'.

Eddie had moved on himself, but he hadn't completely left Ireland and while he was abroad he had exhibitions in Dublin, in 1955 and 1957. Both were in the Brown Thomas Little Theatre, on Grafton Street, a cultural space within the posh department store which held exhibitions and music recitals free of charge. The scrapbook cuttings give a flavour of the time that is quite different to the 1960s coverage, with their grainy photos, small typefaces and formal-sounding reviews.

'With the enthusiasm and energy of youth,' reports the *Dublin Evening Mail* of the 1955 show, 'this young artist has produced the 41 exhibits on display within the last nine months, which is indeed, no mean feat … His palette is more vigorous than discreet. He is certainly not afraid of either colour or experiment. His true gift seems to lie in sculpture.'

'His colours are strong,' wrote *The Irish Times*, 'and he is prepared to tackle a wide variety of themes and techniques, from simple landscapes like the unassuming and attractive *Harbour Harmony* to ambitious religious groups like *The Waiting Room*. It is not surprising, perhaps, that most of his work remains for the moment derivative or that his courage outstrips his taste. There is, at any rate, sufficient evidence of sensibility in his work – in such paintings, for example, as the mobile yet motionless *Head of Christ* – to show him as an artist worth following; the mistake perhaps is his, in holding a one-man show so early in his career. In his sculpture, Delaney seems more assured and his confidence appears more justified. *A Fisherwoman* has dignity and repose and there is a good grouping in the slightly sentimental *Thoughts of Hope.*'

Most of these works have long vanished, but some have not. *The Waiting Room*, a strange grouping of cloaked biblical figures like an early Dali, was rescued from the farmhouse in Farmhill, before PJ's death. This was not Eddie's first public showing of art, incidentally, and another item refers to the Tostal exhibition in 1953, when 'his exhibit and Henry Moore's "controversial" *Reclining Figure* were the only two pieces of sculpture on show'. He was in good company, then, showing with Henry Moore at the age of 20. The item appears under the headline 'The Colonel', explaining that this is how 'for some reason or another, Delaney is known to his friends'.

An Tostal was a nationwide arts festival, set up by the government in the early 1950s to encourage community activity and attract tourists. It has been ridiculed by some historians and even at the time by sceptics like Flann O'Brien and Kavanagh – the festival had a sort of kitsch Celtic-pageant quality – but it was a genuine attempt to create a cultural ferment and, indeed, it still operates in some towns. It also galvanised the growing tourist industry. One of the welcome changes of the 1960s, incidentally, was the disappearance of much of the terrible cynicism of the 1950s.

This cynicism, of course, was due to the economic backdrop. One of the liveliest pieces on Eddie's first show, for example, was by John Healy in the *Irish Press*. Healy knew all about poverty. From Mayo himself, he would write about rural life and emigration in a novel, *Nineteen Acres*, and a book *Death of an Irish Town*, which was specifically about how his home town of Charlestown was emptied of people going to the US and England. (Among those who left was Mary Gallagher, mother of Manchester musicians, Noel and Liam Gallagher of Oasis.) Healy would later become a strong advocate of the political and business culture of the 1960s, which sought to turn this situation around, and in particular of Charles Haughey.

Here is Healy, writing about Eddie:

> A small boy who was 'forever scrawling pictures on the back of schoolbooks' and 'ran away' to Dublin to become a painter has opened his first exhibition in Dublin – and set the art world talking excitedly.
>
> And centrepiece of 22-year-old Eddie Delaney's exhibition was a head of 70-year-old Mary Rogers, an unknown Aran Woman whose striking face the young Mayo man had 'in his mind' for years as a subject. Explained Eddie: 'Mary is an Aran woman who lived beside us in Claremorris for years and is still there. As a youngster I used to watch her face and thought it very expressive. I made up my mind that if I ever took up painting I'd use her as a model. Then one day last Christmas when I was at home I made a model of her and used it for this piece here.'

But could this not also describe the German woman, *Anna*?

> According to his mother, who caught a train to Dublin from Claremorris to see the show, 'he was always at it – when people came to the house they wouldn't be sitting down five minutes before he had them sketched on a piece of paper.'

In the photos, his mother is clad in an overcoat and hat, just as if she had indeed come directly from the train. (It was said of country people in Dublin that they used to keep their coats on at social events: wary, ill at ease, might have to leave early.) Beside her is

Eddie's youngest brother, James, with a black diamond on his sleeve – Eddie's father has recently died: the hunter hunted. But far from looking grief-stricken, Granny seems happy and proud of her son's achievements. They are all looking at the plaster carving *Thoughts of Hope*.

As for the alleged 'mistake of holding a one-man show so early', as the critic put it, Eddie would have another show two years later. He was clearly a man in a hurry. 1957 was also the year his fellow Mayo-man, Charlie Haughey, first entered the Dáil. They were 'on their way', as Healy put it. Meanwhile, Haughey's father-in-law, Seán Lemass, was finally about to replace the ageing de Valera as Taoiseach and, in the Department of Finance, a visionary official called T.K. Whitaker was drafting the First Programme for Economic Expansion which would sow the seeds of the 1960s boom.

In between these Brown Thomas shows, the newspapers gave updates on Eddie's progress. One early supporter was the anonymous 'Tatler' in the *Irish Independent*.

'The finest studio in Schwabing, the Montmartre of Munich, is Number 11A Ainnmiller Strasse and its tenant is a brilliant 25-year-old sculptor from Claremorris. He is the only Mayo-man I know who speaks Irish and English with a German accent and German with an Irish accent. His studio is one of story and tradition, for it was one of the artistic homes of famous expressionists, Paul Klee and Kandinsky.'

Tatler reported that 'Eddie was also studying at the Salzburg International Art Academy with Giacomo Manzù, who had recently, in the face of intense international competition, won the commission to make the new doors for St Peter's in Rome. "I believe him to be the greatest sculptor in the world," said the man from Claremorris. The Salzburg Academy was run by Oskar Kokoschka who had a one-man show some years previously at the Victor Waddington gallery in Dublin. When Kokoschka met Edward he welcomed him with both hands. "Ah," he explained, "but you are solid."'

This is quite in contrast to the farmer we met in the Duck Inn, incidentally, when I was with my father. 'Sure, you have lady's hands,' as the haymaker told him. Is it something to do with an earlier generation, this 'hands' thing?

'An incident that happened at the Academy the same day may explain what he meant,' continues Tatler helpfully. 'Two students from Canada had turned up, one a painter, and the other a sculptor, young folk apparently with no roots of their own. They were not "solid". Kokoschka could not see why they should leave Canada just to go to Salzburg. He knew of an even better place! "Why don't you go to a place like Ireland?" he asked them. "It is one of the best countries in the world, a place where an artist can live, and create, and think and be quite apart from our material world." '

This was quite a compliment to Ireland, and one that bore true for Eddie, but only after he had been trained abroad. Interestingly, also at Salzburg was an American painter, Barrie Cooke, who subsequently did move to Ireland.

According to Tatler, Eddie was already acquiring a German accent. 'Munich has put a German bias on his Irish and English and he loves to mystify Germans by slipping Irish words into the conversation. He agrees on the great practical use of Irish to the student of Continental languages, with its all-embracing range of vowel, consonantal and guttural sounds.' This is ironic given that, decades later in Connemara, Eddie would again mystify Germans, this time tourists, by talking to them in German mixed with Irish. But he wasn't being mischievous. It was more a case of being genuinely mixed up and of not having enough vocabulary in either. The German visitors were utterly confused but, being polite, they simply nodded their heads patiently while trying not to grimace.

But then maybe I am wrong. One can feel overly self-conscious about a fast-talking and unusual parent, and they are often much clearer than we think they are. As I said, it is like hearing their voice – or one's own voice – on an answering machine.

For example, on the occasion of the 2004 retrospective, a journalist from *The Examiner* conducted a telephone interview with Eddie in the nursing home in Galway, 'where he now lives'. Eddie's

Alzheimer's was advancing, but far from finding him confused, the reporter, Marc O'Sullivan, described him as 'witty, mischievous, and extremely well spoken.'

In other words, he hadn't changed. Fifty years on, he was still talking about Manzù and Kokoschka and his stories were almost the same. 'Still Breaking the Mould' was the spirited headline and a photomontage had a cut-out picture of Eddie at the RHA opening, smiling in a tweed cap and glasses, and walking with a stick, and set against a background shot of Tone, bold and upright, in front of his granite columns. *The sculpture outliveth the man.*

> Although his work was the subject of a retrospective, Eddie began by saying that 'he would as happily not discuss it'. But this was false modesty, a playful preliminary to the stories. 'I don't like talking about myself in the past tense,' he cautioned wryly. 'It sounds like I'm writing my own obituary.'
>
> 'We worked on those doors in Salzburg and fitted them in Rome. They were enormous. They must have weighed two or three tons. If one had fallen over, it would have killed me,' he says, adding wistfully, 'though it would have been nice to die in Rome.'

O'Sullivan describes Eddie's time with Kokoschka, 'who had the distinction in 1937 of having his work celebrated in a major retrospective in Austria while simultaneously featuring prominently in the Nazi's "Degenerate Art" Exhibition in Munich.' This was the show in which Ernest Barlach was also included. But at least Kokoschka lived to see himself and the other 'degenerate' artists vindicated.

> 'Kokoschka painted like Jack B. Yeats and couldn't believe I didn't know him in Dublin,' said Eddie. 'When Kokoschka learned I was coming back, he gave me a letter of introduction so I could call on Yeats in

Merrion Square. But when I got there, Yeats had just died. Opening private correspondence between one man and another wasn't done in those days, so I tore up the letter of introduction. Imagine! A letter from Kokoschka to Jack B. Yeats and I tore it up. That's one great regret I have from those times.'

At present, Delaney is being treated for an injured foot at Áras Mac Dara, but he continues to work. He would, he says, like to get involved in training younger artists, as he himself was trained in Germany and Austria, but thinks it unlikely he will find the time to do so. 'I'm getting on, you know. I'm over 70. And I have my own work to do that would keep me busy for another hundred years.'

Reading this cheered me up no end, especially the last line. Also the way the interview opens with Eddie living in Áras Mac Dara but ending with him only there 'for a foot injury', as if the quality of his stories had given him a reprieve. But this is fine: it is all make-believe, after all. As his Alzheimer's continued, the nurses became teachers at the Munich Art Academy, and, more importantly, everything became sculpture. He would sit in the Áras, with its many windows on to the Connemara landscape, and see everything in terms of form and light. And, in his company, believe me, you would do the same: the clothesline, the filing cabinets and the tree trunk outside which, shorn of its top, looks uncannily like an upended torso.

On one visit, I told him I was getting married and would like to use one of his silver rings. Forget about the buried ones, he said, I will make you a new one. But this was another charade, where he checked my fingers for size and spoke about the correct mix of silver. 'Be sure to call me, because I need to get going. I have to make the body first, and then the limbs.' He meant the nude figure on the ring. Despite his frailty, I wanted to look at his own hands and say, 'Ah, but you are still solid.'

CHAPTER 10

Sculpture across Europe

By the time of Eddie's second show in June 1957, he had abandoned painting to focus on sculpture.

The exhibition was called, rather grandly, *Sculpture across Europe*. It comprised 'twenty-three bronzes, two heads and a figurine in copper, one work in French limestone and another in Hamburg limestone, one in terracotta cement and a panel in copper *repousseé*'. The show was opened by Robert Briscoe, the well-known Lord Mayor of Dublin, who made a major impact when he travelled in the US, and especially in New York, where he was lauded as both Jewish and Irish.

In publicity photos, Eddie looks like a man with a mission. In an attic studio, he stands next to a bust and stares at the camera, while on the front of the *Irish Catholic* he is shown welding a crucifix, with goggles pushed back on his head, like a fighter pilot. The *Irish Catholic* was a major family publication then which sold as much as a Sunday newspaper. The photo is credited to the Irish News Agency, an information service set up in the 1940s by the Irish government to give an Irish version of news events. So could we say that Eddie is being endorsed here by Church and State?

The reviews certainly focus on his 'spirituality' and 'sense of country'.

'Studies such as *St Christopher*, *Madonna and Child* and *Crucifixion* show a deep religious feeling,' wrote one critic approvingly, 'while studies like *Donkey's Music*, *Before the Light* and *Weeping* exhibit his power of portraying moods and movements of

145

everyday life. Here is a hard-working artist who has benefited richly from his continental studies, a comparative unknown among us who is destined to became an outstanding known – that is if our country ever gets around to recognising the wealth of sculptor genius it has within its shores.'

Other exhibits are listed, such as the bronzes *The Moon*, *Salome*, *Stillness* and works in copper, *Roma*, *Paris Yesterday* and *Maria Lucia*, as well as the French limestones *St Francis* and *Bended Knees*. There is also a marble *Lonely Goddess* and *Little Feona* in terracotta cement. I have no idea where these early works are, but some appear in old photos, and the titles would explain, for example, those stone sculptures in the 'Living with Sculpture' photos, when I was pictured at the window.

The titles read almost quaintly now, compared to Eddie's more dramatic and existential titles of later. If the 1950s show his alleged 'deep religious feeling', then those from the 1960s reflect an engagement with the country's history and mythology: *Emigration*, *The Famine*, *Queen Maeve*, *Cuchulain*. By the late 1960s, we have moved on to *The Glass Sun*, *Project 24* and *Astronaut's Dream* and by the 1970s we have *Rock Form*, *Destruction*, *Fallen Dog*. There was a run of *Untitled*s through the 1980s until the women's peace marches in the North inspired a whole series of *Women Marching*, *Women Walking*, *Women in a Storm*.

In 1990, Eddie had an exhibition in the Temple Bar Gallery in Dublin (the last show at the old gallery before it was demolished and a new cultural quarter developed). In the catalogue, the terse titles evoke the big steel sculptures against the western sky: *Rising Dawn*, *Wind Ripples No 7*, *Moving Lines*, *The Twelve Pins*. The jangle of the metal trees in the Atlantic winds is suggested by *Shared Rhymes*, whereas other titles capture the vast night sky out to the Aran islands: *Killer of Light*, *Destroyed Tower*, *Descending Dawn*, *Door into Dark*. The show was called *Beo*, which means 'life' and was the name of his new foundry. It was an appropriate last show in Dublin. The symmetry of titles, listed in two columns, is like the chapters of a journey.

However, in 1957, Eddie was only getting started, and in *Irish Tatler and Sketch*, the reviewer put the exhibition in the context of the time. The cutting is unsigned, which is a pity since it is quite personal, even wilfully so. As with the 1955 show, the reviews were often just initialled or coyly attributed to 'Our Art Critic'.

In our isolation, an isolation which is getting more and more intense, it is occasionally pleasant to get a breath of the outside air. Much of the present-day sculpture in Ireland is either pedestrian or uninspired or going to the other extreme, and is forced and eccentric. Delaney's work strikes a golden – or shall we say bronze – mean. It is both lively and decorative; and he has assimilated very well the general principles underlying the present renaissance of sculpture on the Continent initiated by the Italian Marini and others – an inspiration which has been drawn chiefly from the ancient Etruscans. And it is a break away from the Impressionistic School of Rodin and the more realistic Maillol. For sculpture has again become stylised and decorative.

He has also mastered the change in casting. Whereas in the past the stress was on its durability with a texture that was often dull and heavy – as you get with Epstein for example – in the new technique the copper is flashed through, giving a texture that is lively, colourful and attractive. It is brighter in tone and whereas weight was once considered important, the stress is now on lightness and movement – the shell form – as we see in his large torso *Salome* which is both glamorous and decorative.

In 1957, the sense of destiny seemed strong for Eddie. A reporter for the *Evening Press* felt that 'in years to come there will be many who will be proud to say, "Yes, I met Edward Delaney when he was young. He is quite famous now, of course," implying that you can't afford his work. He has a faunlike face, nervous, thin, eager and the dark Mayo face flushes with the effort of his emphasis – he told us of the "lost-wax process" – while his eyes are hooded in concentration.'

Again, Eddie sounds like one of his sculptures of that time – lean, poised, eager – whereas later he looked like one of his craggier, bulky pieces, and then later still he was like a stainless-steel structure, creaking in the wind. It is apparently not uncommon for sculptors to begin to resemble their work.

There is a continuity to the press coverage, so that a few days later a *Sunday Press* writer could report that he 'looked in vain for the nervous, faunlike face described by a contemporary. But when I saw Mr Delaney, he was as cool as the proverbial cucumber. He spoke calmly and confidently of his hopes for the future of bronze casting in this country. As to the commercial possibilities, young Mr Delaney is royally indifferent. His mission is to create art, not dispose of it. One eminent artist was wildly excited by his work. "We must hold on to Delaney," she said. "Surely Ireland can afford one bronze sculptor."'

There was a sense that the state has invested in him and would one day get a return. 'It is unlikely that the Arts Council has done a better thing,' said the *Irish Press*, 'than give a scholarship to Edward Delaney to go abroad to study bronze casting. Now twenty-five, this sculptor has a real creative intelligence and is a fine technician. The Arts Council must feel satisfied that their scholarship has been put to good advantage.'

'Naturally, he shows many influences,' the article continues, 'but they are good influences, such as Greco, the distinguished Italian sculptor, who has a remarkable Etruscan style. One particularly notices how he has absorbed Greco's manner of pressing forward a face, a limb or some other prominence to catch the light and emphasise … the tension of bronze and its relentless living quality. Mr Delaney is the first Irish sculptor to work in this traditional European style, which goes back to Lehmbruck. This is one of the most exciting exhibitions to be shown in a long time, and Edward should be proud of the great advance he has made, the *Irish Press* critic concludes like a kindly school inspector.

Edward was indeed pleased, but he had a 'few niggling doubts', he told Tatler in the *Irish Independent.* 'Should he have held the show abroad, namely in Paris, where he could have made a bigger impact and sold more? This would have enabled him to show his larger works which he was unable to transport to Ireland, because of the cost.' As it was, the exhibits had to come from Hamburg, Vienna, Rome, Salzburg and Munich, so assembly was a considerable feat.

'Still, I think Edward is delighted to have the chance to stake his claim as an Irish artist in his own country (for at soul, he is a practical patriot),' wrote Tatler, 'and I suspect his claim is being treated more seriously than he may know'.

Later that year, Eddie participated in the annual exhibition of the Institute of Sculptors at the Hugh Lane Gallery, a curious body set up to boost public interest in sculpture, and in terms of 'culture' the Honorary Committee reflected the official Ireland of the time. The committee was composed of Anglo-Irish Lords (the Earls of Rosse, Longford and Wicklow) or Catholic prelates (Bishop Lucey and Cardinal D'Alton). The other member was President Seán T. O'Kelly.

Much of the work in the show was religious or spiritual, with exhibits from Imogen Stuart, Oisín Kelly, but also Frederick Herkner, Eddie's former teacher, who had fought on the Russian front for Germany and then returned to his post in neutral Ireland. His exhibit titles are interesting: *Liberation* and *Mask.* For Eddie, participation was a key moment since he was now among the old guard of Irish sculpture. The institute invoked a golden past of Irish creativity, and the catalogue displays an image of the Clonmacnoise Crucifixion Plaque, from the tenth century, which shows a childlike Christ being speared by squat Romans. This native treasure is invoked in a passionate statement about sculpture by the architect Daithí P. Hanly:

There is nothing as significant as behaviour.

You, who love these deeds of valour and wish, not only to remember them, but to make them an inspiration for generations after you … help to give them the elegance of sculpture.

You, who are building, let the aesthetic symbolism of sculpture give a further meaning to the modern structural shell.

You, who have seen this Exhibition, are already half convinced! Now use your voice, your strength of mind, your persuasion, your place in society, your committee, your club, or any of these, to have this generation act in a practical way.

Let our streets, parks, buildings and Holy Places all show that we have pride in our beliefs and the ability to express that pride with the elegance of artistic form.

There is nothing as significant as behaviour.

This is really the same clarion call that Eddie would make all his life. And it would find some fruition in the 1960s when Daithí P. Hanly himself, for example, designed the Garden of Remembrance. In 1966 Davis was also erected. Interestingly, there is also an image in the catalogue of the plaque as laid on the site in 1948, along with a question mark. *Where is Davis?* But it would be another decade before a statue went up, by which time the state had moved on to a bolder modernism. The question mark is thus more significant than they could have known.

Not that the institute was necessarily old fashioned. On the contrary: two years later they held a show which was avowedly modern and included European artists. The catalogue again lamented the 'greater enthusiasm for sculpture in other European countries' and how 'we must strive to justify our inherited treasures of crosses and relief in bronze, silver and gold. Proud of this heritage, we Irish sculptors endeavour to foster a greater interest in our art at home. And so we present our work side by side with the works of well-known European sculptors.'

The list is impressive, including Barbara Hepworth, Jean Arp, Marino Marini, Robert Clatworthy, Henry Moore, Ossip Zadkine and Elisabeth Frink. Among the Irish exhibitors were Seamus Murphy and James McKenna, another young and uncompromising sculptor. Herkner is here again, this time with a melancholic Madonna, not unlike Wackerle's fountain. There are also similarities to Eddie's work in artists one rarely hears of, such as Emilio Stanzani and Rosario Murabito. Eddie's own exhibits were *Dog* and *Rest*, titles which are now much less sentimental and suggest work that is blunt and primitive.

In the institute's 1955 show, Eddie's exhibit had been the *Land of Music*. Yes, those doors which connected to the energy of the *fleadh* and the sensuous atmosphere which (I like to think) gave rise to myself. 'Ever since art began,' wrote the *Irish Press*, 'the cow has been depicted dancing in the meadows surrounded by primitive man and woman playing on the lyre or other instrument. Here a series of panels makes a beautiful harmony of such forms in the manner of modernised Etruscan art.' Ah, how right they are. Chester Beatty, the legendary collector of ancient Asian and Occidental art, is photographed beside it. The King of Copper, as he was known, was delighted to see such sensitive use of the material from which he had made his fortune.

The reference to Etruscan art is significant, for in many ways it was the foundation of modern sculpture. It was clearly a major influence on my father's work and among his books is a handsome art volume called *Art of the Etruscans*, bought by my expectant mum as a Christmas present in 1961. The 'beautiful harmony' of the *Land of Music* had led to marriage and prospective family the previous month. This would have been the snowy Christmas they spent in Luggala. Instead of the polished realism of the classics, the book's colour plates show expressive clay figures with wide eyes and sly smiles.

Like the musicians at the *fleadh*, modern sculptors seized upon the revitalising effect of an ancient source. 'Etruscan art interrupts the smooth flow of historical tradition,' writes the almost disapproving author. 'It has an anarchical sprightliness and is a law unto itself. It lacks an internal historical synthesis. At one and the same time it combines ancient legacies from the past with Greek influences of its own day, together with an uncanny anticipation of the future; from this jumble of inspirations and intuitions, it has managed to derive its own quite novel and highly individual existence.'

It is worth stating here just why Daithí P. Hanly and others felt a need to make the case for sculpture. For a long time there has been a pecking order for the arts in Ireland, and visual arts is not a priority, sculpture even less so. The hierarchy is as follows: literature at the top, especially theatre, then music and then painting and sculpture, design and architecture – anything which involves a visual aesthetic. This is mainly because of our history. A dispossessed people, eking out a living on the land, we didn't have time or affluence to create objects of aesthetic pleasure – as they did in other European countries and kingdoms. We found our expression through our verbal culture and told stories and sang songs. As one politician told me, 'We carried our mythology in our heads.' We also exacted a post-colonial revenge by becoming masters at the language forced upon us.

'And yet Ireland has a tradition of sculpture continuous for over 2,000 years,' James White, the director of the National Gallery, wrote in 1960 when he opened an open-air exhibition of Eddie's sculptures in Cork. 'Even in the darkest years of the sixteenth and seventeenth centuries, carvers made tombstones, and primitive craftsmen made Penal Crosses, so easy to conceal in one's clothing. A note of hope is sounded today for the neglected sculptor of modern Ireland; for Cork talks of creating an open-air sculpture park. Once again we look south for inspiration and initiative.'

It was a sentiment with which Eddie would concur, and having held his own exhibition in Fitzgerald Park he then became part of its permanent display, with *Adam and Eve* and *Torso*, a truncated figure of a dreamy woman. James White was a strong supporter of Eddie's, and in a revealing letter in 1960 he urged the Arts Council to continue to support his studies, saying 'it would be most beneficial to the future of Art in Ireland. But I think it is important to endeavour to put some control on him with a view to getting him to return to Ireland to work. This might be a problem, but a native Irishman teaching the craft in a School of Art is something to be aimed at.'

In 1959 and again in 1961, Eddie was chosen to represent Ireland at the Paris Biennale, in the city's Museum of Modern Art. Sponsored by the French government, the Biennale was for young artists of all nationalities between the ages of 20 and 35. The Irish representatives were selected by a panel that comprised the architect, Michael Scott, a major figure in the Irish arts world, Robert Figgis and Lord Killanin, who was later Chairman of the International Olympic Committee.

Killanin had worked on movies with John Ford and he and Michael Scott later formed a company producing films like *The Rising of the Moon* and *Gideon's Day*. His son Redmond Morris recalls going onto the set of *The Quiet Man* and watching the railway-station scene where John Wayne steps out and asks, 'Which is the way to Innisfree?' Redmond himself went into film and got an Oscar nomination for *The Reader* in 2009. One of his early experiences was working with Roger Corman on *The Red Baron* and experiencing the same frugality as occurred with *Dementia 13*. A staged plane crash was shot from different angles so that it could be used for other scenes.

When his father died, Redmond inherited the title and attended the House of Lords where he was amazed to find he could speak, and even vote, on British legislation. This was just before Labour's reforms in 1999. His father told him that 'going to the House of Lords was like being an extra in a film'. Except that in the case of Lord Oranmore and Browne, it was strictly a non-speaking part!

Eddie's exhibits in Paris included a study of the Irish Princess *Rosaleen* in welded brass and two linocuts entitled *The Land of Yeats*. The titles sound even better in French – *Le Pays de Yeats* and

Roselyne. Even the material – *cuivre brase* – sounds more sensuous. The Yeats drawings are related to the *Land of Music* door. One shows a spiky figure playing a flute to a female figure, with an outstretched arm, sitting on a bench. This is strange, for it is clearly *Anna*, sitting cross-legged and just as she appeared later in the garden in Galway. It is as if the imploring *Anna* has been redeemed from the Munich pavement and restored as an enchanted nymph. By now I have realised that there are many different names to Eddie's works, and many different stories.

The other Irish representative was Leslie MacWeeney, a striking, blonde-haired elfish woman, who painted in a very distinctive style, with strong black outlines, resembling a Rouault or Munch. Her characters have narrow faces, like woodcuts from a children's story. I enquired about MacWeeney and discovered that there may be a reason for her haunted faces and elongated figures. She herself was very small and was born with curvature of the spine. She was put in a mould as a child (an image which obviously interested me) but was taken out too early and remained stooped. But she was a feisty character who eventually moved to Boston where she became so enthusiastic about teaching art that she gave up painting – surely the reverse of the usual situation. In 2008, I acquired her *Head of a Girl* at an auction, and it now hangs at top of our staircase, severely and confidently watching all who pass.

The Irish artists were in good company. Representing the United States were Helen Frankenthaler, Robert Rauschenberg and John Paul Jones, while Italy sent Arnaldo Pomodoro and the UK had Anthony Caro. These are old men now, like Eddie, or have passed on, so it is curious to think of them as young men and women, in the flush of their careers. For, in Paris, it was all about youth, and the catalogue included endorsements from André Malraux, the Minister for Culture, and a spirited, if somewhat confused, salute from Jean Cocteau.

We are wrong to give the youth labels such as 'new wave' or 'black jackets'. The youth is the youth, with the strength to disobey. If conformism is non-conformist, here are the young people who will move back with horror from the old 'avant-garde'. *Vive* the Biennale of Paris, where youth can throw its fortune on the green carpet!

Eddie had indeed thrown his fortune on the green carpet and expressed his pleasure to the supportive Tatler in the *Irish Independent*. But he was also already looking out for the generation behind him – the next 'new wave', as Cocteau would have it – and told Tatler that the National College of Art and Design should be 'kept open during the holidays, so that classes could be taught by foreign masters. This way students who couldn't afford to study abroad could get some chance of learning their craft'. He also urged them to open a foundry. 'Casting is terribly expensive and no student can pay for it himself: so a foundry would be a Godsend.'

The NCAD must have looked askance at this advice from a former student who had bluffed his way through their college and had then allegedly been 'expelled'.

In the spirit of youth, the French put on quite a show for the Biennale and raided their museums for other exhibitions, which were held *en marge* of the main event. The idea was to show the works of these greats when they were about the same age as Eddie and his fellow exhibitors. Thus, we had the Generation of 1900, including Bonnard, Matisse, Mondrian and Rouault, the Generation of 1914, with Derain, Dufy, Klee and Van Dongen, and the Generation of 1930: Braque, Chagall, Kokoschka, Modigliani and Soutine.

Even better, there was an exhibition of sculpture at the Rodin Museum, with works by Bourdelle, Calder, Gonzales, Lipchitz and others. What a treat. Imagine all of these, in a city already dripping with sculpture, from bridges and arches, and filling the precious lawn of the Rodin Museum. It must have been an amazing sight.

After the Biennale, Eddie went home and decided to buy the house in Dublin that he'd been renting. Within a year, he met my mum at the *fleadh*. She became pregnant, and they got married. He would come back to Paris in 1961 for another Biennale. I came back too, arriving in from Morocco for the end of my honeymoon, and I saw all those sculptures again, spread along the Tuileries like oversized toys. Think of sculptures as toys and you'll be a happy man all your life.

In 1960, Eddie had another show in Dublin, in the Building Centre on Baggot Street. By now he had made another major decision: he did everything in bronze.

There would be no more Hamburg limestone or terracotta cement. His work also became highly modern, figurative and abstract, such as *Sea Creature*, *Dancer* and, of course, *Anna*. His foundry was up and running and he was clearly casting like a madman, as can be seen in the *Spectrum* film. Alas, the scrapbooks have no coverage for the 1960 show. Apparently, there may have been another scrapbook, now lost, which is a tantalising and maddening thought. The only coverage of the 1960 show is a photo of the big room, identified by my mother's handwriting. She has taken over the scrapbook from Eddie's mother: a relay system of proud and supportive women.

However, a retrospective assessment of the 1960 show appears in an *Irish Times* review of Eddie's 1966 exhibition, when the critic Brian Fallon referred back to the Building Centre show in some detail. 'He patented his style early and it has remained with little change – unmistakably his own, though with some resemblances to Frick and Chadwick and other sculptors of the 1950s. There is perhaps some faint obeisance to Moore.' (Fallon seemed to find it impossible to describe one artist without referring to others.) But his descriptions of the sculptures are interesting. 'Delaney's ribbed, angular figures sometimes appear as half-human, half-robots, sometimes as organic creatures pitted and lopped like dead trees, sometimes as combinations of all these.'

He refers to the 'taut set' of *Anna*, 'haughty as a goddess and as threatening as a snake', obviously a different perspective on the plaintive woman of Germany, but a recognisable one. Fallon also liked the paintings, but thought they sometimes looked 'more like textural experiments than actual visual ideas'.

However, he finishes on a caution: 'The vitality of this young sculptor is plain; so is his unevenness and occasional indebtedness to other men. One hopes he won't get too set in his ways or, in other words, overwork the style he has hacked out for himself. He is one of the liveliest of his generation in the country; one can only hope the youthful arteries will not harden. At the moment, they are pulsing happily.'

Eddie's big breakthrough was winning first prize at the Living Art exhibition in 1964.

The Living Art was the main event in the country's arts scene. It was set up in 1943 as an alternative to the more conservative RHA, after the latter's continuing rejection of modernist work, specifically Louis Le Brocquy's *The Spanish Shawl*. The backdrop was also the extraordinary rejection, by the Hugh Lane, of *Christ and the Soldier* by the French painter Rouault. In time, the Living Art would itself be challenged, not least by the Independent Artists group, which emerged in the late 1960s and of which Eddie was a founder member. But, for years, it was the main event. It was also a modernist relief from the torpor of the NCAD, with which the RHA was associated, although the art school would plod on, unchanged, until the late 1960s.

The Living Art was ostensibly for 'living' Irish artists, but foreign artists could also appear and the first show in 1943 had Modigliani, Klee, Cézanne and Rouault. The idea was to break free of the so-called national aesthetic, of which the RHA was the principle custodian, and an image of Ireland that was Gaelic, Catholic and rustic: basically, the idealised Ireland of de Valera, reflected in endless paintings of cottages and harbour sunsets. The Living Art would try to reconcile international modernism with the ongoing desire for a national art: it would fashion a modern Irish aesthetic.

And so one of its founders, Mainie Jellet, produced works such as *Virgin of Éire*, which combined her cubist style with a subject familiar to an Irish audience. This impulse to have an 'Irish dimension' is interesting and persistent. Even the international Rosc shows were held in tandem with displays of Celtic treasures. Nor was the idea of reconciling these two impulses necessarily an obligation. It was also an opportunity, which was all about branding. As Irish writers well know, there is nothing as sellable as one's 'Irishness'. They can present themselves as European and modern, but they can also say, 'We have this special extra thing: we are Irish, and draw from the country's rich past and often contradictory present.'

The Living Art was a colourful and eclectic event, and at an auction I managed to acquire a random set of catalogues from the 1950s to late 1960s. They are a fascinating insight into the art scene of the time and the social prosperity from which it drew. There are ads for galleries, artists' suppliers and academic publishers. One is for the Brown Thomas store, with an illustration of the Little Theatre where Eddie had his 1950s exhibitions, but also of their Christian Dior boutique and an 'Information Bureau where bookings can be made for shows in Dublin and London'.

The 1952 catalogue has an ad for Baird television receivers. 'It is possible to view direct from the fireside the leading events of the world, sporting, orchestral, theatrical, etc. being seen whilst they are actually taking place.' What a great early description of live television. It reminds me of how, even in my own time as a child, you'd be watching a soccer game with the word 'Live' on the screen, just in case you didn't know. Or, better still, a World Cup match coming in from Mexico with 'Live via Satellite', flashing across the screen every few minutes: so needlessly dramatic, but conjuring up images of top-class footballers being beamed half way round the planet.

The Baird ad has a drawing of a 'console TV model', which looks like a parlour cabinet with a strange little screen. The early date of 1952 is surprising, for it meant that television was being watched in

Ireland a full decade before the national station came on air that snowy night in 1961. But presumably such TVs, with their pure diet of Anglo-American culture, were for the wealthy, whereas the rest of the population could watch the same fare in the cinemas. They could also watch Amharclann na hÉireann before the main feature where an item on the 1963 Living Art appeared with the camera panning across *Two Wives* (there is no sign of Christina Rundquist).

A year later, the Living Art featured the *Spectrum* programme on RTÉ with Patrick Kavanagh sitting in front of *Cathedral* and reading his poems. The combination of famous poet, early TV and modern sculpture was an inspired 1960s moment and typical of the producer, Jim Fitzgerald. *Cathedral* would take two or three men to move, but it was clearly no bother to Fitzgerald to haul it into the studio. He had, after all, dragged sculptures up to the top of Killiney Hill for his film on Eddie – Garech's *Good Shepherd* is shown standing before Dalkey Island – not to mention bringing them down, and in to, the Dún Laoghaire shoreline.

Kavanagh's pose is particularly satisfying because *Cathedral* is such an abstract piece. Whatever about the public work, this really is modern, like a section of moon rock with a niche in its side or a gouged-out tree trunk. Uncannily, a protrusion at one corner of the piece imitates Kavanagh's hair. Indeed, the whole piece resembles the poet himself: solid, grounded and both traditional *and* modern, recognisable *and* abstract. He even shares the special quality of Eddie's work: brute weight rendered tenderly.

In the RTÉ still, Kavanagh looks directly at the camera, calm and confident in his hound's-tooth jacket. This is quite unlike how he appeared at the Tone unveiling some years later, when he had barely a month to live. The RTÉ image now appears in a *Writers of Ireland* poster, alongside photos of Yeats, Joyce and Behan, and quotes from their work. It is a popular poster, to be seen on the walls of Irish pubs across Europe, which always pleased Eddie, who caught sight of it in Paris and Brussels.

Eddie's first Living Art was in 1961, with *Emblem of Love* and

Eternal Life, titles I find apt given that my parents had met the previous year and were now expecting myself. The 1963 show included major American expressionists like De Kooning, Robert Motherwell and Mark Rothko, and the following year the Irish cigarette manufacturers Carrolls came on board as sponsors and funded a set of awards for Irish artists under the age forty. This was a major boost to the Living Art, and appropriate since Carrolls epitomised the buoyant commercial life of Ireland in the mid 1960s.

The Carrolls factory in Dublin, on the Grand Canal, was a striking block of glass and concrete, decorated inside with newly acquired modern art. The address, Grand Parade, became the name of one their brands. Cigarettes were a glamorous fixture then, as testified by my mother's TV ad for Players, another big Irish producer: *Players No 1 – for the sophisticated taste.* Carrolls, by contrast, were phasing out the old pipe tobaccos, including a strong brand favoured by Seán Lemass, although they took the precaution of sending the Taoiseach a lifetime's free supply before ceasing production. Perhaps as a thank you for planting the (tobacco) seeds of the 1960s boom.

In a globalised age, it is worth remembering, and fondly, just how ubiquitous these Irish brands were. English visitors would comment on the number of products not available in their own country – Jacob's biscuits, Harp lager, HB ice cream. They are, in many ways, as valid a part of Irish culture as poetry and sculpture, and certainly in the 1960s they were a mark of long overdue industry. They were the names you would see advertised on old hoardings in Croke Park, where the GAA policy was to try to promote Irish products only. One of our favourite TV ads used to be for Flahavan's oats, where an Irish family are joined at the breakfast table by their smart father, in a clean white shirt and tie. 'Start the day the Flahavan's way!' was the jingle and, polishing off his Irish porridge, the businessman got up briskly and headed off, presumably to work for the IDA or some big company that was buying sculpture from our dad.

Carrolls would also build a landmark factory in Dundalk, with a large outdoor sculpture by Gerda Frommel, a stainless-steel mobile suspended over a pool of reflecting water and gleaming like a silver sail against the brown glass of the factory. Eddie was very impressed. It had all the elements he yearned for: steel, size, space and water. (Today the building is the Dundalk Institute of Technology.) To celebrate the Dundalk area, and the nearby Cooley Peninsula, with its connection to the ancient Irish legends of the Táin, Carrolls commissioned Louis Le Brocquy to do his famous tapestry *The Hosting of the Táin*. This was on the cover of a new translation of the Táin by the poet Thomas Kinsella, a source of inspiration for many artists, including Eddie.

With awards on offer, the Living Art invited international critics, such as Sir Ronald Penrose and David Sylvester, to become adjudicators. For the 1964 show, the judge was Dr Brian O'Doherty, the Irish-born critic of the *New York Times*. O'Doherty is an interesting figure. He would later become an artist himself and change his name to 'Patrick Ireland' because of events in the North and especially Bloody Sunday. In 2008, in a somewhat strange public ceremony, he had his 'Ireland' persona buried in the grounds of IMMA. Peace was now finally secure, and ushers in white gowns placed his plaster 'death mask' into the ground at the old soldiers' hospital. Not far, indeed, from where *Anna* was due to be situated. More interestingly, from the 1970s on O'Doherty became a major theorist in the world of conceptual art. Like the filmmaker James Coleman, he dealt with theories of perception. Both came from Ballaghdareen in County Roscommon, not far from Claremorris. How strange is that?

However, in 1964, the selection of winners drew caustic comment from *Quidnunc* in *The Irish Times*, who was upset that the prizes didn't go to one of the existing panoply 'such as Norah McGuinness, Anne Yeats, Colin Campbell and Nano Reid, all of whom seemed to have more value than the prize winners'. This drew a stiff letter from the chairman, Michael Scott. 'May I point out that these artists are all over 40,' wrote Scott, 'while our judge was asked to adjudicate the best works by Irish artists under that age. *Quidnunc* quotes a Dublin comment: "Maybe they'll go really wild next year and appoint a judge from Europe." I suggest that such insularity today is merely sad. In order to ensure that the Carrolls awards could not properly be criticised as biased or controversial on the grounds of their being selected by a prejudiced or insular group, the distinguished art critic of the *New York Times* was invited. Opinions on art will inevitably differ but it must be stated that the *New York Times* is uniquely respected in America and in Europe for its knowledgeable interpretation of the visual arts.'

It is a stunning put down, reinforced by repeated reference to the *New York Times.* But it also marks the changing of the culture. Whereas other broadsheets just accepted, and even embraced, the changing art forms as part of a new national energy, *The Irish Times* was still quite traditional – ironic for a title that has now become most associated with the arts. The quoting of a 'Dublin comment' was another way to pour scepticism at a remove, like deigning to the wag at the bar counter. *Quidnunc* offered a 'typical Living Art opening day story', for example, about an American woman who'd 'gone to a kinetic art exhibition and had spent the best part of twenty minutes looking intensely at a raised circular relief set in one edge of a rectangular frame and pondering its significance. And then she realised that she'd been contemplating a doorknob!'

The sculpture that won Eddie first prize was called *Flight*, which, in an unexpectedly poetic account, the *Irish Press* described as 'a tense abstraction of a bird's wing standing upright as a monument to the achievement of muscles and feathers conquering the light and invisible. The upper tapering section is thin and hollow in contrast to the base. Scanning up and down one can almost sense movement. The sculptor is a sure judge of providing just enough dynamic elements for an observer to participate in bringing life to his construction.'

Eddie is pictured with his finger pointing upwards, 'explaining a detail to Mrs D.S.A. Carroll', a striking elegant woman in a coloured print dress and chic hat. She and her husband Don owned the company. They were still the 'quality', but at least they were 'our quality', and not some high-pitched grandees with a country seat in England and an empty seat in the House of Lords. They may not have been the gentry at the RDS Horse Show but, don't worry, they would soon be sponsoring the event.

The headlines – 'New frontiers', 'Living Art is 21, and lively' – suggest a coming of age for the art show, and for the country in general. The Lemass reforms had paid off and Whitaker's economic programmes were bearing fruit. Jammet's restaurant was full, Garech was sipping champagne in the Shelbourne and Haughey and Lenihan were holding court in Grooms Hotel. Meanwhile, the Dubliners were playing to packed houses, while Séamus Ennis had gone further afield, attending that year's *fleadh* and playing at the Newport Folk Festival, where a young Bob Dylan would cause a stir by going electric. Yes, indeed, the times they were a changin'.

'Space-age theme wins arts prize' was the headline about *Flight* in the *Daily Mail*. 'Edward is an artist with his "feet on the ground" and his thoughts on space. He explained: "My work at the moment is in the form of space. We are trying to get off the ground with our work. I am striving for the open air, not interiors. We want vastness … freedom." '

Eddie and his generation were restless and, in terms of his work, it was a prophetic statement. But it would take another 20 years for him truly to achieve this space, with his open-air sculpture park in Connemara.

The newspapers gave personal detail on the winners, stressing the ordinariness of their backgrounds – except for Anne Madden, 'an expert horsewoman who competed successfully at the RDS and is now living in the foothills of the Alps with her husband, Louis Le Brocquy'. An unfortunate typo describes her work as 'peasant', which is not the effect she would have intended. The other winners were Michael Farrell, 'who does art therapy in a polio unit in West Ham', and Brian Bourke, who 'worked as a barman in London' and in a hospital, where he was 'first in the mortuary and then, following promotion, in the operating theatre'. I love this: Bourke's career path was in direct reverse to life's progress. What would have happened if he'd excelled in the operating theatre – promotion to the maternity suite perhaps?

Both Bourke and Farrell were later familiar to us: Farrell with his bawdy humour and those memorable inflatable seats in his house, like huge sweets, and the bearded Bourke who visited us in Connemara and ate all the unwanted spaghetti off our plates: truly a starving artist, especially after the long drive out from Galway. We regretted he didn't visit us in Stone View and he could have finished our *speck*. Farrell also visited, trundling down the boreen in a Volkswagen full of French-speaking kids, with whom we played on the windblown beach, as well as at the Living Art, a fact noted by the *Evening Press* reporter who described Varnishing Day as 'always distinguished by the tumbling presence of little toddlers, the children of the artists'.

In the same report, Eddie returned to an old theme and wished 'that here in Dublin we could safely organise a pavement exhibition of the more impervious works of Irish sculptors, mentioning that such an out-of-doors show had been held in Cork with success. "But then I think they threw the benches into the Lee," he said.

'"Had the benches been mistaken for exhibits?" someone asked, and it was time to change the subject.' This was a predictable jibe, like the story of the woman looking at the doorknob. But Eddie's attitude to vandalism was interesting: keep replacing the objects until they stop being vandalised. (He also had a constant desire to get sculpture into the deprived areas of Dublin and other places.)

'We shouldn't jibe at the moderns,' warned the reporter. 'Remember the scorn that was heaped on the impressionists and other pioneers of new frontiers in painting. There came a day when the scorn turned to adulation.' This, of course, was the historic 'mistake' after which the public and critics were terrified to ever again question 'modern art'. To such an inhibited extent that even to the present day art critics will challenge very little.

The report concluded that 'the whole exhibition radiated an

almost tangible vitality which had the effect of leaving you slightly exhausted (or was that the *vin rose*)'. Vitality: that was the key word, and some European refreshment, for the *Evening Herald* noted the 'very good *vin rose* which circulated liberally'. But it wasn't for everyone. One newspaper, temporarily missing its art critic, sent along one of its racing correspondents, but the giddy atmosphere of it all – the glamorous women in miniskirts, the sophisticated chat about art and the follow-on session in the pub – went to the poor fellow's head, and he promptly got sick and was known forever afterwards as 'The Vomiting Art Critic'. Not that he was ever let near an art show again.

Winning the Living Art was the final breakthrough for Eddie and he had now arrived as a national sculptor. With it came all the publicity and interviews, the sort of coverage it is hard to imagine now for a visual arts award. Perhaps for theatre or music awards, but not for the visual arts, and not on the news pages.

There was even a newspaper photo of Eddie being blessed by his younger brother, John, outside the church in All Hallows where John had just been ordained. Eddie is wearing a smart suit and is on his knees. It is hard to believe that he'd go on his knees for anyone, but he is smiling, as is John, and their demeanour suggests that it is all a bit tongue in cheek. *Verily, you have arrived* (both of them). There was also some private joke, to do with Eddie not allowing himself to be photographed near some garish statue of St Patrick, and so the blessing was done on a gravel path instead.

Although now accepted by the establishment, Eddie was not a real part of any group and very much ploughed his own furrow. He became, early on, an associate of the Royal Hibernian Academy, with all its rituals and red gowns, but he was also a founder member of the Independent Artists Group, which sought to connect art to contemporary society, although he then resigned from the group for reasons which are not clear. Certainly both of these were more compatible to him, and to each to other, than much of the more elitist group which came to dominate the Irish arts scene, which dealt in a sort of cool minimalism. By contrast, Eddie was seen as a bit of a hustler, whose work could be raw and emotional. It didn't help, of course, that reporters played up his humble origins. 'It was intriguing to learn,' wrote one reporter, 'that he had trained as a barman in his native Mayo, and still treasures a reference stressing his talent as a window dresser.' Well, this was a new one, and surely 'treasures' was a bit of an exaggeration.

'The fifteen year career of young Eddie Delaney,' wrote a *Daily Express* reporter, 'has been so spectacular that is it comfortable to remember that he is only a gossoon. It could be that, like Picasso or Van Gogh, the man may become several men, before his creative ability ends.' Several men, indeed. Is it any wonder then that, by the mid-1970s, Eddie was 'slightly exhausted'? By 1964, he had already been an artist for a decade and half and yet he had still to experience the controversy of the big public commissions for which he was best known. But he was certainly on his way.

In her catalogue essay for the 2004 retrospective, Roisín Kennedy writes that 'Delaney's modest rural background is markedly different to that of the earlier generation who had lived and studied on the continent prior to the Second World War. Artists such as Mainie Jellet, Evie Hone and Louis Le Brocquy all came from wealthy, middle-class, urban families. Delaney held a particular position within the Irish art world of the 1960s – midway between the traditionalists and modernists such as Hilary Heron and Gerda Frommel – but his background and the sense of risk in his work put him in a category of his own.'

'There was a robustness and daring to his larger figurative pieces of the period which seemed, at some level, to reflect the country's new-found confidence,' writes Kennedy. 'He was able to cross the accepted boundaries of high and popular culture when his work made its way onto the record covers of the Chieftains. His reputation as outspoken and unconventional fitted into an image of the artist, recently established by Brendan Behan and Patrick Kavanagh, and Delaney, young and bohemian, offered a new and exciting image for the visual artist. The state, like many of Delaney's corporate patrons, saw in his work, and in the personality of the artist, a spirit of enterprise and modernity ideally suited to its new self image.'

But there is no doubt that there was a paradox at the heart of his ambition: the more success he achieved, the more uncomfortable he felt. But this was also the paradox of the state. The more it sought modernisation, the more it felt the need to hark back to the past, or an idealised past. It was a contradiction that Thomas Davis knew well. As Eddie told James Ryan, he just wanted to get back to the fields and the rabbits and the circus. But first, he had to reward the state for its investment and help it to build modern monuments to its heroes. His mission was only beginning.

To give an idea of his world, Eddie did an article for a *Sunday Press* series called *Growing Up.* It had an illustration of a key with '21' upon it. In fact, Eddie was now 34, but such is the freshness and wonder of the articles, that he could have been 14. Editor that I've been, I feel like smoothing the jagged text and gathering it into paragraphs, but that would be to take away from its extraordinary vitality and staccato directness, a directness that I, with my education and literary knowingness, could now not hope to achieve, or more accurately, ever recover.

The headline – 'I wish I'd never come to Dublin' – reflects Eddie's *faux* protest at his success (on the reverse are all the cinema ads and a city teeming with life) but there is no doubting the nostalgia for his childhood. I suspect that the piece was written and not dictated and I am glad that the now departed editor has put it in verbatim, as I have. It would be a shame to break it up, so here it is in full:

> Falling over a bucket of water and getting up and saying 'I won't die' is the first thing I remember. Looking back I remember things that happened but I no longer understand the meaning of a child's freedom.
>
> More than anything else I was thrilled by the circus

when it took over the Brook Hill mansion for the winter and the long line of coloured wagons passed amongst the reeks of turf on their way to the meadows. The elephant wagon sunk to its axles and they took out the elephant to lighten the load. It sank into the turf as well and all night they dug by the light of the lanterns shining over the back of the grey elephant.

That year for the first three weeks I stayed with the circus all day and late into the evening. I always had a story when I went home and I'd say that the teacher kept me in for catechism, because everybody knew I hated it. I was always good at scheming from school. It was the first thing I could plan well and I never had any regrets.

The circus had a painter who painted jungle scenes on all of the wagons. He copied from a book while the animals howled. When he tired of the jungle pictures he made Punch and Judy puppets. I bought some and hid them in the turf shed. The teacher found Punch and I got a terrible beating. Judy escaped and when I was taking it home the other boys tore it to pieces.

I remember a circus trainer making a horse sit down on a steel girder and the horse fell over and broke a leg. He was shot in the slaughterhouse and the next day I saw his ears in the lion's cage.

When the circus started printing their posters before they went out on the road again I carried them out to the grass to dry the ink. One afternoon the wind blew the posters up on the trees and there was a lot of shouting and I ran home. When the wagons left there was nothing in the meadow except bones and horse manure.

There was a tinker's camp on the way to school and we stood on the road and sang this song:

Said an old tinker woman
To an old tinker man
Will you go and have a rattle at the old tin can
With a hole at the bottom and a hole at the top
And the devil only knows
When ye will ever stop

One day the tinker woman, Maggie Moynihan, ran after us with her bare arms sticking out from under her shawl. She shouted, 'I'll tell the teacher, ye pups.'

Next day the teacher came to the school. No matter who knocked at the school door, I always got red in the face. The teacher knew this and I was always the first to be questioned, guilty or not. I was beaten for Maggie Moynihan.

In the summer the tinkers broke bottles at the camps so that we couldn't go near with our bare feet and we had to walk on the railway line to pass by. Maggie Moynihan died one night and teacher said to visit the corpse house and say a prayer. The tent was full of candles and there was fresh straw from our barn. The tinkers put up a cross where she died but it was knocked down by the cattle scratching it.

I remember the boys shouting, 'The train from Baillinrobe is coming. Put the halfpennies on the track and make pennies.' The policeman came to the school and the teacher said, 'Get out your Catechisms.' He thought it was the priest. The policeman asked one question, 'Who are the people buying slices of bread and jam with flattened halfpennies?'

He looked around and waited. Nobody spoke and I got red. 'Ye'd be making half-crowns if your fathers were rich.'

We tried sixpenny pieces but they stuck to the train wheels because the metal was too soft. My uncle said that a trainload of the Black and Tans went up on the train one morning and came down on the same night, dead. It was a hot day and they took off their coats in the Partry Mountains and they were shot by mistake for Irishmen by some of their own.

Some body threw stones at the Great Western Railway sign and chipped the enamel letters and the policeman came to the school again without wearing a hat.

I never liked greyhounds. They held their greyhound meetings on Sunday afternoons. They propped up the back axle of an old Austin car and the wheels had no tubes or tyres. When the car engine was started it dragged a stuffed hare up the field and the rope wound one of the rear wheels. One Sunday the hare went too fast around the wheel and there was big bang and the smash of glass and the greyhounds were battered and some died. They went for a spade to bury them.

I went to Dublin and I wish now that I had never gone. Once during the school period I went and stayed at Monkstown. I bought a small book and I decided to start carving in stone. I got a lovely piece in a builder's yard and there was no way to take it home except in the bus. It was heavy but I could roll it and I got it to a stop. I asked the conductor of the first bus to take it to Monkstown. 'What do you think this is?' he said and banged the bell. I watched it go down the road.

Eventually I wrapped the stone in a big piece of brown paper and some people helped me to lift it on to the next bus and I got it to Monkstown. A messenger boy on a bicycle said he'd take it for me but it fell through his basket and he wept. I gave him sixpence but he went away still crying. I tried to roll the stone all the way but it was too much and I slipped and my shoulder hurt. I ended up in St Michael's Hospital and they wrapped me in bandages and sent me away.

About that time I got a job in Rathmines cutting glass and it was only temporary. One the second day an old lady asked for a pane of glass for a lead window. I was a failure at cutting glass and I broke every bit on the premises – but with good intentions. The old lady waited and then she became annoyed. 'You should have told me you were so busy and I could have ordered it from George's Street and they deliver it free.'

She was angry going away too. I was fired that night and I left Westland Row to the Galway Races and home.

CHAPTER 11

The Wearing of the Green

A year after he pulled the cloak off Thomas Davis, President de Valera unveiled Wolfe Tone in St Stephen's Green. It was another major event, captured in TV coverage and newspaper photos. We didn't get to the Davis unveiling, but we went to this one, buttoned up in the small tweed coats we got from our grandmother's shop in Cavan.

Tone was possibly an even more important statue than Davis. If Davis was the founder of the Young Irelanders and organiser of an ill-fated revolt in the famine-enfeebled country of the 1840s, then Tone was the godfather of Irish Republicanism, whose United Irelanders fomented the rebellion of 1798 and got Napoleon to send his troops over. He was the originator, the rebel to whose grave in Bodenstown all strands of competing Irish nationalism went to pay homage. As someone said, never was a man *less* likely to rest in peace.

We got the full story about Tone as kids, about how French war ships tried to land at Cork but were held at bay by the storms (the 'Protestant winds') although the French did land earlier on the west coast and drove their way inward, assisted by Irish rebels until they were defeated by the redcoats at Ballinamuck. Tone tried to repeat the invasion and landed at Lough Swilly in Donegal, but the French were intercepted and the operation failed. On such occasions, the French were treated with respect – there were even sporting dinners between opposing officers – whereas the Irish were taken off for harsher treatment. As was Tone, the 'class traitor'. As soon as he stepped off the boat, he was immediately recognised and arrested by a fellow Trinity graduate, now in the king's army.

The British wanted to hang Tone, but Tone argued that as a soldier he should be shot. He was in French uniform and an adjutant general in the revolutionary army. He was thus entitled to be shot by firing squad, a more dignified exit. But the British denied him this. It was the age-old insistence of the Irish rebel on 'political status'. In his cell, Tone tried to cheat the hangman by cutting his own throat, not very successfully. So the British, with extraordinary pedantry, stitched him up so he could be properly strung up. Afterwards, the surgeon told Tone 'not to move his head to the left, or he'd be done for', to which Tone replied, 'Sir, I can't thank you enough for that,' and slowly turned his head to the left, with a crack. It wasn't strictly true, but as children we loved this, like the closing scene from an old movie.

But even before Eddie got involved – long before – the project was controversial. In fact, right back to the original proposal in 1898, the centenary of Tone's death, after which the efforts were protracted and even deadly. The British didn't want a statue of Tone going up in Dublin, but the planners were determined and a special Committee was set up, sponsored by the Fenians. In fact, the attempt to put up his statue was itself bound up with revolutionary activities, as if it was an act of irreversible defiance – and a prelude to creating the Republic. And, indeed, the tale of its erection and the subsequent use of the memorial is, in many ways, the story of our country and its evolution into a modern state.

Before the statue, there was the laying of the foundation stone, itself always a major event. The laying of the stone for O'Connell's statue drew hundreds of thousands, and the crowds were nearly as large for Nelson's base in 1808 (presumably a different sort of crowd). For Tone, a stone was quarried out of Cave Hill in Belfast and delivered to Dublin in an extraordinary ceremony.

According to Judith Hill in *Irish Public Sculpture*, the stone 'lay in state for two nights on the site of the old Newgate Gaol in Harcourt Street before it headed a vast and tortuous procession' past Tone's birthplace and then his death place and then the site of Emmet's execution. John O'Leary performed the ceremony at the top of Grafton Street, where it was intended to erect the monument. Then, with an ornate trowel sent by Wolfe Tone's American granddaughter, 'who had found as many of his descendants as possible to lay hands on it before sending it to Ireland, O'Leary tapped the stone six times, once for each of the four provinces, once for the United States and once for France'.

It is like the delivery of a body – or a sculpture: an unmade sculpture, from which a body, or figure, will be wrestled. Even the reverence for the tools, such as the ornate trowel, is like something out of pagan ritual, or sculptor's studio. The presence of John O'Leary is the missing link here. He was an original Young Irelander, like Davis, and then a legendary Fenian and inspiration for 1916, the man about whom Yeats would later lament, in a famous refrain: 'Romantic Ireland is dead and gone/ It's with O'Leary in the grave.' More connections, more graves. Another head.

And there is the symbolism of place, passing Emmet's execution spot on Thomas Street. Indeed, the execution block itself has been given the status of a holy relic and, in a famous newsreel from 1920, during the War of Independence, Michael Collins is filmed, smiling and defiant, signing Dáil loans for the public upon it. The scene is in the garden of St Enda's in Rathfarnham, Pearse's school for young Republicans. Symbolism was crammed in. The British took Emmet's head off on a block, and now Collins was bringing the Republic into life upon it!

Axe-scored wood and uncarved stone. And even before Tone's stone left Belfast, there were exciting connections. In a letter to a co-organiser in Dublin, Patrick Flanigan describes his discovery that William Agnew, from whom he bought the stone, is – 'now for the fateful surprise' – 'the great grandson of William Orr who was hanged at Carrickfergus, by the mother's side (sic), and the grandson of William Agnew of Agnewstown, Co Antrim who was transported for life for carrying arms against England in 1798 ... Is this not very strange,' said Flanigan excitedly, 'strange as a romance of the rebellion invented for the purpose of giving the tale a roundness, creating excitement and fully expediting the realms of imagination in its adhesiveness to the evolution of one hundred years? We should all feel proud of being a portion of the mechanism which completed the whole century round story?'

His description itself suggests an emerging sculpture or the sort of memoir in which I am here engaged. Flanigan's letter appears in a souvenir booklet issued for the unveiling by the Wolfe Tone Committee. It has a modish 1960s cover, with a duotone of green over the sculpture's face, but inside the contents are of the most traditional variety: a wild speech by Pearse, a foreword by de Valera in Irish and a homage from Terence McSwiney. The only levity is provided by some diary extracts by Tone, which give a lively flavour of the man, scheming in Paris, and an essay by Eddie on the sculpture's creation, a rare piece of writing about his work.

In his letter, Flanigan describes the recovery of the stone as something akin to a military manoeuvre, or rebel sortie. 'We had to blast three times before we got the stone we wanted. But it was about 5 tons. We had to remove it on bars to the edge and managed to do so when it was landed on the floor of the quarry ... I attracted the attention of men all over the quarry. Then I said,: "Men, are you going to disappoint me after all my anxiety and trouble?"' One can see Flanigan walking around, firing out instructions, like Tone himself in Paris, gathering men and assistance. Or on the prow of his burning ship, doomed but fighting on heroically against the odds. 'We had to jump a hole to blast away the upper beds which would not suit our purpose,' said Flanigan firmly.

Although the two documents were written a century apart, Flanigan's letter appears to mimic Tone's diary, as if the planning of a statue and the planning of a rebellion – better still, the planning of a republic or state – were somehow similar.

This is Tone's diary: 'And as many officers as desired to come volunteers in the expedition. The people have been urgent more than once to begin, and at one time eight hundred of the garrison offered to give up the barracks of Dublin if the leaders would only give the signal' (1797). It is breathless stuff: decisive and impatient. 'The militia were almost to a man gained over, and numbers of these poor fellows have fallen victim in consequence.'

And it seemed that Eddie was getting in on the act. His Tone essay is purely about the mechanical aspects of the statue's creation and doesn't go into anything about artistic intent. But it is worth quoting, for its vivid and dramatic description of the casting process. At first this might seem out of place in a book intended for patriots and ageing rebels, but, on the contrary, it has the same quality of determination and derring-do as the rest of the essays.

'There was no bronze art foundry in Ireland,' begins Eddie, so in 1954 he decided to learn the craft. 'Otherwise I would always have to depend on foreign foundries to cast my work which meant that for me, it would be impossible to continue as a sculptor. So I set out with the help of the Irish Arts Council to study this craft. I was also helped by the German and Italian governments.'

One can imagine the die-hard separatists nodding approvingly at this aim for independence and self-sufficiency, aided by native sources and friendly foreign governments – just like Tone himself.

'It generally takes the enthusiasm of one person to push over any pioneering work of this kind. In this case, great credit is due to the efforts of Professor Heinrich Kirchner. His great dream is of developing the art of *cire-perdue* casting that it might be advanced to a high standard with the great progress in metallurgy and chemistry.' Enter Kirchner, the wise old revolutionary, the John O'Leary figure, tapping the stone with the trowel and mixing the smoking elements.

However, Professor Kirchner – and his new Irish protégé – had 'little time for the accomplishments of most European foundries, which were limited by their inherited traditions'. Their methods were 'inevitably the same, passed along for centuries from father to son, old ideas which to some foundries are professional secrets well guarded'. Well, *this* is news: I had hitherto thought that such secrets were 'the best ones'. But obviously not.

Kirchner had 'no time for this, so he being a sculptor gave me the great push that I needed,' said Eddie. 'Leaving Munich and Kirchner in 1959, I worked in seven different foundries carrying the secrets from one to another. I now found it easy to be employed because of the places that I had worked in. I was useful, a type of spy carrying the ideas and well-guarded professional secrets. I kept nothing to myself; I was prepared to pour out knowledge if there was something in the foundry to be learned.'

Again, a dramatic image that would surely be approved of by the old-timers: the sculptor, like a Fenian agent, moving incognito through Europe and seeking allies. Although Eddie seems to be somewhat contradicting himself: if these traditions were so 'old' and 'limiting', then surely they were not worth learning?

'Founders belong to that prima donna breed of craftsmen who combine great skill with somewhat fiery temperaments,' continued Eddie, in what could be the description of some moody rebel leader (or something of a self-portrait).

As an illustration of just how problematic the process could be, Eddie describes going to France to help a friend cast a horse. The friend's equipment 'was very limited' and as they lifted the mould out of the drying-oven, it fell and broke across the middle. 'My friend, in a trance, letting an occasional roar, ran away into the street.' (It sounds like Uri.) But Eddie had previously worked with 'a very old German craftsman' and, using techniques he'd picked up there, he 'repaired the mould and poured again, getting a perfect cast'. The friend was overjoyed because 'his future as a foundry man depended on this horse'.

Eddie then describes the making of Tone.

> When Wolfe Tone was completed the statue became a vast shell of wax about 2 inches thick. The inside being hollow, it was filled with a plaster mixture. When I had completed the surface modelling of the figure, additional coats of plaster were carefully applied, as the plaster must withstand a temperature of 600 degrees

Centigrade. The figure is now in the middle of a large block of plaster. A brick wall is built around the mould, leaving a small hole in the wall where coke could be pushed through. The fire was lit and, as the heat penetrated through the mould, the wax figure becomes liquid and burns away until the inside became negative. The empty spaces left by this molten wax are actually the forms of Wolfe Tone into which the subsequent molten bronze is poured and left to cool and harden: hence the name '*Cire- Perdue*'" or "Lost-wax" process.

Is this not a perfect metaphor for the birth of a state – especially after turmoil?

Then the outer layers of the mould were broken off, the core shaken out thoroughly and the bronze cleaned.

Or the real state emergent from an idealised republic?

One can imagine the old boys reading this: the creation of their hero, the 'unique process', the fiery crucible. Eddie goes on to describe the amount of molten metal that went into the memorial: 'three quarters of a ton and, with the famine group, a ton and a half'. But on another level, he seems to be deconstructing the great man: 'a vast shell of wax', the 'inside being hollow'. Tone's ingredients are listed: an 'alloy of from 85 to 90 per cent copper, 7 per cent tin and 3 per cent zinc' all of which will ensure 'a quality metal, with a good colour and a very good durability for out of doors. When made in this manner there is only one bronze and the unique process automatically destroys the original figure modelled by the sculptor.'

'There are no original models in plaster,' he stresses bluntly, 'as the wax original figures burnt away in the moulds and were replaced by bronze.' As if to say, I have replaced the 'subject' with a 'sculpture'. This would confirm a later point by some critics that

Eddie was not really interested in these commissions as portraits of national icons, but merely used them to pursue his interest in the human form. And then just pursued 'form' itself, in its purest, sculptural sense.

The dream is over – *gentlemen, you have a country*. What a paradox: to create something, you have to destroy it. The original model has to be dissolved to make way for its 'unique' embodiment, something lasting and tangible. And this is what Thomas Davis had asked for in his poem 'Tone's Grave', also included in the booklet. It is the title of one of the panels in College Green, so in a curious way one public sculpture of Eddie's has pre-figured another. And it gave instructions not dissimilar to the plan eventually accepted:

> *But the old man, who saw I was mourning there, said*
> *'We come, sir, to weep where young Wolfe Tone is laid,*
> *And we're going to raise him a monument, too –*
> *A plain one, yet fit for the simple and true.'*

Is this not a strange coincidence of prediction, as the stone-holding Patrick Flanigan might put it? The panel shows a huddle of animals and elongated figures, with their heads hung in mourning, although they might just as much be relaxing, in the manner of the *Land of Music*. Somewhere at the centre is a cross denoting a grave.

In all, Eddie's contribution to the Wolfe Tone booklet has a refreshing practicality, compared to the other essays, with their solemn talk of heroism and sacrifice. The most high-pitched is an extraordinary oration by Patrick Pearse in Bodenstown in 1913, which is almost sacrilegious in its rapture. Tone's grave, says Pearse, 'is the holiest place in Ireland, holier than the place where St Patrick sleeps in Down': *this* about the man who brought Christianity to Ireland.

It is exclamatory stuff and a preliminary to his graveside oration for O'Donovan Rossa in 1915, which set the scene for the Rising. There is also an essay on the 'Heroic Wife of Tone', by Terence McSwiney, the former Lord Mayor of Cork, and another man whose phrases went into the language. 'It is not those who can inflict the most, but those who can endure the most who shall prevail,' he said and, true to his word, in 1920, McSwiney died on hunger strike in Brixton Prison, after 74 days. Pearse was executed in 1916. All these deaths and graves.

Another piece describes how the grave of Tone's widow had become a shrine in Brooklyn, New York (of all places) and was visited there by shadowy groups of rebel veterans, known as 'Tone's Men', who travelled from different parts of the US to pay homage. After her husband's death, Matilda had fled to France with her family and then to the US, where she was joined by other United Irishmen. They 'cherished her and the memory of her husband', and as they themselves died they were buried in the 'Irish Rebel Plot' in New York. When Matilda died, in Georgetown in 1849, she was buried among them and a memorial erected over her grave by Clan na Gael, the powerful Irish American organisation that was busy fomenting another round of resistance against England. America was the crucible for Irish rebellion against Britain. As Dev knew when he went there to unveil the Emmet statues in 1919.

The only levity in the booklet is an essay about Tone's writings by the scholar Roger McHugh. And, of course, the diary extracts of Tone himself: impish and colourful, as he flitted around Paris drinking with revolutionaries. 'Put on my regimentals for the first time: as pleased as a little boy in his first breeches. Foolish enough, but not unpleasant. Walked about Paris to show myself: huzza! *Citoyen Wolfe Tone, Chef de Brigade* in the service of the Republic!' (August 14, 1796).

And yet despite all the rhetoric in the booklet, Tone's statue was very slow to get off the ground, or onto it, and the booklet acknowledges this fact. Funds were not forthcoming and the Republicans missed their chance when the intended spot at the top of Grafton Street was taken instead for the Boer War arch in 1900. The arch celebrates the British (and, by extension, Irish) campaign against the South African rebels. Not everyone was for the Republicans. Far from it.

A walking Giacometti: de Valera arrives to unveil Tone, 1967
Photograph © *Irish Press*

Mum, Colm and I at the
Tone unveiling
Photograph © *Irish Press*

The front row at the unveiling. De Valera and a sulking Patrick Kavanagh are at opposite ends. Charles Haughey is next to my parents.
Photograph © Lensmen Photo Agency

With Haughey and Montague Kavanagh, at the unveiling of *Fisherman* in Lansdowne House, Ballsbridge 1967
Photograph © Lensmen Photo Agency

My parents with painter Sean McSweeney in the Hendriks Gallery, 1969
Photograph © *Irish Press*

Colm and I showing our bronzes at an art show in Dún Laoghaire
Photograph © *The Irish Times*

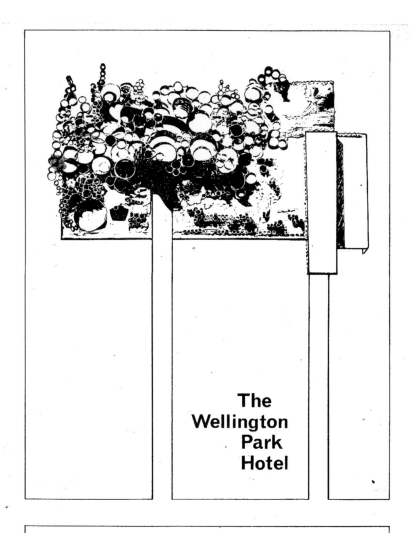

The Wellington Park Hotel

MENU

Menu card for the Wellington Park Hotel Belfast, with an
illustration of *Integration*

Tone after his bombing by Loyalists, 1971
Photograph © *The Irish Times*

The Delaney family
by *King and Queen*

Portrait of the sculptor by Colman Doyle for *The People of Ireland*
photobook 1971
Photograph © Colman Doyle, National Library of Ireland

Drawing for *The Samson Riddle* by Wolf Mankowitz

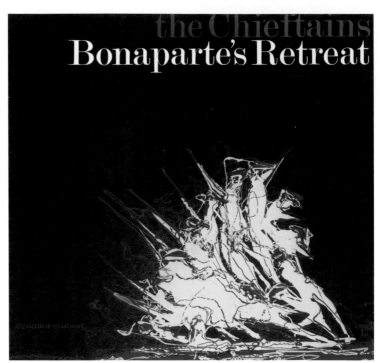

Bonaparte's Retreat, album sleeve for the Chieftains, 1979

Beyond the Pale Eddie in his sculpture park in Connemara, 1994

Today, the arch still bears the chips of stray bullets from 1916, a mark of revenge by disgruntled rebels perhaps, although they could just as likely be from British bullets, aiming for the rebel-held College of Surgeons nearby. Specifically, the arch is for the Royal Dublin Fusiliers, the famous regiment drawn from the Dublin working class and celebrated in *Ulysses* and in countless songs and stories, including a rousing salvo by The Dubliners. It was mostly Fusilier families, for example, who had jeered the 'extremist' rebels when they emerged from the rubble they'd created in 1916, a hungry populace outraged that Republicans could pull this sudden stunt while their men were off fighting in the trenches of Europe. This was the initial reaction to the Rising, but it lasted for some time.

In a haunting photo, for example, which is rarely shown, a sombre crowd has filled up College Green to attend the erection of a memorial to the 16th Irish Division, a poppy-bedecked wooden cross placed exactly where Davis would later stand. It is late 1916, and by now the entire 16th Division, including the Fusiliers, has faced devastating losses on the Western Front. The crowd look stunned and confused. People are on roof of Trinity, gazing down. The pendulum of history has swung against them. The small cross would soon be removed and the event, and the huge sacrifice it commemorated, swept away from the official memory. It is the sort of picture we never saw in our school history books.

But the 1916 Rising changed everything. It decimated the Wolfe Tone Committee and their records were seized in a raid by British forces on their Parnell Square office, including some original proposals for the statue. These would have been interesting. One was by the sculptor Willie Pearse, who was executed along with his brother – mainly because he *was* his brother.

Almost all the committee were caught up in the Rising. Many were killed and all the others, except James Stitch, the treasurer, went to prison. He escaped arrest and managed to keep the financial records intact. One notable casualty was the old Fenian Tom Clarke, who had organised collections at football and hurling matches in aid of the Memorial Fund. This strikes me as particularly poignant, perhaps because it adds to the general pathos of Clarke, a little white-whiskered man with his tobacco shop (and den of sedition) on Parnell Street. And before that, his nine years in British jails, much of it in solitary confinement. Illustrations in our school books showed Clarke with his arms chained behind his back, and forced to eat his dinner 'like a dog'. Not only did these men face death and execution for their cause, but long prison sentences: Clarke did fifteen years, and O'Leary another fifteen, again much of it in solitary confinement. In 1916, Clarke was among the rebel leaders executed by the British.

After Clarke's death, his widow, Kathleen, took over the project and, with the release of prisoners, the committee was re-constituted. But, according to the booklet, the 'force of events during the War of Independence and the subsequent Civil War prevented the fund raising activities needed to complete the project'. This is a coy way of putting it. In fact, the Republicans – or hardcore Republicans – lost the Civil War and, with it, the impetus, and public support, to put up more Republican statues. The pendulum of history had swung against them.

In 1927, a new committee was formed, with the old IRB funds. In fairness, the committee crossed Civil War boundaries, and involved Free State figures, such as Generals Richard Mulcahy and Seán Mac Eoin. Safely dead before any bitter Treaty differences, Tone could now be a unifying figure. But with more committee members dying, the project ran aground and did not really come to life again until decades later when it was proposed to put Tone down on Mary Street, near where he was born, and specifically inside the church yard of St Mary's Church where he was baptised. The Protestant Church of Ireland generously offered the disused cemetery for a memorial park and the infamous 'stone' was transferred there. In 1929, it had been ignominiously transferred to the Corporation Yard, after it was dug up from the Grafton Street spot where it had been so elaborately laid but then supplanted by the 'traitors arch' of the Boer War.

By now, however, the government had got involved and the Minister for Finance, James Ryan, decreed that the park was not central enough, nor funds sufficient to finance a 'memorial worthy of the Father of Irish Republicanism'. It was the 1960s and the state was flush with cash and confidence. They wanted to do things properly, and eventually the Taoiseach Seán Lemass intervened and proposed that Tone should go back up onto St Stephen's Green, next to the swanky Shelbourne Hotel. Despite such glamour, the link to armed Republicanism was still strong among the statue's movers: both Ryan and Lemass were War of Independence veterans, as was Todd Andrews, who sat on the Competition Committee that picked the eventual design.

Eddie was triumphant in the competition, and newspapers show him and the architect, Noel Keating, looking down at their maquette and smiling at the figures, as if they were toys come to life. Tone seems to be waving back at them, with his hand saluting upwards. Beside them are three middle-aged men in dark suits and ties and prescription spectacles: the unadorned look of Irish officialdom, and of officialdom anywhere, in the 1950s and early 1960s. They are handing the prize-winning cheque to Eddie and Noel Keating, who look very young by comparison, Keating with a beatnik beard and Eddie with short hair and a dark open-neck shirt, which is, at least, buttoned up neatly.

At the announcement, Minister James Ryan was also triumphant, and even a touch scathing. 'From time to time attempts had been made by little men to denigrate Tone,' he said. 'Little men are often jealous of great men and this is not confined to any one generation.' Was this a sideswipe at his political opponents of the day? Tone's detractors had 'tried to remove him from the pinnacle where his countrymen had placed him,' added Ryan, 'but his fame will live.' The phrasing was doubly ironic given that the sculpted Tone was not going to be on a pinnacle or pedestal, and even if he was, he would later be spectacularly removed from it by his Loyalist 'detractors' – using the very methods he himself championed.

Ryan then extravagantly claimed that Tone was 'honoured, not only as an intellectual statesman and a philosophic revolutionary, but as an ecumenical Christian'. This was stretching things. Tone may have been a political ecumenical, aiming to 'replace the labels of Protestant, Catholic and Dissenter with the common name of Irishmen', but to call him an ecumenical Christian conjures up an image of some clap-happy vicar, quite at odds with the libertine Jacobin that Tone actually was. But, by this stage, Tone has become Everyman and it is hardly a wonder that his grave in Bodenstown was so constantly visited by different parties.

The statue had been 'a long time coming', agreed Ryan, but 'this was not for the want of enthusiasm or effort but principally the want of funds.' The implication was that the country had now finally come into prosperity. And it was now very much a state project. Through the government's contribution, 'every taxpayer and citizen would help to perpetuate the memory of Tone, and that's how it should be,' said Ryan firmly. This made the project much more compulsory than it had been, but no one was complaining. Everyone was a 'Republican' now, especially since real Republicanism had been bedded down and had had its teeth extracted.

As Minister of Finance, Ryan was 'glad to be in a position to help this worthy project'. Ryan himself is an interesting character. A 1916 veteran, he was apparently the last man out of the GPO. He was also a thorough moderniser, who despaired of de Valera's protectionism – Ryan was a major advocate of free trade and inward investment – and of Dev's close relationship to the Catholic Church. Ryan took seriously his Irish Republicanism – as he saw it.

Ryan then praised the earlier efforts to get Tone erected, and again there is a parallel with the independence struggle. 'More than one group was interested,' said Ryan, 'but all had but one objective. Eventually they all coalesced into one group and pooled their resources.' In the case of Kathleen Clarke, the parallel is explicit. 'Despite the many setbacks and disappointments she never ceased in her efforts to see the memorial realised in her lifetime. And with it, the ambition of bringing to fruition one of her husband's cherished dreams.' If Tom Clarke's most 'cherished dream' was a free Irish Republic, then a statue of Tone was a secondary but related one. And here we are now, suggests Ryan, with state *and* statue.

But Ryan's eulogy is full of the contradictions of Irish nationalism. Having praised Tone as an 'ecumenical Christian' he then goes on to describe how the same Tone helped to found the United Irishmen in Belfast – a group which 'saw the futility of constitutional action on behalf of Catholics and, encouraged by the revolutionary methods in America and France, emerged as a secret society working for complete independence'.

These words would come back to haunt the Irish government three years later, when armed militants emerged to claim the mantle of this tradition – and challenge the credibility of Ryan's bourgeois state. The state would spend the subsequent thirty years trying to fight the historical 'legitimacy' of the modern IRA. After all, if 'constitutional action on behalf of Catholics was futile' in 1796, then maybe it was also futile in 1969?

Historically, the statement is also completely untrue: most of the gains made for Irish independence before 1916 were made by the Home Rule movement. And who could describe the work of constitutionalists like O'Connell and Parnell as 'futile'? O'Connell was probably more effective than a generation of doctrinaire rebels. Not for nothing is he known as 'the Liberator'. And not for nothing do the statues of him and Parnell mark our capital's main thoroughfare.

But no one saw the need to question such easy platitudes in 1966. At the sculpture's announcement, General Seán Mac Eoin was in attendance, having been on the Memorial Committee. He was now a Fine Gael icon – in 1959, he challenged Dev for the presidency – and was still known by his jovial *nom de guerre* of 'the Blacksmith of Ballinalee': strong-handed, folksy and very good at 'taking out' Brits. Or the rebel Irish, as the subsequent Civil War would prove. The main opposition party also had its roots in rebellion. But so unquestioning was this official line that no one saw fit to talk up the broader, parliamentary tradition. It was an omission which would come back to haunt them, but such are the distortions of history.

CHAPTER 12

Raising the Tone

After the long political struggle to get the Tone memorial finally commissioned, there was then the row over what it should look like. And many of the aesthetic arguments were a re-run of the controversy about Davis a year earlier.

For a start, it was proposed that a corner of the Green be taken over and the conservationists were not happy about this. Just a month earlier, a large Henry Moore sculpture in honour of Yeats had been installed in the Green, with a raised rockery around it, and the public were only getting used to that. 'The wearin' of the green', the newspapers called it.

For Tone, the setting would be more dramatic. The corner gates were to be removed and replaced by an open plaza, from which the statue, set back from the street, would be visible from many angles. The plaza would be backgrounded by a row of granite columns, with an overlap into the Green itself and towards the other sculpture, the *Famine Group*, which would be just inside. This was originally to be just two figures, but on his own initiative Eddie developed it into a full family, with an animal or dog. Both of these features were controversial: the addition of a famine group and the inclusion of an animal. Tone, meanwhile, would be an imposing 11 feet tall and would stand on a sort of flat rock made up of further granite slabs.

In fact, the design by architect Noel Keating was ingenious. It opened up the Green 'to the people', a subconscious political note for a former colonial playground which was so often gated and locked. As the judges put it bluntly, 'The piazza becomes part of the streetscape rather than part of the Park.'

'For once, a major Irish sculpture will be neither shrouded in traffic nor locked up after sunset, said *the Irish Press*, 'inswept railings will ensure a 24 hour long viewing point.' This is very thoughtful, as if the statue was indeed not an inanimate object but a sensitive living man who shouldn't be locked in after dark. It also suggested that people might want to come and look at Tone at around 3 am. Which many did, including revellers coming back from the nightclubs on Leeson Street, often pausing to put a scarf around his throat or a flower in his hand. Or, on a few occasions, a glass in the hand near his mouth, as if he's having a final drink or even cutting his own throat, just like he tried to do at the end. But now, jauntily: *I'm having the last laugh, I'm back in bronze*. This 24-hour viewing point also gave the public the sort of access we had, as children, when we looked out the window in the middle of the night and saw Wolfe Tone, under the moonlight, standing next to the clothesline.

As for the statue being shrouded in traffic, Davis was indeed besieged, and letters to papers protested about this. The Irish were as bad about traffic in the 1960s as they are now, and, as the letters pointed out, the authorities were just as bad in allowing it. O'Connell Street was like one long car park, as was College Green. 'Surely, after all the effort and expense involved,' wrote D.G. Fitzgibbon in a letter to *The Irish Times* 'the automotive monster should not be allowed to engulf once again, something aesthetic.'

Happily, Tone would be further back, away from all the traffic. Futhermore, the fact that he was at ground level meant that he was approachable, as opposed to being up on a plinth extolling the people below. You could touch him and people do, which is why to this day his codpiece is shiny, as is the hem of his coat. You could stand up beside him, or under his arm, as tourists do for photographs. Tone was thus monumental, with a proud and haughty expression, but he was also austere, and even modest, with an austerity and purity appropriate to the space. In a sense fulfilling the 'simple and true' suggestion of Thomas Davis's poem.

Also, the base was reversed. At the last moment, Eddie told the workmen to turn the stones over, so that instead of the flat polished granite, we got the lumpy, craggy side, as if Tone is standing on a good old Irish rock, like something in Connemara, or hewn out of Cave Hill in Belfast. Or standing on his own tomb, as if he's been resurrected and come back to life, despite what the British did to him – and despite being later blown up. (Davis incidentally also looks like he's risen again and is standing surprised on his upended coffin – like a big toy out of his box. His base is of white granite, a nine-foot-high single block quarried in the Dublin Mountains.)

'Wolfe Tone was a man who put Ireland on the ground,' Eddie told the *Irish Press* 'and he should be down on the ground among the people. The idea of a figure on the ground is not a new one. Rodin did it, for example, with his statue of Victor Hugo in Paris, though I think it was eventually put on a pedestal because the authorities wanted it on one. But Rodin himself envisaged it down on the ground, 'walking' on the ground, if you know what I mean.'

The other subtext was that Tone would not be on a horse. An Irish hero should never be on a horse, lording it over the peasants, or tenants, below. Brendan Behan's famous demystifying definition about the Anglo-Irish comes to mind – 'a Protestant on a horse'. And, in fact, equestrian statues have been among those most attacked by angry Republicans: King William in College Green, King George II in St Stephen's Green and Viscount Gough on his magnificent charger in the Phoenix Park. All of them are gone, and visitors have commented on Dublin being one of the few capitals in Europe without an equestrian statue. Which is particularly ironic for a country in love with the horse, but again such are the erasions of acceptable history.

What is also extraordinary is the level of violence directed at these statues. Queen Victoria may have been moved peacefully from the front of Leinster House, but Lord Gough and his horse were repeatedly attacked, and King William was assaulted so many times that a security guard was put beside it. Nor has the official attitude been any less antagonistic. In 1986, when the state finally sold off the Gough statue it was on condition that 'the sculpture left the country'.

And yet despite this problematic tradition, Eddie told Terence Connealy in the *Evening Press* that he'd love to do a mounted figure, not of a colonial toff, but of the nineteenth-century Land League leader Michael Davitt: 'just as he used to travel the Transvaal exhorting the Boers to resist their oppressors. Imagine a one-armed rider?' (Connealy helpfully informed his readers that Davitt had lost an arm as a youth in a Lancashire clothing factory.)

Imagine, indeed. Nelson was one-armed, of course. But one-armed and riding? Now there's heroism. But, in fact, Eddie was just riffing here. After Davis and Tone, and their attendant controversy, he would never do another representative portrait again. But he liked to get expansive in the long interview: Connealy's feature was called *Friday Focus*.

Also Davitt was something of a hero, back West, with his struggles over the land. And Eddie himself grew up near horses and loved watching them and sculpting them. He was like Haughey, who also had Mayo roots and aspired to bigger things, such as bloodstock and art. It is interesting that when I visited Haughey for the RHA show in 2004, almost all of the work he had of Eddie's were horses. In fact, Haughey is the only Irish politician I've ever seen portrayed on a horse, in the 'secret' paintings of Eddie McGuire. The paintings were never shown in public, and partly for this reason. He had often been accused of wanting to ape the Anglo-Irish, but he was also a man with a bit of grandeur and a wild streak, just like Eddie himself. In fact, it is hard to look at the paintings and not detect an element of tongue in cheek, a rakish touch, as if he's sending up his own vanity, and theirs.

To have a statue on the ground, of course, meant that it would have to be large, and Tone would be over eleven foot tall. This too was controversial and a dramatic departure from the usual life-sized, or near life-sized, depictions of heroes. But then Eddie had already broken with tradition the previous year with his towering Davis. Nor would Tone be a realistic statue in the conventional sense of the word. Although quite traditional in sculptural terms, and certainly in comparison with Eddie's other work, it was a very modern interpretation of a national hero, with little period detail and huge booted legs which look like tree trunks coming out of the ground.

Again, the straight-talking Minister Ryan was in no doubt about this when he announced the commission. Looking at Eddie's maquette, he predicted, with satisfaction, that the statue would be 'sturdy and virile', i.e. not some hook-nosed coloniser in a poodle wig. The sculpted Tone would, presumably, be one of the 'great men' of whom Dr Ryan suspected 'little men' were constantly jealous. And it wasn't going to be literalism: Eddie argued for something monumental, something beyond effete realism – a large-scale figurative work was thus befitting of this ambition and of the state, the sculptor and of Tone himself.

But not everyone supported it. The debate rehashed the arguments over Davis, about conventional realism versus modernism and expressionism, a debate that goes on almost everywhere, and still goes on today. In terms of public art, it is a contest which, in many respects, has been lost by the modernists. Recent statues erected in London, for example, of Nelson Mandela and John Betjeman (in St Pancras station) are not just conventional realism, but pure literalism. There has been a retreat in the face of populism and a loss of nerve by the authorities. Things aren't much different in Paris. You can walk the length of central Paris and not see a single piece of modern sculpture, presumably for fear that it would blemish the imperial capital and distract from *the past*.

Basically, many people wanted conventional realism – and they still do. In Dublin, they wanted Edmund Burke or Oliver Goldsmith outside Trinity College, with all the buttons of their jackets captured. Or best of all, Horace Plunkett on Kildare Street who is so precisely captured in stone that his finger is 'holding' the page of his book, while he poses 'momentarily' for the sculptor –

an amazing conceit of public statuary – while his free hand fondles his chin in ecclesiastical contemplation.

Many nationalists also wanted pure realism, but of the gaudy kind: Tone with a cockade and sword. Or a pike, or gun. In some interviews, Eddie said that he toyed with the idea of a French uniform. Tone was, after all, an adjutant general in Napoleon's army and there was the appealing idea of having him standing there in the uniform that the British wouldn't shoot him in. But this would be to erect a statue of a 'French soldier'. And anyway, it was not a soldier who was being honoured but a man, a leader and thinker.

Eddie would later have some extraordinary encounters with Republicans for other memorials. In one proposal, for his native Mayo, some Irish Americans wanted a gunman leaning over a stone wall with a green neon sign over his head saying 'He died so that Ireland might be Free'. They came down our lane in Dún Laoghaire in a big black limo and arrived in wearing trenchcoats and fedoras, almost happy to fulfil the image of Chicago hit men.

'But you'll frighten all the children,' protested Eddie when he heard their crass neon-lit proposal, and he argued instead for some abstracted subtlety. A heated discussion ensued during which my mother could hear, through the kitchen door, the immortal words: 'You'll take your instructions from us!'

The project was not commissioned. Worse still, the limo got stuck at the end of the lane, and it was with considerable relief that we saw the fedora-hatted men eventually get it free.

The other argument against realism was that there was no totally accurate image of Tone. Eighteenth-century drawings were stylised and enhanced. Grattan for example, did not look nearly as groomed or heroic as his statue on College Green. Drawings of Tone suggested a slim feminine face, with a button nose, but these were usually in profile. Ironically, the most accurate reference is Tone's death mask. Despite his torment towards the end, the mask shows a smooth-faced, sleeping man, but this is possibly because all death masks essentially look the same, be they of Austin Clarke, Séamus

192

Ennis or the tortured Tone. With the perpetual rest of death, they settle into being generalised corpses.

The more Eddie was pressed on these questions, the more provocative his replies. 'Tone figured life-size in a park setting would look like a leprechaun,' he told Terence Connealy in the *Evening Press*. 'The normally true proportion is that the head should be one-eighth the size of the full man.'

'Actually, I have lost out,' added Eddie, 'because I was originally commissioned to make a life-size statue but realised it would look ridiculous instead of monumental.' This value-for-money argument was popular with journalists, who had their tax-paying readers to think of. He also said that he was only supposed to create two famine statues. 'Ireland got four for the price of two,' he said with a smile, as if he was trading people or bringing the dead back to life.

Connealy's is a feisty interview, which again shows the colourful reaction Eddie provoked in journalists, but also the impact of modern art at the time. 'Delaney is a confirmed individualist, who is rapidly creating a culture-splitting cult with his near-grotesque symbolisms, but he is not repelled by controversy.' Connealy's prose is almost gothic as it describes 'the months of foundry casting, cleaving the mutinous metal into molten shapes and sinew; months made wearingly tense as arguments grew about the structure of the final design'.

Again, as with the Tone booklet, one can't help thinking of a new treaty, or state, being hammered out, but also the sense of combustible, rebellious material (nationalism, the sculptor himself) which must be harnessed and tamed.

'When I put it to him that one distinguished critic had dismissed Davis as an 'elephantine-footed monstrosity', writes Connealy, 'Edward's simple reply could have been foreseen: "Truth lies in proportion, not size."' Tone was 'a slim, springy medium-sized man', adds Conneally, and a 'few of the thousands who flocked to see the national tribute to him pointed this out with scathing reference to the tall statue'.

Connealy also asked him about the addition of a 'famine family', behind Tone. Many felt that this took from the purity of Tone's memorial and was from another era (the 1840s, fifty years after Tone) but the unease was also because it struck at something deeper, and that was the shame of the famine, an event which was only selectively used in nationalist mythology and represented a low point in terms of poverty, trauma and colonial subjugation. Indeed, in many ways, it was not until the 1990s that the Great Famine could be properly and openly commemorated.

'Tone's is not a victory monument,' said Eddie, in his own historical summation. 'He wanted all Ireland independent and united. The failure of Tone's expeditions led to a decline in national morale and presaged the famine or Great Hunger. If Tone had succeeded, I doubt if the famine would have been allowed to happen. Grain stocks would have been kept at home when the potato crops failed.'

The famine group is thus not a representational, realistic piece. That would be too direct and painful, and even sensationalist. It would be reproducing, and intruding upon, human suffering. It would also risk an element of self-pity, which was the very quality people wanted to avoid and which they feared would undermine the heroic status of Tone. Instead, precisely because the group was a modern, figurative sculpture, the figures could appear to be skeletal, yet also abstracted, distended and mythified. They have a worn dignity and transform their subject matter. One figure stands with arms upstretched towards the sky, while another weakly holds a cup of running water to the mouth of a seated figure. But the water is running over, out of the bronze cup – a sculpture cannot drink, obviously. This adds to the poignancy of it all: the water trickles outwards and down over the base of the monument, suggesting wastage, or aid coming too late, or a stream of tears.

There was further controversy over the inclusion of a 'dog'. Critics said it was undignified and diminished the idea of human suffering. Eddie was particularly impatient with this. First of all, it was not a 'dog', he said, but an 'animal': a sort of generic creature, in keeping with the non-literal, expressive nature of the overall piece. If Tone was a generalised hero, then the dog was a generalised animal. However, in the cut and thrust of discussion, he eventually settled on 'hound'.

An intriguing defence, offered by one critic, suggested that the general animal represented a general Christian and so united the specific, divisive categories of Catholic, Protestant and Dissenter, just the way Tone wanted to – in a single beast. Labels were no longer required. The common name of Irishmen was grounded, and symbolised, in a prone but determined animal. This really baffled the commentators and infuriated others.

And anyway, asked Eddie, what was wrong with such an animal? They starved too. To exclude them was to detach the people from their economic context, which Irish history often had a tendency to do. That the natives were in with the animals and had a closeness to them would be unthinkable now: the cows inside the cottages to keep people warm, the pigs eating scraps, the horse tethered to the gable. It was almost as if Eddie himself came from this time, and from a region, Mayo, which was particularly rife with famine memories.

Indeed, the animals add a lively and affirmative quality to his human groups, such as with *Land of Music*. In the stylised disintegration of Eddie's treatment of the human figure, the family was not an actual family but attenuated beings. They have been transformed into sculptures and thus made permanent. They transcend their suffering, as we have. In the prosperous 1960s, we were now confident to commemorate the famine, and this was the appropriate way to do it. In a sense, it is a victory monument. We have triumphed – despite this.

The memorial was also enhanced by its setting, with the famine group inside a stone screen and away from Tone, in a separate space. The screen itself is an enduring feature, a piece of striking modernism which echoes the ancient Irish past: long, slender columns, made up of two to three pieces of granite, and often with the heavier sections on top, in the daring manner of a dry stone

195

wall. The columns are of differing widths, with the gaps between them big enough to see through, but not get through, unless you are, indeed, skeletal thin.

The granite stones have been left rough, and some still bear the claw marks of the diggers on their edges. It was rumoured that this was ogham, the ancient Irish lettering, but this is incorrect. One delightful phrase was 'micro chips for the Stone Age'. By leaving the stone craggy and unpolished, it suggested raw modernism but also that the national project was something unfinished and ongoing. Sculpture was an evolving form, and so was Irish nationalism.

Indeed, such an 'unfinished' quality was almost a prerequisite for Republican memorials, and a newspaper editorial in 1963 warned that the sudden flurry of Republican memorials should 'not be presented as representing finality or the consummation of the age-old ideal'. Hence, for O'Donovan Rossa, there is a large rough-hewn boulder in St Stephen's Green. In the case of Tone, the surface of the stone reflected the sculpture itself. Or as Judith Hill wrote about another such memorial, of a rebel pikeman in Tralee, 'The surface of the clay is rough, expressive, the essence of vigour,' and the intention is, 'to project an image whose essential liveliness was not dissipated by a detailed attention to surface detail.'

There was one thing left unfinished with Tone, however, which shouldn't have been, and this was the chiselling of his details on the base. The job was done by Frank Morris, the sculptor and husband of painter Camille Souter. Morris had actually been a runner-up for the commission itself. Second place went to Hilary Heron, the mixed-media sculptor, who has a distinctive spiky style. These are interesting choices, for they prove that if the commission hadn't gone to Eddie, the memorial would have been no less modern or experimental.

Morris had already chiselled 'Wolfe Tone' into the granite, but didn't realise that he was also to chisel in Tone's year of birth and death. For a short time, Tone had neither been born nor died. According to Eddie, Morris had already been paid and so Tone's years have a much shallower indent than his name. But as the leaves collect around his bulky feet, his large chiselled name is deep enough to hold water: recompense for the dribbling water being lost to the famine victims behind him.

Finally, to integrate further with the Green, the memorial was echoed by nearby trees: weeping ash for 'sorrow' on the famine side and an elm for 'optimism' next to Tone. Their presence encouraged notions about ogham lettering, since the ancient Irish alphabet is based on trees. However, the elm was later removed, to the relief of many who felt that they hindered a view of the statue. Generally, however, trees are an excellent complement to sculpture. They are, indeed, sculptures themselves, which is why in Japan whole families go into the countryside to stare at them as such.

So in summary, the statue, and the overall memorial, was not about Tone as a person, but about his legacy and beliefs. And about his actions, through which he has transformed himself from a 'slim, springy figure' into a big striding hero. Tone was an icon, and it was better to have an imaginative, inclusive version that would be closer to the true spirit of Republicanism. His statue was a mirror in which each man and woman can see themselves as equal and valid, and larger than their human potential. Eddie would do a *generalised* Tone, a broadly figurative Everyman.

And, if there was no accurate image of Tone, then who did he use as model?

Himself, he told the startled interviewers. Each morning before he went out to work on Tone, he had a good look at himself in the mirror. If Tone was Everyman, then Tone could be him, so he would model his subject on himself. De Valera only 'had to look into his own heart' to see the patriotic wishes of the Irish people, but Eddie only had to look into the mirror. And when you see Tone's face close-up, you can indeed see my father's expression, at Tone's age. As you can with Davis, indeed: both statues have similar faces. And given my own close resemblance to my father – the very image, people would say – I had the ludicrous vanity of people telling me that I had two statues of myself in my native city. If Joyce could model his heroes on himself, and have them walk about the city, then surely I could do something similar: accept the image of a father figure and have him stand there every day, before the swirling traffic. The place where Wolfe Tone was. *Here comes everyman.*

CHAPTER 13

Here Comes Everyman

So, to unveil this archetypal Republican, this mythic man and evergreen rebel – not to mention self-portrait of sculptor (and his eldest son!) – President de Valera came along in his old Rolls Royce. In the photographs, you can see the hushed awe as Dev emerges from the car and walks up the plaza towards the waiting ceremony: truly, a walking sculpture. It is only a year after the Davis event, but he already looks older, his aide de camp walking close to his side, just in case he lists.

Dev had won re-election as president, but only just. Incredibly, he won by a margin of just one per cent. He lost heavily in Dublin and among young people. 'Sure I'm a countryman at heart,' he said, afterwards, 'and Dublin people have always been flighty.' Some say he also blamed Haughey for the closeness of the election but there is no evidence for this. Haughey, after all, had secured him the clever TV deal and got him elected in the face of a robust Fine Gael campaign. The reality was that many people saw Dev as a relic of the past and wanted him to move on.

Nevertheless, precisely *because* he was a relic, he was treated with great respect and the crowd at Tone's plaza opened into a 'V' to see him in from the kerb. Old men stand with their medals and the banners of old brigades: small men in overcoats, just like the little fellow with his wife at the Davis unveiling. Dev's car is still the old Rolls Royce, but behind it are the shiny bonnets of new Vauxhalls and Hillman Hunters. Indeed, Dev's car was also treated as a relic and, after his death in 1975, a Department of Justice official queried if it could be considered an 'archaeological object' given that Dev was a 'historical person'. (It wasn't, and the car was sold.)

The Tone unveiling represented a wonderful crossover of 1960s Ireland. In the background, also, an office block, Huguenot House, is going up, clad with scaffolding and named for the little Huguenot graveyard next to it (ironically, Protestants who fled to Ireland to escape Catholic persecution in France). Mingling around afterwards are smiling Trinity students, in long scarves and Buddy Holly glasses, while my mum and us pause to have our picture taken. Colm and I are in our tweed coats and short pants from our granny's shop in Cavan. My mum is in a cape and white tights and buckled shoes. In other photos, next to bemedalled veterans, my father is in a tweed overcoat and Mr Fish tie from London and is talking to Haughey, the Minister for Finance, in his French raincoat and neat haircut.

The same element of crossover is evident in the other photos. In one shot, the people in the front row are all standing solemnly, presumably for the national anthem or the dedication. Heavy, serious women, like something from the Soviet era, stand awkwardly in their big fur coats. Among them is Jack Lynch, the Taoiseach, with a booklet pressed against his chest, James Ryan and then Haughey who watches it all closely. Since the Davis unveiling, he had been thwarted from becoming Taoiseach. Instead, Jack Lynch was appointed, a compromise candidate to prevent the party from tearing itself apart. But Haughey doesn't seem too put out. On the contrary, he gazes at the ceremony with great determination, as if he is merely biding his time. He is, after all, now Finance Minister, having succeeded Lynch in the post. And he has just helped get Dev re-elected, even if it was a close-run thing.

In almost all of the pictures, my mum's white fishnet tights stand out dramatically, even racily, as a '60s call to arms – a Mary Quant cry for a bit more glamour. In other photos, it is Dev whose long legs stick out, especially when seated, his hat and cane dangling from his knee. In one photo, their crossed legs echo each other.

Meanwhile, my grandmother, up from Mayo, is still wearing the customary heavy hat and overcoat, with a fur collar around the neck. This one has animal's paws still on it, possibly something shot by her late husband.

Next to her, we have, bizarrely, the poet Patrick Kavanagh. Indeed, these are the last pictures taken of him. He is not a happy man and is in the midst of a row. This is not the 'rock form' of the *Spectrum* TV still, but someone quite different: obviously cranky and bloated from drink. He even looks shorter, with an expression of mild alarm, as if he is shrinking. Eddie had invited him to the party afterwards in the International Bar on Wicklow Street, but Kavanagh had come to the actual unveiling, a state occasion where gold harp invites were required. Naturally, there was a commotion. The stewards didn't recognise him and took him to be a street wino, until Haughey went over and intervened, saying, 'Let this man through, he's a poet. Why don't you go and take the children out of the trees?' Some kids had climbed up into the trees to get a closer look and were perched precariously in the branches, like over-sized pigeons. (Whether the children were hanging on the 'sorrowful' willow or the 'optimistic' elm is another question.)

Kavanagh at least had a seat. Better still, it was a front-row chair left empty by the sudden absence of Donogh O'Malley, the colourful Minister for Education. There is a nice irony here since O'Malley was the husband of the beautiful Hilda, the unrequited love of Kavanagh's life and inspiration for his masterpiece *Raglan Road*. O'Malley was possibly absent preparing his famous education reform of that year, which introduced free secondary education and sowed the seeds for the future boom. The schools would soon be studying the poetry of Kavanagh and Austin Clarke.

However, this was of little consequence to Kavanagh. Having settled down, he erupted again when he saw de Valera, feeling about the Long Fellow the way half the country did, as was evident from the presidential contest. But my grandmother quieted him by talking to him about farming. They came from the same small-holdings background. He told her that the *Farmers Journal* was the only paper that told the truth ('all the other papers tell lies and half truths'). But the poet remained unhappy and didn't show up in the International Bar, going home instead to his wife, where he apparently cried, took to the drink and died a fortnight later.

Meanwhile, Tone's relatives had arrived from the US. In the days before the ceremony, the newspapers showed a parade of young boys and girls coming off an aeroplane in cream raincoats, like very young Beatles coming in to tour. Literally, Tone's descendants *descending*. We were fascinated by these American kids with their neat clothes and haircuts and eerie confidence. They had names like Livingston-Dickason, Goodale and Rassweiler, the sort of names you'd hear in a TV detective series. It was as if the widow Matilda and her shadowy group of 'Tone's Men' had gone out to America as veterans and come back, centuries later, as young boys, de-aged and re-energised by the New World superpower.

In general then, there was great excitement, and in the days before the unveiling Tone was pictured being hoisted into place by forklift and workmen, and looking like he was getting the hanging the British couldn't give him. The statue even tilts to the side the way a hanged man does. What is a dead man but a statue now, a sculpture in the making?

A contact sheet from the Lensmen agency shows the ceremony as it unfolds – literally *unfolds*, with the colour-party undraping flags and Tone's shroud falling away. As with College Green, Dev appears once more in front of a covered patriot, but whereas Davis was drenched in a heavy satin, Tone seems to be covered in something stiffer, like raw silk. It looks boxy, as if there was something underneath trying to get out. Again, the artistic resonance is of Christo and his covered objects, but there is also an echo of an earlier era, with the covered Tone looking like a rough column of Carrara marble, carved down to the core, the way a sculptor's assistants do before the *maestro* can come in with his finishing chisel and 'free' the man from the stone.

As de Valera presided over the ceremony, he was faced by a colour-party of equally stiff men, standing in military formation and holding the Republican flag. This is the 1916 flag which, coincidentally, is very mod and 1960s, with a Japanese-like sunburst and yellow stars. The photos then show de Valera pulling the cord, but whereas the Davis sheet fell smoothly and dramatically to reveal to the crowd the unexpected colossus underneath, this one comes off uneasily and catches on the jagged bronze half way down, as if reluctant to be exposed. For a moment, it looked like Tone was wearing a sari, or having his modesty covered by a windswept sheet.

Eventually, the sheet falls free, and the statue stands exposed. The colour-party now switch their attention from Dev and turn to face Tone, giving him homage, as if he is, indeed, no longer a sculpture, or a mere statue, but the real thing come back to life. As if, indeed, they have gone back through the years to give the poor devil the military help he begged for back in 1798. Tone is a young man again, reborn through a statue, and they are the veterans, rejuvenated by remembrance.

At first, the men stood with feet together, passively, respectfully. But now they stand with feet apart, and the pose looks much more commanding and even confrontational. (Not unlike the statue itself, it must be said.) Indeed, on closer inspection, the colour-party are not so old at all, but bulky middle-aged men who looked like the Irish American group which visited Eddie about that garish commission. Many more of these men appear throughout the crowd and, basically, they were all IRA. Or what was left of the IRA. The giveaway was again the raincoats and fedora hats. But here, at a modern 1960s state ceremony, they look like an anachronism, a throwback next to the business suits and Mary Quant outfits. But, of course, in less than two years, Northern Ireland would erupt, and the militants would come back to life. Except, instead of old men in trenchcoats they would be joined, and supplanted, by new Republicans, in leather jackets and long hair: young Northerners who had come through the rioting and wanted to get the war going again.

But, right now, militant Republicanism was something from the past. It was something romantic but outdated – the 'whiff of sulphur' – with old rebel ballads being sung, now often, half ironically, in prosperous pubs. It was like the Dubliners' little ditty for Nelson's Pillar, a respectful 'call to arms' which no one really heeded. Blowing up a monument: that'd be about the height of it.

Dev, meanwhile, is oblivious. With the formal ceremony over, he greets the veterans and American visitors. He is animated and smiling broadly, not the demeanour we expect of de Valera but these are the moments he lives for. It is like during an amazing film of Yeats' funeral in 1965, where one very quick moment reveals his character. He is walking along the street in Sligo, following the coffin, with the crowd of mourners, when someone in the crowd puts their hand out to him. Dev nods obediently and leans forward to shake the hand: at your service. In that moment, he is a true politician – and a human being. And so it is here.

The crowd is mingling now, and more relaxed, and in the midst of it all, we see Haughey smiling tigerishly and caught in profile. He appears conspiratorial, confiding to a huddle of listeners. Or do we just say these things now because we know what is to come? But people do stare at him here with curious awe, as if he already evoked that compelling mixture of fear and admiration which would become so familiar. Within a year, he would be convulsed in controversy over the importation of arms for use in then erupting Northern Ireland.

It is curious to look at the photos now and think of what was to come. For this reason, and perhaps other more valid ones – Kavanagh's scuffle, the lugubrious IRA men – there seems to be a certain awkwardness or uncertainty in the pictures, even tension. As if the country was at an awkward crossroads and didn't know where it was going. It was a year after Dev's re-election, and the Summer of Love has just passed. There were student protests in UCD, the so called 'gentle revolution'. The first Rosc exhibition had opened, but it was also the beginning of the Civil Rights movement in the North, and there were already hints of the violence ahead. On the day before Tone's unveiling, for example,

Ian Paisley led a march in Belfast, which inevitably ended in disturbances with the police.

In the Green, the crowd came up to see the statue, just like in College Green, and touch the bronze and walk on the plinth. Others went round the back to check out the famine figures. The American kids had left, as had Paddy Kavanagh. Those local urchins, young Sweeneys, were now down from the trees and posing stiffly and impudently for photographers beside the marching Tone.

Meanwhile, my father took us to shake the hand of the Long Fellow who was indeed long, especially when you're a small boy looking up at him. In retrospect, it was nice to have met a man, the casting of whose head paid for at least some of my maternity fees. His hands too were long and worn, like those of Séamus Ennis, except these were from freeing and running the country, and handling guns and pens, as opposed to pipes. We also met Haughey, who was very convivial.

'Some day you'll have a medal just like those men,' Haughey told us, pointing to the wizened old veterans with their War of Independence medals. This excited us. For we had started collecting coins, to go along with our stamps, but medals were even better: whether holy, military or for the school sports day in St Joseph's Orphanage. Could Haughey really get us a war medal? We were intrigued.

In Cavan, we used to be shown our grandmother's medal, taken down from its hiding place on the kitchen dresser, next to the stamps for the Missions. Our maternal grandmother was active during the War of Independence and Civil War, and there were many stories. Our paternal grandparents, working happily on Lord Oranmore's estate and tending his hunts, showed no such rebel inclinations (which was a pity perhaps, given all the guns they had).

Although there was a quiet sense of satisfaction and achievement to the occasion, in the media there was some disquiet; the triumphalist air of the previous year had been replaced by a much more critical attitude. *The Irish Times* was particularly withering.

'The President has unveiled a memorial which a forgetful and only partially Republican country has puttered with for decades and in his speech urged them to read what Tone had written. But how many of his cabinet have really absorbed Tone's work? If they had taken in his thinking, they would not be so limited in their outlook on that part of the country where Tone spent much of his native political life and which he so enjoyed and understood.'

The latter was a reference to the North. The paper also suggested that Tone's memoir be put on the senior school syllabus, a mischievous proposal, since Tone's diary is often a radical and Godless document, which had already been famously abridged to exclude some *risqué* Paris interludes. 'There is an excellent selection edited by Seán Ó Faoláin,' added the paper dryly. The editorial continues:

> Everyone claims in Tone a justification for his own particular views, but while Tone would, no doubt, have much cause for rejoicing in the relative freedom we have so far achieved for a portion of the country, can anyone who has read his writings believe that he would have anything but contempt for some of our fumblings – like the excesses of our censorship and other pussyfooting – or that he would have been able to contain his wrath at the fact that a century and a half after he wrought for the Catholic Committee, members of that Church were still under disabilities in part of the country?

What is interesting is how similar the editorial line is to today's *Irish Times*: pluralist, progressive, with a tinge of Republicanism – of the leftish sort, as opposed to the Catholic nationalist version of Fianna Fáil. For example, in castigating the 'limited outlook' of the government on the North, the paper was calling for a less crudely nationalist approach to Unionism, but also a proper engagement with the grievances of the growing Civil Rights movement.

In short, the newspaper's politics were not unlike those of Tone himself: well-heeled, Protestant and liberal, which probably explains the sense of kinship with the man. The Belfast angle is also important. Unlike other Irish titles, *The Irish Times* was an all-Ireland paper, preceding partition. The paper thus compares the two states unfavourably with the fine example of Tone himself. 'There is so much to admire in Tone, his easy advocacy of the "common name of Irishmen" for all who live in this country, an approach which has become less popular since the settling down of the new Irish states, his fidelity to men and causes; but it is probably his gay courage which leaves the clearest stamp on the mind.'

It is admirable, idealistic stuff. As they saw it, the problem with Irish Republicanism was that it wasn't Republican at all. And they were right. The point was echoed a day later, in a letter from George Gilmore, the Republican Socialist, and Protestant, who agreed with the editorial but went further:

> Tone would undoubtedly have raged at the attempts to preserve a Protestant ascendancy around his beloved Belfast, but would not a few sparks of that rage have been aimed at President de Valera who – at the unveiling – enthused over Tone's attempt to 'substitute the common name of Irishman in place of the denomination of Protestant, Catholic and dissenter' but who in the Constitution of 1937 left it, at best, doubtful whether the substitution had in fact been made. Would it not be a fitting tribute to Tone's memory to amend and clarify the relevant parts of it so that it may become a clearly apparent reality that the question of religious beliefs does not affect any man's standing before the law?

This is a reference to the 'special position' of the Catholic Church in the Constitution, a sectarian clause that would be removed in 1972. In reality, the Constitution, and the whole Catholic ethos of the state, would not change until the early 1990s. We had the torturous battles of the 1980s to go through yet, the rows over divorce and family planning, and Garret FitzGerald's attempt at a constitutional crusade. Ireland was not a republic in the French or American sense, the way Gilmore would have wanted or *The Irish Times* advocated. But those supporting this secular plurality were in the minority. Most people were Catholic nationalists, like Dev, and were broadly happy with the independent state that he and his generation had created.

In reality, true Republicanism would have scared many Irish nationalists. Which is why another letter, in the *Irish Independent*, attacked the event from the other perspective, saying that Tone was a Godless revolutionary, opposed to the Vatican and therefore not fit to be honoured in holy Ireland. 'Tone's unveiling a "sad day for Ireland"' was the headline. According to B. McDonnell (no gender given), Tone 'was a man whose love for Ireland was secondary to the dictates of a secret society condemned by the Catholic Church. The true story of this fickle man is so distorted in our history that he is now known as the father of Irish Republicanism. But by his own diary, he shows himself contemptuous of the programme for order as laid down by the Mystical Body of Christ. Anything contrary to this order is contrary to freedom itself.'

McDonnell had at least read Tone's diaries and alerted the readers to an extract from March 1798.

'An event has taken place,' wrote Tone excitedly, 'of a magnitude scarce, if at all, inferior in importance to that of the French Revolution. The Pope is dethroned and in exile. Bonaparte accorded a peace, and a generous one, to the Pope; it was signed at Toletino. Many people thought at the time, and I was one of them, that it was unwise to let slip so favourable an opportunity to destroy for ever the Papal tyranny.' Are we to believe, asked an incredulous McDonnell, 'that the man who wrote this, so hateful of the Papacy, and so much in accord with the Satanic principles of the French Revolution, could possibly have any respect for the rights of Catholics in Ireland?'

'His feeling for Ireland is one we can well do without,' declared McDonnell, adding that 'the memorial is a manifestation of the ignorance of the Irish people, who apparently cannot see anything wrong with the principles of Wolfe Tone, despite the warnings of many Popes of the evils which can only result from the acceptance of such principles as Tone's. At the rate we are "progressing", isn't it nearly time we reserved a spot for Karl Marx? I suggest a suitable spot would be between those of Yeats and Tone in the "Green".'

In fact, true Republicanism offended, and this was a dilemma Ireland would not resolve until recent times. In reality, theirs was only a nodding consent to Tone. As Peter Lennon put it in his seminal *The Rocky Road to Dublin* film: 'What do you do with your revolution, now that you've got it?' But then, as Kevin O'Higgins would have told them back in 1922, 'We were the most conservative revolutionaries in Europe.'

In 1967, however, there were other fish to fry. A week after the Tone event, there was the opening of Lansdowne House, a big new office block in Ballsbridge, for which Eddie had done a large lobby sculpture called *The Fisherman*, a much more modern, abstract piece made up of bronze, wire and welded copper, and festooned with quartz and coloured perspex.

The two events are on the same Lensman contact sheet, but they are quite different: we've gone from old men with medals to young men in business suits. These were busy months for Eddie. The five men in dark suits are lined up in front of the sculpture and a plate glass wall, all attentively 'listening' while the artist 'explains' his piece. They look like the famous Las Vegas Ratpack. The group includes a large, older fellow on a sturdy cane while beside him are two white-shirted executives and then Haughey, who gazes at Eddie with pursed lips and an appropriate frown. Perhaps because of his size he stands with his legs apart, like a wiry terrier, or like those veterans standing for Tone.

The sculpture was very modern. Ostensibly it represented a

man, or creature, fishing but it also looked like a crane, with a long arm like a barnacled beak and a wire suspended from it on which hung another piece, a harp-shaped lozenge, which sat on the floor. The surface detail of wire and welded panelling echoed the shellfish and anemones that we'd see in the rock pools along the Galway shoreline. *The Fisherman* had become the place where he fished. Its process and entrails are exposed, with the belly an actual kitchen colander melted in. This is visceral sculpture, and again it is the celebration of something natural in a modern setting. It was also wired so that its coloured glass and quartz could be lit from within.

The photos are an endearing example of how humans interact with sculpture. In one shot, the executives look away from the piece and into the mid distance, as if they were hapless humans finding themselves in the presence of a strange creature: *stay absolutely still, and nothing will happen.* Haughey, however, is at ease and considers the hanging lozenge with almost mystical satisfaction. The sculpture itself appears animated and real, with its long arm perfectly overhanging the group, as if to say, *look at these men I've assembled for you: these captains of government, art and commerce. They made me but now I have come alive for them.* Truly, an extra terrestrial is at work.

The photos also reveal the seeds of our more recent boom. Montague Kavanagh's son, Mark, would later become a property developer himself, and chairman of the Custom House Docklands Authority, while Haughey would be the politican who saw most clearly that area's potential, steering it towards being an international financial services district, transforming the old quays and filling the skyline with towers and cranes, just like *The Fisherman.*

The 1960s were an earlier version of this expansion, and the city was starting to change dramatically, with new buildings such as O'Connell House and Liberty Hall. Not all of it was positive, of course, and major battles ensued between conservationists and developers. It was partly echoed by the debate about sculpture. If conventional realism was regarded as colonial, so too was Georgian architecture in comparison to the new modernist brutalism. In fairness, many of the new buildings were exciting additions. We can't live in a colonial stage-set, after all. Lansdowne House, for example, won architectural prizes and has aged well, with an outside mural of grey concrete, which resembles a circuit board of cogs and wheels – the machine age, technology – as well as a large white crag, or dolmen, cut from the same stone as the building's marble cladding. Again, the 'process exposed' and a link to the natural elements.

However, there was a slight paradox here. Although Haughey lauded modernism and change, he himself lived in a Georgian house in the countryside in north Dublin, designed by James Gandon. However, he did have Innishvickillaune, a rugged Kerry island, with a modern house, just as Eddie had a country retreat in Connemara.

De Valera had neither and, in reality, he and his generation were out of touch with this thrusting new business culture. But not Eddie. He relished it. He told Terence Connealy (*Friday Focus*) that he preferred portraying young heroes, 'not old fogeys', as if Tone and Davis were thrusting young businessmen, not like the old committee types who were putting up their statues. 'He sees the country shaping ideally for the junior optimists of commerce,' wrote Connealy, 'and welcomes a closer association with Europe among our artists.'

Eddie even described his work in industrial terms, and in a way to which these business fellows could relate. 'Irish artists don't work hard enough,' he told Connealy. 'On the continent, a 14-hour day is not abnormal for creative artists. Here too many are content with little industry and a lot of talk about problems. I make about 20 bronzes a year myself,' he added, which was surely an understatement.

Clearly then, Eddie was not some leisurely effete swanning around with a cravat and an easel, but an ambitious visionary with a practical, 'can-do' attitude. 'The six-foot experimenter is Ireland's most exportable, and perhaps most prolific artist,' wrote Connealy. 'He is a determined enthusiast, who overcame early struggles – he started work as a five-shilling-a-week assistant – and insists that his real education began in Dublin, where frequently unemployed one year, he spent most time poring over National Museum treasures.'

This humble background was also part of the required narrative. In reality, Eddie's background was not that deprived. All of his family had secure employment on the Oranmore estate and did well in later life. They certainly had a better start than those who grew up in the Dublin slums. But then 'Dublin' didn't come into the picture. Except for the songs of Luke Kelly and the wit of Brendan Behan. They all loved Brendan, but his world was not really theirs.

Instead, the new entrepreneurs and developers came from the same background as Eddie, and often the same part of the country, namely the West of Ireland, and specifically Mayo. There were lots of Mayo connections with local boys 'made good'. Eddie referred to them favourably as the 'Bohola mafia', as if all the connections went through this small town. There were even Bohola links to New York, and Paul O'Dwyer, a candidate for the city's Democratic nomination for Mayor. It was all written up by John Healy, who had vividly described the emigration of 1950s and was now on hand to witness the country's economic recovery and to celebrate the mohair-suited men who drove it, especially Haughey.

Another Mayo man, Charlie Kenny, was starting to put up office buildings around the city centre and built a large complex at the top of Harcourt Street, in which he put a sculpture of Eddie's entitled *Tower of Babel*, a big column of welded cylindrical copper. It is now in the offices of Ernst and Young. On Lower Mount Street, a formerly Georgian street now full of office blocks and apartments, Kenny built the Clanwilliam Court development. Outside it, Eddie erected a steel column or tree entitled *Celtic Twilight*, a rare departure from his usual bronze but an anticipation of later work in stainless steel. If *The Fisherman* was clustery and organic, this was clean and cool.

Eddie also did the fired-enamel panelling inside the lobby of Clanwilliam Court and a wall sculpture inside Ferry House, further along on Nassau Street. Further on again, around Trinity and into College Green, is the Davis memorial. This meant that, at one stage, his sculptures punctuated the Georgian city in a line from Ballsbridge to the city centre, a visual motif for a generation reclaiming their capital. And a source of oedipal frustration for myself. At the base of *Celtic Twilight* are bits of Tonehenge, put into an arrangement like the steps of the Giant's Causeway. These are leftovers from the stone columns behind Wolfe Tone.

'If you can send a truck down to the Green, you can have it,' said Eddie. The granite stone was not his to give, but this was how things were done. It was all nod and wink, help yourself, ask no questions.

In 2007, the site was completely redeveloped and the owner David Arnold donated *Celtic Twilight* to UCD where it was splendidly relocated and dedicated to his late father, John F.V. Arnold. It totally befits the high-tech campus of Belfield and the spirit of the Celtic Tiger. Meanwhile, Trinity had finally managed to find *The Gymnast* in Dartry and put her back up on her shiny high bars, turning over in the sun like Olga Korbut.

For Haughey, artistic commissions such as that in Lansdowne House should be a pattern and not necessarily a once off. At the unveiling of another piece of Eddie's work, this time a large wall sculpture, *Integration No 2*, inside an American bank on St Stephen's Green in 1969, he called on more private sector for the arts, especially the visual arts, and the commissioning of such work as a 'point of principle'. But Haughey was a lone pioneer in this, and few other politicians supported his case.

His track record on the arts, incidentally, continued to be impressive. He would introduce tax exemption for artists and later create the artists' body Aosdána, with an annual stipend for its elected members. In time, he would also help establish an Irish Museum of Modern Art (IMMA) as well as assist the National Gallery to complete their new wing.

'Large commercial organisations,' said Haughey at the 1969 unveiling, 'must today take the place of the wealthy individual patrons of the past. Many of them had been adventurous, in commissioning painters and sculptors, but it should be universal and standard business practice. No major building should be erected that did not include as an integral part of it a major work of art and it should be by an artist living and working in Ireland today. This is something that is of considerable importance for the future. In terms of making a living the artist still has to contend with a general view that his art is a luxury that can be afforded only by the very rich.'

Haughey, who knew many artists, painted a sympathetic picture of their situation. 'There were few painters or sculptors in Ireland today who could make a satisfactory living entirely out of the sale of their work, and fewer still who can make a living comparable to what their colleagues in industry or commerce can achieve. This puts undue pressure on an activity which requires, in a very high degree, the combination of technical ability and vision. How much more pleasant and agreeable would life be for all of us if the public buildings to which we recourse during our working day provided us with something to pause and appreciate.'

Newspaper photos show Haughey with Eddie, standing comfortably by the piece and looking into its perspex coloured circles. The scene looks international and corporate.

'The Minister congratulated Mr Delaney and commended the First National City Bank for its initiative. The sculptor described his work, constructed of bronze, glass and glass fibre, as *Integration No 2*, and said that he tried to make it as a sculptural vision of a building seen as a dream. "I tried to construct a sculpture with delicate and spatial vibrations in colours which call into play both the relations and the movements of the forms: a type of vision contrasting immobility with mobility."'

Haughey's appeal was welcomed by editorials, especially after what the *Irish Press* referred to as 'a week of sometimes bitter political debate'. This was the growing Northern Ireland crisis which would consume Haughey and his early career. 'It would not be too much,' said the newspaper, 'to expect the bigger business corporations to fill the part of encouraging the arts and subsidising artists once filled so magnificently by the Renaissance merchant princes.'

Could they be cheekily referring to Charlie himself and his expansive lifestyle? Either way, it was a farseeing speech and anticipated today's Per Cent for Arts scheme which commissions art for new public spaces. In the 1960s, the corporate world was impressive in its support of the arts and was, in many ways, much more adventurous than during the recent more affluent boom. It is one of the disappointments of the Celtic Tiger years that private sector support for the arts was often so grudging, certainly by European standards. Instead, it was the state which provided most of the support.

Earlier in 1969, a sister work entitled *Integration No 1* was unveiled in the Wellington Park Hotel in Belfast, an event covered by Tatler in the *Irish Independent* who described it as 'the largest sculpture of its kind in Ireland, or in these islands'. It is '26 feet high and, since it was unveiled in the forecourt of the hotel, it has kept those who have seen it guessing. Its title is "Integration", a quality fairly relevant to current Northern politics because of its lack, but Mr Delaney has not been politically inspired. Over the 18 months during which he has been working on the sculpture, he has been more concerned with achieving an artistic unity of colour, shape and light.'

This is interesting. As Eddie moved away from figurative work, he also moved away from matters national and political.

'The work looks like a few dozen camera lenses of varying sizes welded together at random,' wrote Tatler in a good description. 'Actually, the material is bronze, and while some of the circles are hollow, others are filled in with coloured fibre glass. Because of this, the sculpture reflects colour on the brick wall behind it in daylight, and there is a unity between bronze and brick. At night, the work looks a great deal different, for it is lit from within. The built-in lighting is, I gather, very impressive when it illuminates the coloured circles. By night or day, there is an effect of stained glass.'

215

Again, Eddie's desire to bring illumination to sculptures. Almost thirty years later, his audacious *Blue City* proposal was an attempt to bring such an inner-lit addition to the centre of Dublin.

'Although Mr Delaney feels the reaction in Belfast has been very good, there are those who have been puzzled. "People kept asking me why it was there,' he said. "But I kept on saying: 'You don't ask why a tree is there. In a way, *Integration* is like a tree, because it gives the impression of growth – a solid form developed in a growth of circles." Apart from the sculpture, the owners plan to have original paintings by contemporary artists in all of the bedrooms, a type of development that Mr Delaney would dearly love to see in hotels everywhere.'

The Wellington Park unveiling was also attended by the poet Seamus Heaney, who had just published his collection *Door into the Dark*. Once again, Tatler sets the scene. 'If you do not associate the word "furious" with poets, you could be wrong. I listened to poet Seamus Heaney talk about poetry and sculpture, poets and sculptors, at the unveiling of *Integration No 1*. He linked them both with what I might call "furiosity" and, in choosing a poem for recital on the occasion, he said he didn't have to write or compose a new one. He had one already, which he believed was very apt. Just as the blacksmith, with furious might, hammered out of the red-hot iron the creation he wanted, so too, was it with the sculptor, and with the poet'. Heaney then read from 'The Forge':

> All I know is a door into the dark
> Outside, old axles and iron hoops rusting.
> Inside, the hammered anvil's short-pitched ring,
> The unpredictable fantail of sparks.

There is a nice symmetry to this. After Heaney's daughter Catherine Ann was born, Eddie, who was around in their house, did a drawing for her, 'to the as yet unnamed child'. I do like this, a poet who is given to the naming of things has not yet named his daughter. In the true spirit of artistic cooperation, Heaney also helped out at the unveiling of *Integration*: apparently, the piece was somewhat unsteady in its installation. 'I'm just helping a friend,' he told an onlooker. But *Integration* didn't survive the Troubles and the owners, fearing bomb damage and the cost of insurance, took it down, and today it has vanished.

The Northern crisis was growing, but Eddie kept out of it. He may have done nationalist monuments, but he tried to avoid any comment on the renewed conflict. Haughey, however, became directly involved and in 1970 he was sacked from the cabinet over a conspiracy to import arms. Eddie's only real Troubles-inspired work was the Peace Women marchers series, which he kept making for as long as he was working: women marching, always marching for peace. In 1976, he was approached to do a memorial to Billy Fox, a Fine Gael Senator from Monaghan shot dead by Republicans – the only member of the Oireachtas killed during the Troubles. Eddie was interested, but nothing came of it, and there was some tension about the memorial, with organisers having to meet secretly 'in snowy fields'.

Eddie enjoyed visiting Belfast. He had a major exhibition in the Whitla Hall in Queen's University, and in 1969 my parents attended the opening of the city's new Lyric Theatre, along with the Heaneys and the poet John Hewitt. The foundation stone was laid by Austin Clarke and the first production was Yeats's *The Cuchulain Cycle* for which Eddie did the set. According to Ray Rosenfeld in *The Irish Times*, the production was 'acoustically and visually magnificent', and 'the light did justice to the possibility of the rock-like slabs with their encrusted organ-pump ornamentation'. In the first of the cycle, *At the Hawk's Well*, the sound of the chorus 'melted into and emerged from the slabs, like spirits of the rock intermittently made visible' and the overall effect 'conjured up the quality of doom of Cuchulain'.

CHAPTER 14

'For the Vital Form'

Despite the eulogy of 'The Forge' by Seamus Heaney, Eddie was taken to court for the use, or 'misuse', of his foundry and workshop. This was hardly surprising. Not everyone in Dún Laoghaire shared the wondrous attitude of visiting reporters to his Vulcan-like activities.

Actually, the immediate neighbours were fine and no one in Stone View Place objected. In fact, some were occasionally employed as helpers. John Connolly, who lived next door, was a plasterer, back from the sites in England, the classic builder of that era, carrying home his batch loaf and pint of milk. He was a gentle soul whom my mother insisted should come and eat Christmas dinner with us, which he did with a grateful muttering. He was equally pleased to be called in to help carry sculptures down to the seafront to be photographed.

Better still, Tommy Hynes, from the bottom of the lane, was employed to cut strips of wax to go into a multi-headed bronze group. Eddie thought him a fine cutter. 'You're a sculptor, Tommy, there's no doubt about it.'

'Ah, jaysus, you'll frighten the life out of me,' said Tommy, cutting away. 'Will I be on the *Late Late Show*?'

'Maybe you will Tommy, sure why not?'

'And what about the money?'

'Oh, you'll definitely make money.'

But the Sharpes, who sued Eddie, were different. They were an electrical suppliers on George's Street, whose premises backed on to the foundry. They were the classic Dún Laoghaire merchants: quiet, hard-working Protestants who held great store by paperwork. According to Arthur Reynolds, who worked in the foundry, it was no great surprise that someone objected. They would spend up to 18 hours getting the ovens up to top temperature and the heat was tremendous. Between Sharpes and the workshop, there was an upstairs warehouse, one part of which stored cosmetics, and the lipsticks were constantly melting. Another part of the building housed a snooker hall and fellows would hang out the windows, bare-chested, shouting, 'What the hell is going on? We're boiling up here!'

'Relax, it'll cool down,' Eddie would say, 'in about 18 hours.'

Reynolds' other memories included searching all over the town for two famine figures which had been stolen and which were eventually found near Crosswaithe Park, right behind Bob Geldof's house, in fact, which is sort of appropriate. He also had to bring Eddie to hospital after he drove a nail through his foot (another injury) and was impressed to see Mother Mary Martin arrive in to darn his socks. The commission for the hospital in Drogheda was underway and Mother Mary was anxious that it not be delayed. But Reynolds found it strange that, on admission, Eddie would not give his profession as sculptor, but as building worker. Perhaps it was a sense of solidarity with Tommy and John Connolly.

However, in his court case with the Sharpes, Eddie was anything but a 'building worker'. 'Sculptor's work is not "industrial" ' was the headline in the *Irish Press*. This was not just vanity. It was a clever get-out, on which the whole case hinged. His other angle was reflected in the *Irish Times* headline, 'Delaney may give up sculpting'. This was a threat which showed his growing arrogance, as borne out by the court reports.

Judge Wellwood in Dublin Circuit Civil Court concluded that his work was not to be treated as an industrial undertaking. The injunctions sought against Mr Delaney were refused, but the Judge allowed damages for "a technical breach" of the covenant. When the 35-year-old sculptor stated his preference to be described as an artist, the Judge said, "Though I don't pretend to understand art, I concede that people who do have given Mr Delaney his proper niche in the artistic life of this country and Europe. Therefore, I do not consider his use of the premises to be a strict breach of the covenant which this lease was intended to guard against.'"

According to the report:

> Cyril, Robert and Herbert Allen Sharpe of Upper George's Street had sought an injunction restraining Mr Delaney from using the premises contrary to the lease, and a mandatory injunction directing him to demolish all buildings and structures erected by him on the premises. In his defence, Mr Delaney stated that his workshop was merely a replacement of an existing building which became dangerous and which was replaced in consultation with the surveyor for the local authority. The workshop was built only partly on the property comprised in the lease; the remainder was on freehold land, his property.
>
> However, the Sharpes said that a covenant in the lease provided that he was not to erect any building on the premises without written permission, use the premises as a factory or carry on any offensive trade. Under their own lease, the Sharpes were responsible to the head landlord to ensure there was no breach of the covenant or suffer a fine or forfeiture.
>
> Diarmuid O'Donovan, counsel for the Sharpes, said that, shortly after he moved into the premises, Mr Delaney knocked down an existing building at the rear and erected a larger one in its place. He installed a furnace, which he used for casting metals. When the Sharpes became aware of this, they instructed their solicitors to write to Mr Delaney asking him to desist. He did not answer the letter.
>
> In evidence, Mr Delaney said he was a sculptor, and

not an ironmonger or businessman. He had learned casting in Munich, Rome and Milan, and had worked with such world-renowned sculptors as Henry Moore, who did their own casting. There was no one else in Ireland who could do this. 'I poured metal in a seventh-floor bed-sitter in a very fashionable part of Rome,' he said. Saying he was not a manufacturer, he added, 'This is an important work of art; it is culture. I cannot make reproductions of anything I make. I cannot employ people because they do not see art as I see it.' He had made it clear he would be working with metal in the studio.

It is as well then that John Connolly or Tommy Hynes didn't come forward as witnesses. To distract from all this talk about planning infringements, Eddie issued a broader threat – to withdraw his artistic services from Ireland and the world.

Mr Delaney said he was no longer interested in sculpture but was more concerned with painting and might give up sculpture altogether. He would follow his conscience in this. He told Mr O'Donovan he was doubtful if he would even now execute art even if he got a good commission. He felt his talent now was in painting. At present he was doing metal welding and fibreglass works.

Mr O'Donovan said that the matter could have been settled if there had been any goodwill on Mr Delaney's part. But he had taken the attitude that he was above mundane matters that affected lesser mortals, and would not be dictated to by architects or anyone.

Judge Wellwood agreed that the evidence established that Mr Delaney, in reconstructing the building, had covered a portion of the leasehold premises. Because of the small area involved, it would be unreasonable to grant a mandatory injunction requiring it to be demolished. On the application for the other injunction, the Judge did not think that Mr Delaney's work could be referred to as 'offensive art' within the meaning implied in the covenant. He had established himself in artistic circles in Ireland as a virtuoso exponent of his particular gift.

The *Evening Press* flagged the case on their front page, along with a file picture of Eddie, wearing a smart tweed coat and Mr Fish tie. It's from the Tone unveiling, but he looks like he's dressed for court. Underneath is the pull quote: 'Poured metal in a seventh-floor bed-sitter in a very fashionable part of Rome.'

Years later, I was speaking to the son of Lord Longford, Thomas Pakenham, having just rowed across Derravaragh Lake – the magical lake of the Children of Lir – with him and his daughter, Eliza. 'Did you know Eamon's father?' asked Eliza, meaning from the social whirl of years ago.

'Well, yes, I remember we had a dispute in Dún Laoghaire,' he said. Clearly a different sort of memory.

'Oh, did you have the ground rent for that part of the street?'

'Oh, no, we had the ground rent for that part of the town.'

'Did you, indeed,' I said tersely, and I thought, my God, we let them off lightly. Perhaps in class-bound England it was okay, but we were supposed to have had a revolution here. As opposed to what we did have, which was a bourgeois transfer of power. Otherwise, we'd have taken all the land off them. But then we'd probably only have built some eyesores across it. Thomas Pakenham is a famous arborist and I was glad to hear that he'd bought yet more land at the other side of the lake. In fact, this was the spot to which we had rowed. He had lined it with new hardwoods, to save it from ribbon development.

Talking to him, in his castle in Tullynally, was an insight into how things used to be, and sure enough, the placenames of Dún Laoghaire, and its adjoining suburbs of Monkstown and

Glenageary, are all of Eliza's cousins: Longford Terrace, Silchester Park, De Vesci Terrace, Pakenham Terrace. Coming from the West of Ireland, with its struggles over land, Eddie quickly bought out the freehold on Stone View, so he wouldn't be beholden. The letters are headed 'Kingstown Estate'.

Eddie's counsel in the case was Hugh O'Flaherty, later a Supreme Court Judge, and he was paid with a standing figure. It is now with his son in New York. These payments in kind were not unusual. Eddie also used sculpture to pay his dentist, who was also Dev's dentist, we were told proudly. De Valera was never far away. If Eddie was casting the Long Fellow's head, then his dentist was fixing the teeth. Indeed, if my father had later got the okay for Dev's death mask, he could have had advance warning on the jawline. The dentist was also a close friend of Jack Lynch, apparently, and with the pressures of the Arms Trial and the North, the Taoiseach was happy to take solace in his company. Sculptures or drawings could pay for a lot of things – which was ideal really in an era when 'cash was king'. One time, in Galway, we bought a new TV, urgently needed for the upcoming World Cup. Eddie didn't have enough money on him, so, with the agreement of the shop owner, he took out some paper and did a drawing on the bonnet of our car.

However, despite the legal dispute, Eddie got the use of further land: a disused storehouse and yard at the back of Murray's Record centre, next to Sharpes. Murray's also had a basement club, into which long-haired guys and girls used to stoop. 'There's pot in there,' someone said, and as kids we imagined some bubbling cauldron with all these hippies around it. Perhaps they too were making sculptures? The club was written up in some detail in Bob Geldof's memoir *Is That It?* He describes how Murray's saved his life, providing an escape from suburbia and introducing him to blues and rock music. Later, Geldof describes dropping acid and going up to Killiney Hill for views of the sea.

This is interesting for it was often said later of Dún Laoghaire that the drugs 'came down from the hill', meaning from affluent

Killiney and Dalkey, where rich kids dabbled with them before they trickled into the pubs and council houses of the main town. The implication was that rich kids were protected from arrest and serious addiction, through private rehab. But the reality is that cheap heroin arrived into Dún Laoghaire in the late 1970s – even before it appeared in Dublin city itself – and it never left. Dún Laoghaire, after all, was a busy harbour town, with a ferry to Britain and a very mixed population. As well as the faded colonials in their deck chairs facing the sea – the 'disappointed Brighton' atmosphere – there were also side streets of dockers and railway workers and, of course, the occasional struggling painter or hippie.

In this context, Eddie told Donald Connery, he had more empathy with working people. 'Out here, the people – the man on the street – they think I'm a scrap merchant. I do my own casting, and they see me buying off the tinkers and piling up scrap metal. In the pubs they know I back horses and follow football, and that's all we talk about.' It was certainly a better rapport than he had with some of the merchants. One day he was in the local sweetshop when he overheard the owner, a servile and pompous gossip, mutter to one of the customers, 'Now there's another one of those artists who doesn't pay their taxes.'

Eddie turned on his heel. 'Always remember,' he said sharply, echoing his comments at the court case. 'I am unique, and if I am gone tomorrow, I cannot be replaced, whereas if you were gone, what would replace you? Just another man in a sweet shop.'

It was a stunning and audacious put down. And obviously we couldn't go back to the shop anymore. This didn't bother Eddie. Such feuds sustained him. After a row with a petrol station in Connemara, he didn't go back for 35 years. However, it was more awkward for us, since it was the only shop that sold the Batman cards with the little squares of chewing gum. But then we didn't openly complain, since we weren't supposed to be chewing gum at all.

We would also go into the city, especially at the weekend, and get that wonderful quotidian sense of a Saturday, which never goes, and which connects to Saturdays everywhere, be it in London, Paris or New York.

Eddie would smoke a cigar out the window of the Renault 12, the sweet smell drifting back, as he sang soft tunes like 'The Blooming Heather' or 'The Three Flowers', a ballad in honour of Tone and Emmet. If he wasn't smoking Henri Wintermans, plucked from flat tin boxes, he'd be chewing something, gum or Charms: multi-coloured sweets like bits of stained glass or the coloured Plexiglas he embedded in his mid-1970s abstractions. How come it was okay for him to have gum and sweets, we'd ask our mother. But then she wasn't going to be telling him off, not these days.

In the city, we'd park by Emmet's statue on the Green and go across the road into Emmet's house, the first floor of which was now the David Hendriks Gallery. Where once it was paced by an excited young rebel, it was now presided over by a cool Jamaican art dealer, sitting behind a desk and sucking on a cigarette holder, like something from James Bond. Eddie had a few exhibitions here and while we roamed the Georgian house, with its white-painted interior, he would chat to the suave Hendriks about money and commissions, always a bit of a ritual as they talked 'around things', with Eddie pacing about the room in his leather sports jacket and Chelsea boots with the elasticated sides.

Once done, we'd go around the corner, where he'd drop in on the Project Arts Centre, which was then on South King Street, next to a cluster of gay bars, or half-gay bars, as things were in those 'pre-outed' times. There was Rice's, and King's, and Bartley Dunne's where my mother was recruited for a cigarette ad by a man in a silk cravat. Beside King's, there was a side entrance to the Gaiety Green and the Dandelion Market, with its Aladdin's Cave of record stalls and clothes shops. This would later prove a formative hunting ground for me and my teenage generation, just as Murray's was for Geldof, but that was a long way off yet.

On Saturdays, but more likely in mid week, we would also accompany my father to warehouses or builders' yards or scrap merchants, where we'd witness the ritual and banter, as deals were done and assistants happily interrogated about their tools and produce. It was the same in artists' suppliers like O'Sullivans, where other artists were encountered. By contrast, we might also pop into the National Museum, where Eddie needed to consult something. Taken around the glass cases where he'd been inspired as a student, we'd be shown the gleaming gold torcs and bangles of the Irish past and the preserved bodies of ritually slain bog people, bound and curled. Later we'd go to sleep in our beds thinking about them being asleep: permanently asleep, with the wax seeping out of them, like our sculptures in the ovens.

On walkabout, Eddie often wore sunglasses and an Aran jumper under his leather jacket, although never a white one. That would be too 'Irish', too much like the Clancy brothers banging a bodhrán. No, instead it was a bottle-green jumper, or purple, and not worn baggily like some pipe-smoking *Gaelgeóir* or academic, but tightly like a body armour and set off by yellow corduroy pants.

On these trips, he would make site visits, checking up on Tone and Davis, and on other sculptures. He loved such visits and could not get enough of them. He enjoyed looking at his work, once it was in place: photographing it and thinking of what might have been. Workmen would watch him respectfully, like he was a matador pacing a bullring, or as if something might 'happen'. It was a workman's thing. Most of them were delighted by the unusual assignment. It was a distraction, but it was also connected to their world, and it was an artistic activity that was intensely physical. That is, a physical art that wasn't a performance (although, of course, it *was* a performance). My father got a great contentment from physical labour, a satisfaction unknown to me. You see it in building workers, high up on the half-built floors of new buildings, tramping down steel fixings like they're flattening hay, and just gazing out over the city, with hammer in hand.

Do many artists go back to look at their art? It can be hard to. What novelist can bear to re-read their own books? Or what director watches their old films? Visual art is different, however. You often see photos of painters sitting on sofas and proudly looking around at all their work on the walls. In a documentary, *With My Back to the World*, the painter Agnes Martin described how one artist used to bow to his work as he left his studio. Asked what her own favourite moment with her paintings was, she said, 'When they went out the door.' But then, in the same film, Martin is shown sitting serenely among her work, in the zone she's created: her own space and spirituality. Eddie was the same, which is why he held on to so many of his favourites.

These site visits were also often accompanied by a photographer or journalist, during which reporters were not only taken with Eddie's verbal energy, but also with his very appearance.

This is how Terence Connealy opens his *Friday Focus* feature in the *Irish Independent*: 'Craggy face cleft like an Achill cliff, deep lines prematurely furrowing into a brooding frown, he lopes into Stephen's Green, shoulders hunched in ancient black gansey, like a lonely fisherman looking for a lost mooring. The talent of Edward Delaney, Ireland's most controversial sculptor and pioneer of metal abstracts, has not yet found a secure anchorage with the public, though it has won harbours in the patronage of four governments.'

This is 1968. But how similar it is to a piece in the *Galway Advertiser* written by Jeff O'Connell in 1993 – all of 25 years later. Except by now the restless young sailor has become an old sea captain.

> Edward Delaney looks like a sculptor. As a matter of fact, he looks, from certain angles, like a piece of sculpture himself. If you haven't met him before, as I haven't, the physical impression you get is very powerful. With flicks of unruly salt-and-pepper coloured hair jutting out of under the band of his broad-brimmed cap, piratical side-whiskers trailing down below his ears like ivy on an old wall, his splendidly hawk-like nose defining the planes of his weathered, craggy face, it is not difficult to see him as

a free-booting sea-captain, taking orders from no one
and heading off on stubborn and perilous journeys.

Eddie is even pictured by the fireside of a Galway hotel, looking
up at the camera, just like a salty old seadog come to rest. He is
even wearing an old seaman's hat. From the 1980s on, he was never
without a hat, inside the house or out: a long succession of baseball
hats, of varying peaks and colours. Again, the journalist here is
more insightful than he imagines, for Eddie was, indeed, at this
stage, 'taking orders from no one' and heading off on some
'stubborn and perilous journeys'.

When he was with Connealy in 1968, he was surveying Tone,
unveiled only a few months previously. 'Shaking an unruly mop
and plucking at unbuttoned shirt collar and superfluous tie, he
mopes restlessly over his latest work. "It's just a lot of muck," he
mutters with startling acerbity, pointing to the paving that fronts
his 11-foot statue of the 1798 patriot. Fingers flutter,
deprecatingly. "Don't think I asked for this jumbo jet runway," he
said, warningly, "it's not in proportion to the statue or the granite
wall surround."

Actually the Tone memorial looks better now because it is set
back from the traffic. Far-seeing planners! As one *Irish Independent*
reporter predicted, generously, 'The memorial will come into its
own when the area is surrounded by modern buildings, and both it
and Davis will represent the twentieth century to visitors in the
distant future just as the O'Connell monument represents the
nineteenth.'

While in the Green, we'd also go to see the Henry Moore
sculpture of Yeats in its raised rockery. In latter years, Eddie
dismissed Moore's work as 'like the back of a Jaguar', meaning
predictable and formulaic (the Jaguar was also posh and English).
Did Moore not want to change his aesthetic, felt Eddie, or
deconstruct his own legacy? But he was also a great admirer of
Moore and of the way he managed his career. He also felt a kinship
given that Moore had equally taken stick for a public sculpture in

the Green. When Moore came to Dublin, they both adjourned to the Russell Hotel where Anthony Butler, in a news piece headlined 'Moore Power!' describes the pair of them 'very fiercely swapping anecdotes about castings I have known'. Butler 'found the English sculptor to be an amiable and kindly man – small, rather plump and certainly not the man one would expect to wield hammer and chisel or stoke furnaces under budding bronze.' Proof then that one doesn't have to be a macho man to be a sculptor. What would Kokoschka have said, 'Ah, you are not solid?' Or those farmers in the Duck Inn, talking about ladies' hands?

In a homage to Moore, Eddie named a large three-figured sculpture *King, Queen and Daughter*, after Moore's piece of (almost) the same title – except he had added a daughter. The piece is of standing, haunted forms, with see-through torsos, as if frozen in disintegration, and later he renamed it *Famine*. For years it stood in Jack Toohey's back garden in Galway, before being donated, along with *Anna*, to the Irish Museum of Modern Art. In October of this year, it was sent for resale at Adams auction house. Incredibly, in 1980, it was shipped to London for the *Sense of Ireland* exhibition, a huge cultural showcase which nearly bankrupted the cultural section of the Department of Foreign Affairs, and no wonder.

After our visit to the Green and the shops, we might go to Neary's on Chatham Street for sandwiches and tall glasses of orange with the brims dipped in sugar and cocktail sticks speared with cherries and slices of real orange. What a treat. We would sit up on high stools in the snug, with curtained windows into the main lounge, where people were gathering after a Saturday in the city. One time we met The Dubliners, about to do a matinee next door in the Gaiety. A back door of the pub led to the stage entrance, off Tangier Lane.

Luke Kelly bought us crisps and we got their autographs, to put in among the maul of Lions rugby players. A cry might go up that Garech was 'down in Hibernian with a merry crew,' but Eddie would as often give them the slip. He had kids in tow and work to get back to – work was always forefront – and before long we'd be back on the coast road to Dún Laoghaire, with thoughts of bog bodies and the winking lights of the harbour coming up on the sea.

On occasion we would pop into Davy Byrne's on Duke Street, where Leopold Bloom goes on his own for a sandwich and where his visit is commemorated by a large wall of sculpture of Eddie's, similar to the *Integration* piece in Belfast: a welded panel of interlocking copper circles of fragments, silverplated and resembling a broken honeycomb. Its overlapping cycles echo a central idea of Joyce, which is the repetitive nature of experience. Or, better still, let Eddie explain it, since it is one of the very rare 'explanations' he did for his work, and possibly the only one.

At the time of RHA retrospective, I suggested to the owner to put up a nametag next to the sculpture, along with this 'explanation'. But the owner, Redmond Doran, produced a letter from my father which explained the origin of the text. His own father had asked for some background to the work when he bought it, so Eddie sent him this written text, but on condition that it not be quoted from or shown in public.

'So there you are,' said Mr Doran on his high stool. 'I'm afraid your father has thwarted you. He must have known you were coming.'

'He must, indeed,' I said grimly and then I asked him about the secret doorbell. This was something from later, when we'd used to go looking for a late drink after hours, and Eddie would go over to Davy Byrne's and press the 'secret doorbell'. It was allegedly one of the many brass buttons along the doorframe and only known to insiders. After a pause, we would be ushered in.

'There is no secret doorbell,' said Mr Doran, smiling again. 'I'm afraid that was a story also. It seems your father had the better of you there too.'

'Fair enough,' I said, but what I didn't tell him was that actually the 'explanation' had since appeared in a catalogue, and so its confidentiality no longer applied. Clearly, Eddie had changed his mind and probably felt that if it was given to one person it could be given to all. But I didn't say this to Mr Doran, for he had otherwise been very helpful. Anyway, here – *again*, and in print – is the contested text:

> You will appreciate that no artist should be obliged to explain his work. It should be self-explanatory and evocative in the most personal sense of the word.
>
> However, you might like me to say a few words concerning the Joyce sculpture, *Finnegans Wake*. The Italian theorist of history, Vico, had an extraordinary influence on many great intellects of this and the past century. Michelet learned Italian so that he could read Vico in the original. He, in turn, influenced Marx and Engels. W.B. Yeats in his philosophical attitudes was similarly influenced. The whole of *Finnegans Wake* is based on the Viconian cycle. Joyce gives indirect acknowledgement to Vico in the first line of *Finnegans Wake*: 'commodius vicus of recirculation'. The theme of the original ballad 'Finnegan's Wake' is concerned with the revivication of a dead man. Joyce also likes to play upon the theme of the return of the heroic era 'Finn Again'.
>
> Personally, I am disturbed by the present travail of the world, and I sometimes fear that we may be approaching chaos. This is the Joycean theme I have sought to express in my sculpture. Joyce symbolised it in many ways, including the original 'fall' of man from the glory of perfection. Joyce's chosen word for the fall is also on the first page of *Finnegans Wake*. It is the title of my work.

It is a striking piece of writing, and I don't know where Eddie did his research. It also echoes his line about *Anna*, about realising 'as

Joyce did, that every great river is an old woman and every river, on which towns live and grow and die, holds in itself, as old age does, the mystery of simultaneous life and decay'.

CHAPTER 15

The Samson Riddle

Consistent with his support for artists, Haughey decided to make them exempt from income tax in the budget of 1969. Hence the annoyance of Mr Kelly in his sweet shop behind his jars of bull's eyes, an irritation and envy which was reflected in some of the coverage. 'A haven for artists – or hippies?' is the headline from one cutting, an *Irish Independent* article by Xavier Carthy.

> Some see the measure as an open invitation to the tax-loaded writers, artists and musicians in other countries to come and live in Ireland, which was once the Island of Scholars as well as Saints, and which has so often sent her greatest geniuses abroad to earn their living. Others fear an influx of penniless, long-haired artists who will be a burden to the taxpayer and the government and flood the home market, taking the bread out of the artist's mouth. Ireland seems to have been the first country to give this recognition to her creative artists.

The cutting reports that Mr Haughey also announced the re-organisation and strengthening of the Arts Council.

> Mr Delaney 'agreed whole-heartedly' with the minister's decision and said last night that during the

last six months he had been 'seriously thinking' of going abroad, but that it was now likely that he would stay at home. He had underestimated the government and had not expected anything as good as this. He hopes that it will also encourage foreign artists to come to Ireland. They would not flock in on too large a scale because they would still have to be earning a decent living from their work before they would normally come into the tax bracket. They would not destroy the home market because a lot of their work would be sold abroad.

He pointed to the uneven way in which an artist can be got through taxes. For instance, he may work for two or three years on the preparation of an exhibition, but sell nothing. One the other hand, he might sell a very successful work which has cost him the same time and be taxed on it as one year's work instead of having it spread over the period that it took to make. Mr Delaney thinks that one great benefit of the tax concession will be that sculptors will not save the money which would otherwise have gone in taxes, but use it to produce more work.

There was a broad welcome for Haughey's initiative and today it still stands as an imaginative and progressive measure, although not without controversy. It has been availed of by wealthy rock musicians and its income limit is now capped. But it was attacked on its introduction too and Maurice McGonigal, the RHA president, said it would only benefit the 'art nits of Dublin and the art parasites of Europe', which showed just how out of touch he was with the actual arts community. McGonigal also resigned that spring from the NCAD because of a 'lack of discipline'. Student unrest was finally shaking up the moribund college.

The Tax Exemption Act did bring in foreign artists, but mostly established figures, many of them well known. It was said that

Haughey introduced the measure to get a superior sort of guest at his dinner table, and so it was with Eddie. He struck up a big friendship with Richard Condon, the American author of political thrillers like *The Manchurian Candidate* and *Winter Kills*. Condon even put a fictitious 'sculpture' of Eddie's – in an office in California – into one of his novels.

Eddie got on well with Americans, especially American artists and sculptors, robust fellows like Richard Serra or David Smith, who were more like industrial workers. Smith had been an automobile worker before embracing the aesthetics of welded iron and steel. In the many issues of *Sculpture* magazine lying around the Galway foundry, almost all of the men and women featured remind me of my father: sculptors in yards, or pulling on chains, or hammering out iron in the snowy wilds, usually in places as beautiful and desolate as Connemara: Vermont, Oregon, New Mexico.

Time magazine came to Ireland to do a feature on the tax exemption and interviewed writers like Frederick Forsyth, Len Deighton and J.P. Donleavy, many of them living in old country houses which they were doing up. Richard Condon worked 'all day in an 18-room salmon-pink mansion' and said he was 'spiritually conditioned to come to Ireland, where writers have the same status as priests'. If so, what is the status of sculptors? The article spoke of the general public support for the measure which one writer, Peter Driscoll (*The Wilby Conspiracy*), did not think would have happened in the UK. He also linked this to an Irish respect for people who can 'get away with it', which is an interesting perspective.

The headline was 'A little bit of haven' and Eddie, one of the few natives featured, is pictured sitting by the *Famine Group*, in a check shirt and Chelsea boots. 'In the long run, the public benefits if the artist's output is greater,' is his quote beneath. The photo is by Terence Spencer, who had extensively photographed the Beatles and the Vietnam War: an internet search is usually revealing on these people. The *Time* writer was Dean Fischer, who was later an assistant secretary of state for US President Reagan, and later still was nearly killed by his own government when US jets bombed Gaddafi's Tripoli (a fate not dissimilar to Hitler's half-brother in wartime Liverpool).

Eddie's most fruitful relationship was with Wolf Mankowitz, the English author, who came over from London's East End, where he had drawn from the area's rich Jewish heritage, and settled in Ballsbridge and West Cork. Their main collaboration was on a project called *The Samson Riddle*, a play and a book for which Eddie did the drawings.

Mankowitz was a multi-talented figure: a screenwriter, dramatist and even an expert on porcelain and Wedgwood (he published an encyclopaedia on the subject). But his main output was stories and screenplays. He wrote *Expresso Bongo* and the Bond movie *Casino Royale* but had his name taken off the credits for the classic *Dr No* in the belief that the film, problematic in production, would damage his reputation (the actor Patrick McGoohan turned down participation for the same reason). His son, Gered, meanwhile, became an acclaimed rock photographer and is responsible for some of the most iconic album covers of the 1960s and 1970s.

Mankowitz came to live in Akahista, in West Cork, and his first project with Eddie was a small book called *The Akahista Fables*, a series of romantic parables – a sort of modern take on mythology and the Bible. Eddie did the drawings, small ink sketches of assertive naked women, surrounded by besotted (or baffled) men and assorted animals, just like in *The Land of Music*. A selection of the sketches and stories appeared in the 'New Irish Writing' page in the *Irish Press*, which was edited by the paper's pioneering literary editor David Marcus. The sketches made an excellent distraction from the farming coverage and the militant nationalist editorials on Northern Ireland.

Eddie met Mankowitz through Gerry Davis, an artist and gallery owner who lived in the heart of Dublin, in Capel Street, where he had a narrow old house with a winding staircase. Off its many floors, there was a small cinema, a music-session room – Davis also played jazz – and living quarters overhung with paintings. On the ground floor, there was a stationery shop, which also sold artists' materials. Davis was an engaging character: moustachioed, Jewish and the quintessential Dub, who appropriately used to get dressed up and have himself photographed as Leopold Bloom in an Edwardian three-piece suit, watch chain and bowler hat.

On our Saturday visits to the city, we loved calling in on Davis: Gerry, not Thomas, although him too. We would buy Rotring drawing pens downstairs and explore the rest of the rambling house, as well as the surrounding Capel Street area, with its distinctive mix of theatre suppliers, DIY stores, pawnbrokers and old clothes shops with Jewish names like Millets and Flittermans. It was, and still is, a busy street, full of local life and mercifully free of UK chain stores. At one end, there was the Liffey and nearby was the fruit market, where Eddie stocked up on spuds and fruit, and where we got empty orange crates to use as lobster pots in Galway.

Through Davis, Eddie's work became exposed to many collectors in the Jewish community, many of them with the same family names that occur in *Ulysses*. The prominence of such collectors is an interesting feature of Eddie's career. The former Mayor of Cork, Joseph Goldberg, was a keen supporter and added many of Eddie's early works to a significant collection that included Matisse and Picasso. After his death, an auction was held of the collection, including bronze menorahs that Eddie had especially sculpted for Goldberg and which now became the subject of a fierce bidding war between Jewish collectors in New York and Cork. (New York prevailed – but only just.)

Why were Jews drawn to his work? One reason may be Eddie's timeless, mythical subject matter, evocative of the early Bible, as well as a rural dimension reminiscent of the *shtetl* life depicted by Chagall and Soutine. But the broad fact is that Jews are known for their attraction to modern art. Possibly because, for centuries, conventional art forms triumphantly reflected the established gentile culture – think of all those horses and lords and castles –

and so the expressive freedom of modern art and, better still, its tendency to abstraction must have been a great liberation. This is also the case for the Irish, especially when it came to political art.

The other reason may be more simple. Many Jews were both cultured *and* moneyed, and curious enough to seek out modern art. This is also the case elsewhere, especially America. Modern art is new territory and advances a staid national culture. There were wealthy Protestants in Ireland, but most of them were conservative and clung to a classical past. In addition, most of the native Catholics were still not affluent, nor perhaps confident enough, to become serious purchasers, although by the 1960s, of course, this was changing. But so little were Catholics in Dublin associated with company ownership that many people assumed that Eddie's brother Tim, who had done well in the plastics business, must be Jewish. In fairness, he also had dark colouring and was, by Irish standards, an unusually quiet and thoughtful man.

This appetite for art provoked a curious sort of benign anti-Semitism, with frustrated onlookers declaring that Jews could 'see things' in abstract art that the 'rest of us' couldn't. One man told me that Maurice Fridberg was crafty enough to 'get' modern sculpture and 'knew that it would make money later on'! This backhanded compliment was despite the fact that Fridberg was himself an artist, with evocative photo studies of tree stumps and roots. But this would be probably dismissed as yet more 'profitable weirdness'. In fairness, the same observer lamented the loss through emigration of so many Jewish families, who added well-needed colour to the Dublin of the 1950s. Fridberg himself eventually left but returned when he couldn't handle the heat in Israel.

In 1970, Gerry Davis opened a gallery in his building, and his first show was an exhibition of Eddie's drawings, many of them studies for Davis and Tone. The show was opened by Cearbhall Ó Dálaigh, the Chief Justice. Ó Dálaigh was a *Shabbas goy*, or 'friendly gentile', who lit fires on the Sabbath and did the tasks religious observant Jews could not. He would later be the subject of major controversy when, as president, he was attacked as a 'thundering disgrace' by the Minister for Defence for referring a government security bill to the Supreme Court. Ó Dálaigh was uneasy with the state's growing powers to curb the spillover of Northern violence.

'He has split the atom,' said Ó Dálaigh of Eddie's work. 'Here is a dynamism in his work, a three-dimensional quality, a unity which is part of the free-standing character of sculptural figures of groupings. These are great gifts and this new gallery could not have a more dynamic opening.'

In the *Irish Press*, Anthony Butler was again eloquent.

> In an important essay in 1966 on Drawings and Sculpture, Mervyn Levy noted how a sculptor thinks in terms of form. This is particularly true of Delaney who uses his graphic instrument as chisel and welding torch. The figures have disciplined tension, something that Michelangelo described in one of his sonnets, 'I am a Syrian bow strained for the pull.' There is no excess emotion in the figures and they are assured and authoritative archetypes of a cosmic aristocracy. They imply a necessary environment and a stylised culture. Identity is not important and they have rejected and sloughed the hide of self. It can be noted as well that the heads are shrunken and diminished, an important point since the face is the ultimate signature of ego.

'Sloughed the hide of self': I do like this. The last two lines could precisely describe the statues of Davis and Tone and what it was that made them controversial.

'There is something too of Henry Moore,' writes Butler. 'The suggestion of forms shaped by an erosion of wind and rain; the planes of mountainsides juggling with lights and shadow. One can also shift one's vision to find architectural elements but this is only natural since buildings divorced from utility are but massive sculpture. The drawings stimulate the viewer to a creative response and underline the paradoxical truth that the ultimate artist is the percipient, the person who enters into dialogue with the artefact.'

Eddie would have further shows in the Davis gallery into the 1970s and was then back in the Hendriks Gallery in 1976 for an exhibition of sculpture.

He also had a big show in the Project Arts Centre in Temple Bar in 1975, which was opened by Charlie Haughey. This was a nice gesture since Haughey was still somewhat in the wilderness after his sacking over the Arms Trial and doing penance amongst the party's grassroots with countless (but productive) chicken-and-chips dinners. Eddie was anxious to give him a more glamorous event to preside over. But he need not have worried. By the end of that year, Haughey was back on his party's front bench and by the end of the decade he would be Taoiseach. As a return gesture, and perhaps also as a way to curry favour with the party faithful, Haughey tried to arrange for Eddie to do de Valera's death mask when the Long Fellow finally died, also in 1975, but nothing came of it.

The Davis Gallery shows heralded a concentrated period of drawing and painting for Eddie, along with the design of book covers, stamps and illustrations.

He also represented Ireland again at the International Biennial Exhibition of Prints in Tokyo. This was a major show held in the city's Museum of Modern Art. In 1968, he exhibited *Project 31*, a painting of overlapping colours done with stencils and paper cut-outs. It was like what we were doing ourselves as kids: you lifted the stencils to reveal different egg-shaped patterns. It was Eddie's third time in the Tokyo Biennial. In 1962, he showed three black-and-white lithographs: *Two Lovers*, *Three Step Dancers* and *My beautiful, my beautiful* – titles I appreciate given that it was the year of my birth. Sam Francis and Jasper Johns represented the US, and for the UK, there was David Hockney and Eduardo Paolozzi.

Four years later, Eddie exhibited *Bullets with Love* and *Astronauts Dream No 1* and *No 2*, described as plastic relief prints.

This was layers of perspex painted with bright acrylic colours, again with stencilled patterns. The panels were compacted to create a multi-layered effect, often with a background of shiny aluminium. Eddie said they were 'more sculpture than paintings'. One hung later over the cooker in Galway, and with all the heat and fumes (it was a chaotic cooker, and Eddie was obsessed with charcoaling steaks) it became a wholly different type of painting: blackened, scorched and even melted at the bottom where the heat had melted it, just like Austin Clarke's death mask.

Eddie's 'team-mate' for all three Tokyo shows was the painter Patrick Hickey. Both were chosen by James White, the director of the National Gallery, who was a strong and early supporter of Eddie's career.

The Tokyo catalogues make interesting reading, charting the changes in international art trends from abstract expressionism to hard-edge abstraction to pop art, all of which we found inspirational, especially the latter. In 1968, for example, Roy Lichtenstein and Robert Rauschenberg represented the US, and for the UK, it was Bridget Reilly, with her distinctive spirographs and optical illusions. From Pop to Op – never was art such fun. It was like my abiding memory of the Rosc exhibition, held in the RDS: an open car door with a spillage of hard plastic coming out of it, like frozen cream. It was an image which could otherwise only appear in a dream, or in Luggala, with the frozen scree and the rocks in mid air.

For Italy, there was an impressive team of Burri and Fontana: with their audacious minimal aesthetic of torn fabric and plaster holes. And Pomodoro, whose deconstructed globe sits outside Trinity College Library. In the Tokyo catalogues, much of the work was more like posters than paintings and this was very satisfying, for by this stage, posters were what most interested us. We entered competitions for anti-litter campaigns and water-safety posters, with blocks of colour and lettering. Designing stamps was also an ambition. When Eddie was commissioned to do a stamp for the United Nations – on the theme of international support for refugees – we got busy doing our own. This was obviously very exciting. He was the first Irish artist to do a UN stamp and maybe we could follow suit, since the UN, like Coca-Cola, seemed to offer great involvement for the world's children.

We also made mobiles, a wonderful idea: sculptural forms moving in the air of their own volition, or by the vagaries of air currents. They were obviously inspired by the great mobile maker Alexander Calder – again, an artist with a piece outside Trinity College Library, this one a stabile. And it's from 1967, that pivotal year. Calder, mind you, was that thing I would always want to avoid, despite all the artistic activity of my childhood: the sculptor son of a sculptor.

Most ambitious of all, we made kites. Here were paintings in the air, moving and trembling in the high wind. We flew them on Killiney strand, out over the sea. They were often large, made of wood and plaster-dashed paper, but became light when airborne. The paradox of sculpture was again echoed: brute weight rendered weightless, except this time, literally. But given that the kite was mine, I also think of it as a metaphor for me breaking free of my father, especially since he was often unable to control the thing and ran back and forth on the crunchy sand trying to curb its growing strength. This wasn't like back in Mayo where you could cunningly draw in a big salmon on a tiny fly. Here the kite had a mind of its own and the elements resisted easy manipulation. With this in mind, I later read Seamus Heaney's poem for his sons 'A Kite for Michael and Christopher' and found his description telling: of the kite getting more powerful, and its flight more spectacular, 'although often because of the strain, the string would break and you would lose the kite and even if you eventually found it, it would have been wrecked by the fall'.

Eddie also did further sleeves for the Chieftains. There was *Chieftains 4*, with black disembodied figures like *The Samson Riddle* except against a turquoise background, and *Bonaparte's Retreat*, inspired by Napoleon's ill-fated invasion of Russia, after which he was unable to help the Irish or any more Tones or Emmets. Both sleeves were done with free-flowing acrylic paint, dropping from a stick or knife. *Bonaparte's Retreat* was a brilliant collection of colours, depicting a triangle of French soldiers with blue tricorn hats and raised bayonets, either going into battle or retreating, their colours melting into a sticky red and yellow mess.

Inside the gatefold sleeve was a photo of the deserted Martello tower near our house in Galway, one of many built around the coast to keep watch for a French invasion (the opening scene of *Ulysses* takes place inside one). The picture was taken from a rowboat at low tide. Garech came to supervise the art direction which took a whole weekend in Carraroe. There was lots of music and dinners and swimming, and a London photographer falling out of a boat. It was all great larks.

The music on *Bonaparte's Retreat* commemorated not only the defeat of the revolutionary French but also the Williamite wars of a century earlier, when again the Catholic French were defeated, completing the English conquest of Ireland and the routing of the old Gaelic chieftains and their culture – the so called Flight of the Earls. It was this that the *fleadh*s harked back to. On the drive to Galway, we passed through Aughrim, which was the scene of the last great battle of the conflict and, on its empty flat fields, you could imagine the opposing European armies lining up, just the way they do in Stanley Kubrick's *Barry Lyndon* – for which, indeed, the Chieftains did the music. The making of these movies always created a buzz, with more dinners and parties. Earlier, John Huston had made *Sinful Davey*, a lively caper with John Hurt, who later became a good friend and stayed in Carraroe. Also in the film was Ronald Fraser, who arrived into Stone View in his film costume of Scottish kilt and handed us sweets from his sporran.

Another man who arrived into Stone View in a kilt was the Scottish poet Hugh MacDiarmid, except his was not a stage costume, or maybe it was. Garech brought him for dinner before he was due to appear on TV. After dinner he expounded on Scottish nationalism and lit up many cigarettes from one of our big catering boxes of matches. With so many ovens to be lit, there were lots of these matchboxes lying around. Later, on the *Late Late Show*, he surprised Gay, and us, by pulling out one of the boxes. In those days, of course, you could smoke on television.

Eddie's sculptures were also on TV again, this time as a backdrop to the tenor Frank Patterson, who was filmed walking around the works as he sang. Patterson was an acclaimed tenor, who later sang for the Pope in the Phoenix Park and whose version of 'The Lass of Aughrim' stops Angelica Huston on the stairs in John Huston's haunting version of Joyce's 'The Dead'. However, Eddie was not paid for the service and was understandably annoyed. As with the Coppola movie, it was expected that an artist would be happy just to have their work on television. As recompense, RTÉ gave him free tickets for us to go to the recording of a pop show called *Aimin' High*, with visiting stars like Gary Glitter and the Bay City Rollers. More interesting for us, however, was emerging from the studio and seeing the actual Wanderly Wagon, from the children's TV series, out in a grass field. We ran to see its magical interior, with famous puppets and time machines, but alas there was just a bare wood floor and an empty cigarette packet. We hadn't yet understood that the interior shots would have been done in the studio.

We also appeared on TV on the *Whose Baby?* programme, where two kids are quizzed by a panel about who their 'Irish celebrity' parent was. Or at least Colm and Cathy got to appear; I drew the short straw. The panel tried to tease out who the parent was, through a series of narrowing questions, a sort of genetic version of charades. But Colm was almost immediately recognised by the comedienne Maureen Potter, who then had to feign ignorance. At the end, Eddie came out from behind the set and talked to the presenter about his children and his upcoming projects.

Eddie's work was featured in many TV arts programmes, such as *Aisling Gheal*, presented by the poet Cathal Ó Searcaigh, which was recorded in Stone View, with cameras roaming around the workshop and closing in on wax being sizzled and sculptures fixed. The narration is in Irish and a long-haired guitarist plays during the interludes. A similar programme was made by Bob Quinn, for his Cinegael series, this time recorded around the house in Carraroe, with shots of local *sean nós* singers intercut with images of the bronzes and stainless-steel works, an inspired combination against the panoramic Connemara sea and sky.

A three-way collaboration involved Eddie doing a drawing for a limited edition of Seán Ó Riada's score for *Hercules Deux*, published by Woodtown Music (Woodtown was the publishing arm of Claddagh). Montague did the poetry, Ó Riada the score and Eddie the image. Ó Riada was a gifted composer who had refined traditional music and moved it on from the raucous *fleadh*. But he was also a prickly figure and he reacted badly when he saw the drawing, by which time it was too late for its withdrawal. Apparently, the idea arose when the boys were in a back garden, drinking wine. 'All we need now,' said one of them, 'is a naked woman to come out from behind that bush at end of the garden: Eddie produce a woman!' They expected a drawing on the spot, having seen him do it in Luggala, where his entries to the visitors' book were usually sketches. But Eddie declined and said he might do one later for the score.

It is a pity about Ó Riada's unease, for the drawing is an evocative compliment to the musical notes. It is a lithograph image of two disembodied figures, like naked warriors. It echoes the *Land of Music* and the pair look like they are surrounded by a musical throbbing, as well as the remembered bush. Explaining Ó Riada's mood changes, his biographer Tomás Ó Canainn wrote that '[he] sometimes could not, or would not, differentiate between truth and fantasy, between the world as it was and the world as he would wish it to be. But who is to say that such a contradiction is not a part of the amazing armoury of a composer.' Or, indeed, of any artist.

Eddie also did further stage sets, including another one for the Lyric in Belfast: large perspex panels with vibrant stripes of Mediterranean blue and yellows, like a cross between Matisse and Picasso. They later served as panelling for the bathroom in Carraroe. He also did the sets for an Abbey production of Synge's

The Well of the Saints, adapted by playwright Tom Murphy. The play was accompanied by Murphy's meditation on Synge, *Epitaph under Ether*.

The combination greatly appealed to Eddie. He adored Synge and felt a kinship with Murphy, who was from Galway and of a similar background and temperament. The sets included the dark figures of animals or creatures, like frozen livestock, and were made from an armature of metal and twine coated in wax, just the way he prepared sculptures, such as the famine figures behind Tone. After the production, they ended up rotting in the fields in Galway like the carcass of a cow. 'If they were already in wax you should have just casted them,' I told him.

'No,' he said firmly and then nothing more. I think now that maybe there was something I wasn't getting, something to do with the transitory nature of theatre and Tom Murphy's characters. Or the appropriateness of the fragile figures – Murphy wrote a play called *Famine* – wasting away naturally.

By now we were busy with artwork of our own and used to enter the Texaco National Children's Art Competition. In 1972, I won a prize for a painting of the Crucifixion. It was like an Emil Nolde or Max Pechstein with sharp cruel faces and a bloodshot sky. There was a winner's lunch in the Royal Marine Hotel in Dún Laoghaire, at which prizes were handed out by the Education Minister. The Royal Marine was an old stalwart of the town and epitomised its 'disappointed Brighton' atmosphere, with high teas and over-decorated landings. My mother accompanied me, as did Desmond Mackey, no less, in the absence of my father. My father was away a lot now. But Mackey was a glamorous substitute and mingled in effortlessly with the teachers and nuns. He was quite a hit, in fact, with his cream jacket, fedora and racing binoculars dripping with the tags of winner's enclosures.

If my father could be honoured by government ministers, then so could I, except in my case it was Pádraig Faulkner from Dundalk, handing out a Texaco certificate and an Action Man doll. It was all very exciting. We sat next to a family from Derry and a girl who had won for a picture of her troubled town, with matchstick rioters and buzzing helicopters. In England, meanwhile, the FA cup had been won by Leeds United, a new passion in my life. At the dinner, I noticed men gazing at my mother, who was still very youthful and striking for a woman with four children. I was very proud. By this stage, I had realised that the bond of a son to his mother is much greater than that of a son to his father. The latter is formed during the course of one's life, but the first is formed at birth, and even before. Whereas one's relationship with a father is about curiosity and learning, the other relationship is of overwhelming biological love. It is a kite which can never be separated.

In 1972, *The Akahista Fables* had grown into a play called *The Samson Riddle*, which was performed as a reading in the Gate Theatre, as part of the Dublin Theatre Festival.

Mankowitz had assembled an impressive cast. Samson was played by Hugh Millais, Samson's mother by Miriam Karlin, Manoah by Hilton Edwards and Delilah, the bride, by Susannah York. Zoab was played by Alun Owen, who wrote the screenplay for the Beatles film *Help* and now lived in Ireland. Meanwhile, Noel Purcell, a venerable old Dublin actor who had worked with John Huston and Jimmy Cagney, played a medley of roles including Barber, Scribe and Vinter. The play was to be performed on 'the barest possible stage with the minimum essential props', the costumes simple kaftans, white, black or striped, and the dialogue style was to be 'deliberately eclectic and utilising Yiddish rhythms, but should be played naturally'.

This didn't give Eddie much scope for doing a stage set, but he made up for it with his drawings for the published text. The stark drawings, twelve in all, were done with black acrylic paint, dropped quickly and again capturing familiar motifs: a standing woman with head inclined, a couple embracing, or pulling apart, and a brooding woman, sitting like a queen, with her hair a wiry explosion of black lines. The drawings were inked up as a series of prints, as well as illustrating the book of *The Samson Riddle*, published by Vallentine

Mitchell in London. The book included the play, the original biblical tale and an essay by Mankowitz.

Roisín Kennedy sets the context for Eddie's involvement in *The Samson Riddle*:

> Delaney's treatment of the human form is strongly influenced by his interest in mythology. This is expressed in fundamental and abstract terms in works such as the *Bronze Groups* or *Finnegans Wake*, but frequently it is related to more tangible biblical or literary sources. Cuchulain, a recurring theme, is presented in Delaney's work as vulnerable rather than conventionally heroic. Often encased in a complex sculptural form, the figure does not assert itself but suggests physical and psychological exertion. This expresses in sculptural terms the facts of the Cuchulain saga in which the hero, as in all myths, is trapped between divine and mortal yearnings. It also, of course, expresses a much more universal idea of physical and emotional strife.

These qualities would have major implications for the statues of Davis and Tone.

> Wolf Mankowitz recognised Delaney's empathy with mythology when he suggested that he produce the series of screen prints to accompany his 1972 play. In these, Delaney's highly expressionist meandering black line relates to the complex layered meanings of Mankowitz's text, which revisits the Old Testament story of Samson in the light of modern Israeli and Jewish identity.
>
> Animals, vested in mythological significance, provide another important source for Delaney. His interest in them relates closely to the theme of the

pastoral in his work. An archetypal symbol of vitality, Delaney has treated the horse in particular as an archaic beast whose form is emblematic of human emotion. The body of the horse, like that of human form, provides a focus for the sculptor's exploration of the physical and visual capacity of bronze. Confined to a small intimate scale, such subjects have attracted a close and loyal following amongst Delaney's patrons. While his reputation has rested on his controversial public sculptures and on his at times outspoken personality, a major part of Delaney's legacy lies in his constant quest for a 'vital' sculptural form in which he can express the uncertainties and hopes of contemporary life.

Kennedy refers back to the 'clear anthropomorphic quality' of the work in Eddie's 1969 exhibition:

They are part of his consistent preoccupation with the standing figure, which is shared in the work of other post-war sculptors such as Lynn Chadwick and Germaine Richier. The techniques of bronze sculpture are used to highlight the tenuous quality of the human form. The Thomas Davis heralds appear to be delicately bound, the result of the sculptor tying cord around the wax models prior to casting. The skeletal surface of the *Sword of Steel* appears both protective and vulnerable.

Other works such as the *Bronze Groups* (Hugh Lane Gallery) play on the unstable nature of the wax from which they have been cast. Their stretching forms seem almost to defy gravity. This is an abstract version of an established Delaney theme, the family group, which echoes Manzù's use of the mother and child theme as a symbol of lost innocence. Similar concerns are found in the small bronzes of female figures and shepherds. Delaney is playing in these works with sculptural qualities of weight and balance and they demonstrate a fascination with gravitational pull of the human form – a well-established preoccupation in modernist sculpture.

In 2004, the Hugh Lane published a new catalogue of their collection, with a similar and eloquent summary by their Head of Conservation, Joanna Shepard.

> The *Bronze Groups*, made at the peak of Delaney's career, marry themes that had long fascinated him: the standing elongated human figure, also explored through the figure of Cuchulain and the crucified Christ and the family group. In these pieces, however, the figures are rendered abstract single entities that can also be read as multiple figures. Delaney endows them with a delicacy and vulnerability, the elongated structure evoking a lightness that is at odds with the weight and bulk of the material. The smooth texture of the multiple heads references the soft wax of the original modelling and Delaney succeeds in communicating, in them, a sense of the tenuousness and uncertainty of the human condition.

I couldn't have put it better myself.

In the context of all this, the essay in *The Samson Riddle* is worth looking at.

In his research, Mankowitz said that he 'found nothing in the original biblical story to suggest that Samson had been anything but ordinary physically. He had simply been chosen by God for a special task and so, when the need arose, he was loaned special powers.' The playwright explores masculinity and the condition known 'unamiably as the male menopause, which is particularly critical in artists and other men committed to the grandiose delusion of "purpose".' According to Mankowitz, 'men in their forties, their destinies already deeply committed, struggle to comprehend, twist, turn and shatter their lives in the attempt to break shackles of iron or gold, only like Samson, to bend their heads finally to the forbidden question, offer the secret answer to the implacable enemy and eventually go into seclusion to learn patience and await a clearer vision.'

This must have made interesting reading for Eddie. Mankowitz then talks about various biblical characters and describes how he goes to Brooklyn, New York to seek guidance from a leading Lubavitch Hasidic rabbi. Is this the great Rabbi Schneerson, whom I saw proclaimed as probably the Son of God when I was living in New York? And then, many years later, confirmed as such by devout young Hasidics handing out leaflets at Tel Aviv airport?

The great rabbi reminds Mankowitz that only 'one seed is fertilised and a hundred thousand are not lost but return into the system of which that solitary fertilisation is a part'. The difference between seeds and men, muses Mankowitz, is that each one of us is cursed and blessed with self-awareness. No other species is self-conscious, has an image of itself and continuously seeks identity. We are unable to enjoy so easily being the contribution of a seed to the nitrogen cycle. 'We are not important in the way in which we feel we are important,' the Rabbi tells him, 'and we are important in a way in which we feel unimportant.'

All of this must have fed into Eddie's imagination. It even sounds like an echo of his text on the Viconian cycles, itself about a universal echo, or repetition.

Mankowitz concludes that, 'The task which Samson, the Jew, the Artist, Man is committed to is the witnessing of the Word as best he can. It is a lonely and frequently unhappy commitment: "It is not thy duty to complete the task, but neither art thou free to desist from it." We must do to the extent of our ability, the work that comes to hand. Only then may we achieve the identity for which we are chosen, fulfilling ourselves, like Samson, in spite of our deviations. So it is for Artists and Jews and Men. "Where there are no men, be a man.'"

The Samson Riddle was a popular series and they often come up for auction, in twos or threes, or as a full set, especially when the original purchasers die and the family dissolves the estate. For the RHA retrospective, I visited Gerry Davis one sunny Saturday in Capel Street and, in the midst of a walkabout, he handed me a bunch of artist's proofs of the series, dusty and uncut. 'Here, make money from these,' he said, and I did. It is a tribute to Eddie's work that not only did it raise his children, but it has also helped to raise his grandchildren. And possibly their own children if, and when, they are born. Artists' proofs are just that: prints outside the numbered series which the artist has done as a test or an extra.

The other reason for Gerry's generosity was that he had just got news about the return of his throat cancer and I suppose he was subconsciously clearing stuff out of the house. The maquette of Tone stood on the window, waving at me. Jazz instruments hung next to paintings, and upstairs, his son was under a duvet sleeping off a night out. I got a wave as stiff as Tone's. Downstairs, Davis showed me photographs and told great stories, which got increasingly bawdy as the day wore on, and I thought about when I used to come here as a child.

He was dead within a year. Many of those associated with Eddie's RHA retrospective were dead within months of it: the architect Sam Stephenson, the RHA president Arthur Reynolds, who opened the show with a fine speech, and collectors like Gordon Lambert and Charlie Haughey. Even before the show, they were leaving us and, on one visit, I found myself in the Ballsbridge house of a seafood millionaire, sitting with his recently bereaved widow and looking out at the garden sculptures which Eddie had installed to illustrate the four seasons. How quickly they pass.

The most memorable visit was to Haughey in his Kinsealy mansion. I went across the city on a busy summer's day, passing the gleaming buildings of the boom which he had instigated. But when I got to the house in north county Dublin, the door was opened by a small man, who looked frail and worn. 'There they are,' he said, indicating the small bronze horses which he had brought into the hall like a small boy with his toys. I obligingly took photos and we went into his study for a cup of tea and a chat. Afterwards, standing outside on the steps, he said wistfully, 'Your father: he was some character,' which I thought was quite a tribute coming from him. '*Is* some character,' said Haughey, correcting himself, and he gave me that famous sidelong look. But he would soon be past tense himself.

Earlier this year, most of his collection was sold off, including the horses, although not *Bird Alighting*, a sculpture presented to Haughey by Castlebar Fianna Fáil and which the family presumably wished to retain. A full set of *The Samson Riddle* was sold, and the horses were bought by a young bookmaker and collector who specialises in acquiring Eddie's smaller works. People die, but sculpture rides on. When I left Kinsealy that day, the last thing I saw was Haughey's racehorse, *Flashing Steel*, with his nut-brown coat truly gleaming in the summer sun. It was a long way from the 1950s and Mayo and the hunts of Lord Oranmore and Browne.

Meanwhile, in IMMA, which Haughey had helped to create, it was decided not to put up *Anna* after all, but her sister, *Eve*. One reason was that installing a bench for *Anna* would require a deeper foundation and there was danger of disturbing the old soldiers' graves. Earlier diggings had turned up cap badges, bones and even the odd musket. Sometimes a 'found object' is best left unfound. Instead, *Eve* would go up near the rose garden. She is a smaller sculpture, but one also inspired by German suffering, an emaciated, standing figure with a hand holding out a begging bowl. Or a globe, symbolising renewal and rebirth after the destruction of war.

Mindful of the German background, the installation was kindly assisted by the Goethe Institute and by our own Heritage Council and *Eve* was unveiled last September on a tawny autumn evening. *Anna*, meanwhile, was sent to Adams for auction to continue her interesting journey. People die, sculpture rides on.

By chance, *Eve* is situated beside the 'grave' of Patrick Ireland who, as Brian O'Doherty, chose Eddie for the prize at the 1964 Living Art and who, as 'Patrick Ireland', had his persona of protest buried in the ground, along with a living 'death mask' – a mark that peace had finally broken out in Ireland and that he 'could slough the side of self'. A further offering to the prospect of renewal and rebirth.

As a consequence of their collaboration on *The Samson Riddle*, Eddie and Wolf Mankowitz did a series of small silver figures, mainly of embracing and frolicking couples. The pieces were equally inspired by the romantic stories in the *Akahista Fables* and were mostly made from an ingot of silver that Wolf had given his wife on their twenty-fifth wedding anniversary. There were also solitary figures of flute players and standing shepherds.

Eddie also made some of the pieces from Irish silver, part of the first consignment from the newly opened Tynagh Mine in Galway, and from this he was asked to fashion a special gavel to be presented to David Fitzgerald, the President of the Irish Mining and Quarrying Society, by Irish Base Metals, the owners of the Galway deposit. This was an interesting moment, a connection to an Irish material and the old Celtic past. But it was also a contemporary – and, for Eddie, very useful – connection to the buoyant business community. The mohair suits were getting very excited about the prospect of oil, gas and gold in the Irish land and sea, and the government was handing out exploration licences.

The story of Irish Base Metals is a classic story of 1960s enterprise and adventure. Four men, led by Pat Hughes, had started life as navvies until they went prospecting in Canada and found uranium deposits. Selling these, they moved on to other countries and back to Ireland where Hughes was convinced that lead and zinc deposits could be located. Eventually, the large ore body at Navan was located.

The discovery of silver was equally exciting and newspaper cuttings show the gavel being presented to Mr Fitzgerald at a black-tie dinner in the Shelbourne Hotel. In the absence of Pat Hughes, the company chairman, the presentation is being made by his sister, Mrs Michael McCarthy, a smiling woman with Biba-type earrings. The gavel, which is still in use by the society, is a striking work and looks like a slender arrow that manages to seem both modern and ancient. It was presumably inspired by the Celtic craftworks that Eddie used to examine in the National Museum.

'Young Man Going West' was the headline in the *Irish Independent*, along with some revealing portents for the future.

> Architects usually give sculptors work, but last night, next to his lovely wife Nancy, Eddie Delaney, the sculptor laureate, told me of a competition he hopes to launch for architects. 'I've bought 25 acres of land in Connemara and I'd like someone to design me a house that will fit in with the landscape,' an immaculately dressed Eddie explained between cigar puffs last night in the Shelbourne Hotel.
>
> 'It's the first time that I have worked in Irish silver. In fact, it's probably the first time Irish silver has been used in a long time,' Eddie said, although I know he studied the art of working in silver and gold in Germany. However, he thinks this new Irish silver is marvellous to work with and is only dying to get his hands on the deposit up in Dublin Castle. But then, who isn't?

Incidentally, next to this in the scrapbook is a small cutting from much later, angrily gummed in. It is an announcement from 1982 that, for the centenary of de Valera's birth, Fianna Fáil were issuing a special medal with silver guaranteed from the Tynagh deposit, 'the first occasion in modern times that Irish-mined silver has become available'. Which was, of course, untrue. Eddie must have been raging. Were the late 1960s not the original 'modern times'? But then the 1960s seems to be the decade that official Ireland forgot, including and especially Fianna Fáil, despite it being their period of achievement.

> As far as Connemara is concerned, Eddie Delaney hopes to live permanently in the West – he comes from Claremorris – and his plans are very exciting. 'I am hoping to take over the Comprehensive School in Carraroe during the summer months. By inviting artists and teachers to Connemara, I hope to start a centre for the arts there.' Well, I suppose the successful young Mr Delaney has to go west, because there's very little left for him to decorate in Dublin's fair city.

The remarks show how, even from early on, he was determined to move west, an ambition which would more or less end his marriage. But he was not for turning. The expanded house was to be designed by Paddy Rooney, a skilful, imaginative architect with whom he worked on many commissions. For a large-scale sculptor, the relationship with an architect is crucial. Rooney had trained in Edinburgh with the acclaimed modernist Sir Basil Spence, and was known as one of 'Basil's Bairnes'. Spence had the emotional experience of restoring Coventry Cathedral after its destruction by German bombing.

Rooney collaborated with Eddie on the many commissions which came from this mining connection. One was a panel for the office of Irish Base Metals in Clontarf. 'It's made up of several thousands of pieces of metal,' Eddie told the *Evening Press*, 'in different colours, brazed together at the back, and lit from within. It's a sculpture, but also a map plan of Tynagh.' A similar piece was done for the office of the parent company, Northgate Exploration in Canada, and Rooney still has the model, a lovely little velvet-lined box, with vertical copper strips inside it, like something from Grace's toyshop. Along with his payment, Eddie was given mining shares in another subsidiary of Northgate, an Australian branch called Whim Creek, which held 'prospecting ventures in Western

Australia, covering gold and diamonds and copper/nickel' – the last a material he worked in.

'They'll be worth a fortune in the future,' a mining executive told him with a wink, and later when we were annoying him, Eddie used to say ruefully, 'I'll leave you all behind and head off with my shares from Whim Creek!' Perhaps he foresaw himself prospecting with the boys.

At one stage, we even looked up Whim Creek in the stock listings to see how it was doing, although we weren't sure if we wanted it to be doing well or badly. But there was no need to worry. A financial pundit described it as 'reliably volatile' and, besides, it did not really have the most auspicious title for a share, conjuring up both frivolity and a Wild West image of a sun-baked desert gulch.

Eddie also worked in gold, which Garech had brought back from India. Garech was now regularly travelling to India and he would eventually get married there to Princess Purna of Morvi. Eddie flew out for the event, twenty years after Garech had attended his wedding in Power's Hotel, just as his own marriage was breaking up. It was a memorable experience. He slept in the palace, where every time he moved in his ornate four-poster bed, semi-sleeping servants emerged from the aromatic darkness to give him aid. What impressed Eddie about India, and Hindu culture, was that there was not just one God but 'loads of them': animal headed and multi-limbed – the possibilities for a sculptor were endless.

For the Irish party, it was a lively affair and Eddie later told *Harpers and Queen* magazine that the bride had looked 'absolutely rodent'. He was famous for his mispronunciations and malapropisms, such as accusing certain parties of 'hunting with the hares and running with the hounds', something that would have caused utter confusion back in Castlemacgarret. He also surprised listeners by describing a visit to a well-known doctor in the midlands and noticing that 'the house was full of orphans'. He meant Orpens, as in paintings. At one stage, he told us not to be running around Luggala, because Garech had only just had the place 'restocked with peasants', which is an interesting image. He even improved the title of Coppola's movie, giving it the more meaningful reversal of *The Hunted and the Haunted*.

As for my own engagement in 2007, Eddie didn't make 'the ring', as proposed, although he may well have created it in his head, sitting in the nursing home. Nor did I find the allegedly buried rings, although I did find, in the foundry, a small crucible filled with silver pellets, ready to go, and an old school pencil box filled with the small wax models of nude-entwined rings, many of them broken. This would have been one of his last 'works in progress'.

I could also have waited for Garech to fall asleep in front of me, since his own wedding ring was a more than ample knuckleduster. Instead I decided to start afresh and get a ring of my own. It was time to break the connection with the past. I had already moved to Phibsboro, in north Dublin, a liberating experience, and would soon be married in St Joseph's Church on Berkeley Road, where one of the altar servers used to be Seán T. O'Kelly, the president who had laid the plaque for the Davis statue. You see, the connections endure. The back of St Joseph's goes on to Eccles Street, where Leopold Bloom lived, and the whole area is the heart of Joyceland, with connections to his stories and family in the sidestreets, shops and pubs. It was only when I re-read *Ulysses*, incidentally, that I discovered that the walking ad men from HELYs, whose company made my red scrapbook, actually pass, not only the spot 'where Wolfe Tone's statue was not', but the actual stone, as laid by John O'Leary on Grafton Street. In Joyce's time, it was situated off Mary Street. It is now completely missing, alas, just like the mythical rings.

In the early 1970s, there was an excellent journal called *Aquarius*. It was published by the Servites religious order in Tyrone and it had an imaginative and typically robust Northern approach to arts and politics. One of its articles proposed a southern 'Minister for the Arts' and in it I came across this passage:

We are famous for cherishing our citizens best after they are dead. You would not, of course, have considered Brendan Behan or Patrick Kavanagh while they were among us, but with hindsight don't you agree that they would outrageously clobber a little light into us? There are few Behans and Kavanaghs left. There is, however, Edward Delaney. He talks ungrammatical controversy with great gusto. He would enrich Dáil debates, a contribution which could only be described as a Good Thing. And he is a creator (you know his sculptures, don't you?) who could speak for the artists of the country. He would be the kind of minster Gay would love on the *Late, Late* – a Tam-rater. And this Arts Business must be brought out into the marketplace, away from where the cliques foregather.

This is a fine compliment, but it's a double-edged sword: the link to the 'marketplace' and publicity and television.

In his book *The Irish*, Donald Connery writes of his intention 'to speak in detail of a single poet, or perhaps a novelist, by way of showing some of the problems and pleasures of being an artist in Ireland. Someone successful, yet not numbed by success, who might have something to say about the state of the nation. The poets, writers and journalists I met all said I ought to ring up Eddie – you know Eddie Delaney, the sculptor.'

Connery certainly got plenty of observations. He even got Eddie's views on agriculture, and of 'how the average Irish farmer enjoys the simple life and his small pleasures, and is smart enough not to kill himself with overwork.' Eddie quoted his father's philosophy: 'If it's a great day for working, then it's a great day for fishing.' However, Delaney himself, adds Connery, 'who speaks with sadness about the diminishing life of rural Ireland, wishes that that the farmers were "doing something more constructive. When I go to the West and talk to a farmer and we talk for five or six hours

I become restless. I wonder why he doesn't have something to do. Like cut the hay or something.'"

This is a bit rich. After all, maybe the man was being detained by Eddie's storytelling? And 'five or six hours' – what were they talking about? It's also hard to understand what Eddie means by the 'diminishing life of rural Ireland', since the rest of Connery's chapter is an indictment of just how slow and backward Irish farming had become. Like Thomas Davis, Eddie sought modernity, but he also wanted its laid-back absence.

Connery was taken by Eddie's gratitude to the state. Artists often complain about the lack of official assistance, but not Eddie. The state had helped train him and then gave him the job of building its mythic heroes. But he had grown tired of it by now, and it was time to go west, and into abstraction. He had outgrown 'Ireland' although ironically he would go to the most 'Irish' part of Ireland: Connemara. But his was a European sensibility and an international perspective. He could as easily have been in California, with his by now long hair, blue jeans and windbeaten tan, driving pick-up trucks full of metal and fish boxes.

'I've got it very good here,' he told Connery in 1968, 'but I have this itchiness. I'm trying to get out but I can't because I have all this work to do. I'd like to move out for two or three years and see the place from the outside again. I want to think.' On the other hand, he is not so sure he ought to leave. 'If we're going to go on and do something better than what has been happening in the last fifty years, then I think people like myself have to stay at home.'

So Connery used Eddie as a metaphor for modern Ireland and its cultural development, no more than I did forty years later. He was not a direct symbol, but an illustration, a figurative metaphor, so to speak – just like a sculpture. Eddie had by now outgrown 'Ireland', and in writing this book, believe me, so have I. This is how I knew him. He would spend the rest of his life in Galway, where he was going to recreate a world of pure shape and form. Compared to Dublin, it would be a life of relative social isolation, but it would also be busy – very busy, in fact – and he would soon have a new partner, Anne, and two more children, Emer and Ronan. Yes, new kids to play with. Later, he would install a foundry and a sculpture park, which he called *Beyond the Pale*. It was to be open to the public, all year round, 'from dawn to dusk' and it would comprise a hilltop collection of stainless-steel trees and constructions looking out on the ocean.

However, as a preliminary to this, he would envisage another sort of space, a farm of the make believe. It was called a *Still Life Animal Farm* and would include new animals of his making, just like the 'fantastic animals' he carved on his school desk. It seemed like his whole life was, in many ways, an attempt to recreate the magic of his childhood and the German circus coming into town.

Wolf Mankowitz describes a *Still Life Animal Farm* and how he came to meet Eddie.

> One of the stimulating experiences of living in Ireland for the past five years has been a growing familiarity with the work and personality of Edward Delaney. I met Delaney in the first month of settling in Dublin and was instantly taken by his totally unselfconscious involvement in his work. He seemed to epitomise the sculptor, his physical approach to expression being closer to a wrestler than an intellectual, a feeling corroborated and enhanced by visiting him at his studio and foundry in Dún Laoghaire. There, with the Delaney family always imminent, the children's bicycles standing by to be repaired, the scrap brass waiting to be thrown into the fire, the feeling of the Renaissance craftsman's life was strong. I remembered accounts in *Cellini's Memoirs* of the household furniture being thrown into the furnace to boil more metal to materialise the artist's visions. One feels in Delaney this same fierce single-minded obsession: his life and his work are the same thing, and what one includes, the other cannot exclude.

And so it seems very natural that Delaney, now living in Galway on what he describes as 'twenty-two acres of land which is no use for farming – rocky, made up of small little fields, spotted with large loose rocks', that now these rocks and fields are integrals of his creative life, his work should emerge from and live with them. Thus, with irresistible Delaney reasoning, there emerges the concept of the *Still Life Animal Farm* about which he describes his feelings thus: 'Looking at the few cattle that exist there, isolated in the barren landscape of small fields, imprisoned by stone walls, I feel a direct need to construct animals and perhaps figures which can be compared with the living ones standing there against the Atlantic Ocean.'

To this form of still life sculpture Delaney would try to give the same physical character, directness and simplicity he sees and feels in everyday life. Delaney believes that all art should have this directness and simplicity, and it is to this dominant characteristic of his work that I found myself initially responsive and to which I continue to respond. I believe that Delaney's new project may well turn out to be a great tribute to life against the background of the land of Ireland, a daring, exciting, essentially human and therefore blessedly eccentric project, and very typical of Delaney himself.

CHAPTER 16

Raising the Tone Again

As if to illustrate the tenuousness and uncertainty of the heroic condition, Wolfe Tone was bombed late one Sunday night, in April 1971. The bombing was a consequence of the Northern conflict and yet the media treated the attack as if it came completely out of the blue.

In fact, Loyalist militants had been secretly active in Dublin from 1969. But these are forgotten bombings and rarely spoken of now. For example, Wolfe Tone's grave was attacked by the Ulster Volunteer Force in 1969, and three weeks before the bombing of Tone's statue the 170-foot-high O'Connell monument in Glasnevin Cemetery was attacked. The monument is modelled on an Irish round tower, and toppling this would have been audacious, given all the patriots buried around it. Even more audacious was an attack on the O'Connell memorial, right in the city centre.

It is interesting then that while the Dublin pubs were full of talk about an 'invasion' and a 'united Ireland', Loyalists were skulking around the city attacking monuments and statues. Three years later, of course, they elevated their attacks to people, and with devastating effect, killing up to 33 people in one day in no-warning car bombs set to go off during the Friday evening rush hour. One of the bombs blew in the windows of Ferry House on South Frederick Street, in the lobby of which Eddie had an abstract wall sculpture.

In 1971, however, the bombing of Tone's statue was treated with a curious mixture of shock-horror drama and Ealing comedy. The attack dominated the front pages, along with photos of the sundered rebel. 'Big garda alert after explosion' was the *Irish Press* headline, while the *Irish Independent* had 'Famous city monument is blown up'. The latter's vivid account is worth quoting from.

> An explosion, which was heard for miles, shattered the Wolfe Tone memorial at Stephen's Green [sic], Dublin this morning. The statue was wrecked, leaving only the base, and huge slabs of the bronze sculpture were hurled 20 feet into the air. Windows on the front of the Shelbourne Hotel and of houses in the area were shattered and hotel guests were awakened to find glass showering into their bedrooms. The immediate area was apparently deserted, though some people were in 'the Green' and adjoining streets as the explosions [sic] ripped out. No one was injured. Special Branch detectives and Garda forensic experts were called to the scene to examine the wrecked monument and debris. A Garda spokesman said, 'The statue is a complete write-off. Only the stumps of the legs remain.'
>
> One of the first on the scene was the night porter, Mr Patrick Malone, of Fatima Mansions. He said, 'I was standing in the foyer of the building when there was this huge blast. I looked upwards as I thought one of the upper floors was collapsing. I ran towards the stairs and then I saw the glass from the side window littering the lobby floor. I was waiting for the place to collapse and I dashed out into the street. Then I saw the pieces of the statue scattered around the footpath.'

According to the *Irish Press*, the 'first people on the scene were a group of night students from UCD who were continuing their vigil outside nearby Leinster House on the 'night degrees issue'. The *Press* gives further detail:

The figure of the 1798 patriot was shattered into four large pieces, which lay within a 30-foot radius of its site. No apparent damage was caused to the granite background, but this will be examined this morning by engineers from the Board of Works. Army explosive experts and members of the Special Branch were on the scene minutes after the explosion and all roads out of the city were closed as the gardaí mounted 'Operation Northside' and 'Operation Southside'. People at the scene were interviewed, but no one reported seeing any suspicious movements in the area.

Eddie's career and work was quickly summarised, along with the fact Tone was not on a pedestal, but 'stood almost at granite level – on a foot-high block of granite'. This may have saved him from further damage, it seemed: the higher the hero, the greater the fall. The *Independent* had a cropped file picture of Eddie, who looks like he's been doorstepped for his reaction. In fact, it's from the Living Art exhibition of 1964, when he was explaining *Flight* to Mrs Don Carroll.

Nor did the *Independent* lack drama and self-promotion: 'Shortly after the blast rocked the centre city area, the newsroom of Independent House was inundated with anxious callers. Garda squad cars converged on Stephen's Green within minutes and cordoned off the area as crowds began to gather around the scene.'

According to the *Irish Press* 'one man, who was cycling just past the corner of Hume Street, had a narrow escape. He is Larry O'Brien, a clerk, of Pearse Street, who was returning from work. "The cap was blown off my head," he said. "I went over to see the statue and there it was lying in pieces in the roadway. The explosion was terrific and the blast toward me was very strong. There was not much smoke from the blast. It must have been caused by a timing device as I saw nobody running from the scene – in fact the street was empty."'

The bombing was reported on the TV news in Britain. An Irish historian, who was based in Cambridge, remembers everyone in his common room bursting into laughter when it appeared on the BBC News. But then how people here laughed when Nelson was bombed five years earlier.

The same strange mixture of conspiracy and drama continued with the evening newspapers. The *Evening Herald* reported that 'two cars with Northern registrations and one licensed in Dublin were being sought by gardaí and army personnel on all cross-border routes today'. The special alert 'came before the drivers would have had time to reach the Six Counties. There was a hold-up of traffic across the Border today as customs officers, gardaí and army men examined all cars passing through. Experts from the Garda Technical Bureau were today carrying out an inch-by-inch examination of the area surrounding the memorial. Apparently, the blast was heard as far away as Raheny.'

But there was also the continuing strangeness. 'Mystery surrounding the explosion deepened today with the discovery by gardaí of a pair of men's dark grey pants hanging on a tree only yards from the memorial. While the significance of the pants was puzzling detectives today, it is thought they may have been placed on the tree by the men responsible for the blast as a "practical joke".'

But the newspapers had their own jokey tone (forgive the pun). One had a cartoon of a smiling woman surrounded by rejected shoeboxes and an exasperated shop assistant saying, 'Maybe Madam would prefer something up in St Stephen's Green.' A thought bubble showed Tone's truncated boots.

The next day's *Irish Press* had an update by Jimmy Walsh, with the headline 'Tone didn't lose his head', and the revelation from the sculptor that 'it may, after all, be possible' to repair the statue. 'And ironically, the blasting of the half-ton bronze monument has provided its creator with an opportunity to carry out wished-for alterations to the memorial. The sculptor said that when he saw the memorial erected on the site, he realised that it could have been enhanced by a few changes. The desirability of these changes was not necessarily something that would have manifested itself at the workshop stage. Mr Delaney said that the monument had been cast in five parts. From photographs of the damaged parts, he had concluded that the jointings had given way. If this was the case, it might be feasible to repair the statue. He was glad to note that the head section seemed to be intact because he considered it to be a "good resemblance" of Tone.'

This is cheeky, given that he'd modelled Tone on himself. It seemed a tad hasty to be already awarding the repair job to himself, although this was also done with the caution that all might still be lost. 'Mr Delaney said he still had most of the moulds of the work. It was possible that the repair work might only cost a few hundred pounds. However, he could go no further until he had seen the damage for himself and he expected to do so in the day or so.' An accompanying photo shows Tone's blown arms, lying on the ground like rubber gloves.

Eddie already had experience of repairing a bombed sculpture from the attack on the O'Connell monument the year before. This attack was on *Wing of Victory*, one of the memorial's four angels, or large female figures, which always remind me of Paris and those wonderful proud and buxom women of the Republic.

On that occasion, Eddie assured the *Evening Press* that 'once we have the metal pieces (it is understood that the angel came apart in four sections) the sculpture could be put back together again'. But in an image worthy of a Wim Wenders movie, he said that the angel should not have been 'dragged on to the pavement during its removal'. He also 'appealed to anyone who had taken away pieces to return them to the Corporation, since everything would be vital for the restoration'. Barry Devlin, then of the Horslips rock band and now a film producer, worked on the repair and remembers how big the angel was inside the workshop but how easily Eddie moved around her. 'She obviously felt she was in good hands,' said Devlin, and maybe Eddie knew this. Today, *Wing of Victory*, which thousands of people pass every day, shows no sign that she was ever bombed.

The day after the Tone bombing, another jokey if wistful piece appeared in *The Irish Times*, by Nell McCafferty, then a young reporter. 'Taking Tone by the bronze bootstraps' was the headline.

'He was a great character – he kept his boots until the end,' a Dubliner observed yesterday as two men from the Office of Public Works carefully removed the lower halves of Wolfe Tone's legs from the cement base to which they had been attached. The hollow knee-length bronze remains were freed finally, and laid on the ground, like cast-off Wellington boots.

Who was Wolfe Tone? I asked the workmen who had cut away the legs. 'Ah, sure he was a great Republican,' he informed me. 'He fought the British. He came from the North, in the days when Protestants and Catholics were all the one.' What were his ideas, specifically? I inquired of a woman who was pocketing a bronze fragment. 'Wasn't he a great Irishman,' she told me. 'He formed the new Parliament.'

Where did Wolfe Tone live? I asked some schoolchildren who stood watching. 'Who's Wolfe Tone?' they enquired of me. 'I didn't know he was this near,' a woman said. 'I thought he was buried in Bodenstown.' 'Aye,' replied a man, 'he strangled himself rather than let them shoot him. They found him hanging from a rope. Emmet's round the corner, I suppose he'll be next. They got Dan O'Connell last year. Or there's Davis, across the Green. Though he's a right big pair of feet on him, he'll be hard to shift. He was put up by the same sculptor and he makes them outsize.'

Do you think all the trouble will escalate down here, with all these explosions? I enquired of them. 'Not at all,' a couple assured me. 'Sure, they're only statues. Sure we're hell for blowing up statues in Ireland. And if they're not exploded, the students paint them. Did ye see the placard around the one down at Leinster House? I wonder what they're on about.'

'Now you take Birmingham,' an Englishman was saying. 'Walk down any street, black and brown faces everywhere. But we don't shoot them. Live and let live is the way to play it. Aren't we all citizens of the world?'

'Aye, well that citizen's gone into orbit,' the audience of one replied as the workmen carried the truncated remains away.

Not only did Eddie have to make a statue all over again – or at least reassemble it – he had to do another round of publicity and once more defend 'modern art', a prospect which seemed to both excite and bore him in equal measure.

In one long interview, in the *Evening Press*, the writer was not only challenging and opinionated, but freely speculated about who *really* bombed Tone. It is nonetheless a revealing interview and worth quoting from. 'Putting Wolfe Tone back on his two feet again' is the defiant headline, but the subhead is more questioning: 'Who will pay? asks Tanis O'Callaghan. The country, says sculptor Delaney.'

Last Sunday, in the lonely dark hours of early morning, the downfall of Wolfe Tone took place. Only his massive legs, amputated just above the knees, remained standing. There was one witness: a man bicycling past the Shelbourne.

Others heard the thunder as the bronze effigy of the patriot surrendered to the force of the explosion, set off with a time fuse, planned, so said the rumours, by the UVF. If responsible, this organisation was unwittingly paying the sculptor a left-handed compliment. By engineering the explosion they were acknowledging the figure as memorial to the Irish hero and all he stood for. That's more than some nationalistic-minded people do. Delaney himself views the event with a certain stoicism. 'I'm sorry that so many people just laughed or condemned what happened because it was the destruction of a piece of public property. I'm sorry that so few regretted the destruction of a work of art. Though I have had a few sympathetic phone calls.'

Since the deed is done, Delaney is just going to get on with the job of repairing it. 'It will take about six months,' he said. 'It wasn't just smashed at the joints – it broke off in such a way that there'll be lot of work to be done. And the fountain was damaged. There will have to be repair work on the plumbing too.'

Who will pay for the reconstruction, I asked. 'The country, I suppose,' said Delaney. 'It's malicious damage, isn't it?'

Once rebuilt, the Wolfe Tone memorial could be toppled again by its unknown enemies ... and erected again (unless the public purse snaps shut). And Delaney could find himself with a steady income maintaining a memorial he created some years ago. A position few artists could hope to achieve. That's all hypothetical, however. But there's a school of thought that thinks the UVF had no part in the explosion; that maybe nationalists or historians or students, or even artists, who happened to be explosive experts and who were also unhappy about the enduring characteristic of bronze when cast in the form of a Delaney Wolfe Tone ... decided to end their misery.

The man in the street or the car or the bus seems to take little interest. He was aware of the memorial when it was there. Not as a work of art, more as a curiosity and as a conversation piece ... or the arrogance of the government in allowing some people to take a chunk out of St Stephen's Green. Some reacted angrily to the ten-foot-high figure which wore no uniform. Tone wore a uniform, they said. A famine theme incorporated in the memorial had nothing to do with the patriot Tone, said others. And one humorist looked at the granite hoarding backing the long, narrow figure and said the memorial was a monument to a man answering a call to nature.

Delaney came in for much the same sort of reaction when his memorial to Thomas Davis was unveiled in 1966. At that time, when I interviewed him, he seemed to be concerned about criticism, rather excitable in temperament, on the defensive about his productions, but quite determined to continue producing them.

Now older (thirty-nine), he is more relaxed, his hair is shorter, his clothes neater: he is no longer concerned about criticism and still determined to produce his 'works of art'. This is how he describes his creations, regardless of what other people call them. When I ask him to define a work of art, he says, 'No one should ask what a work of art is.' But I persisted.

'I'd say it's a work of art that has a presence. When an artist produces something he is making a statement. It's ridiculous to ask him what it means. It's his statement. If you like it, you like it. And if you want to buy it, you buy it. I won't bargain. I've no room for people who argue with me and try to make me cut down the price of anything I've done. "You've done something for someone else; it only cost so much. Now, if you do something for me at that price I'd buy it." I've no time for that.'

Who buys your pieces? I asked. 'Mostly wealthy Jewish people,' he told me. Why do they buy? 'Fifty per cent because they appreciate them, fifty per cent as an investment,' he said frankly.

271

'My style has changed,' he claimed. He then said that he couldn't possibly produce something today similar to his work of a few years ago. 'I wouldn't do the Davis memorial now as I did it then. For one thing, the authorities wouldn't allow a statue to go up in the middle of a public street. Obstructing the roadway, they'd say. But in Stockholm, you've got statues of animals right on the roadway for people to look at and touch.'

You think it's important for people to be able to touch sculpture, I said. 'Yes,' said Delaney, 'and I always think there should be fountains and water with them for children to enjoy.'

At the moment he is interested in graphics as well as working in bronze, he told me. And he plans to have an exhibition of lithographs in the Davis Gallery next April.

'I'm always drawing,' he said. 'When other people take up a book late at night I start drawing. I never read. I can't read. I read three pages and then skip along to the middle of the book and can't finish it. But sometimes I start drawing something I intend to put into bronze. And when I've finished drawing I think that there's no point now making it into bronze. I've done it. I'm quite happy with it.'

'One of the best things I have done,' said the sculptor, 'is the work commissioned by the First National Bank of Chicago in Dame Street – two bronze figures in the main hall. I did a Joycean theme … Finn's return, you know from *Finnegans Wake*. The figures are on a scale with their environment,' he told me, 'and they harmonise with the modern design of the building's interior. That's what sculpture ought to do. I'm also pleased with the bronze I did for the Wellington Park Hotel in Belfast.' He described this as being part of the structure of the building … 'as a work of art should be. It divides the car park from the main building. But most of the architects don't work at the outset with an artist as they should. Even when they know a piece has been commissioned they think about it when the building is already completed.'

With two public monuments on record and numerous works commissioned by private patrons, he is highly successful. Most major art shows also include several of the grasshopper type figures easy to identify as his. In being immune to criticism he is unusual, he told me. 'Many of my friends are badly affected by criticism. I know many artists who took it so seriously they just gave up working.' Delaney bears no grudge against critics who have slated him. 'These critics expect me to hate them. They're surprised if I buy them a drink.'

According to Delaney he never went to art college, nor were there any drawing classes at the primary schools he attended in Mayo until he was fourteen. 'I was a rebel at school,' he said. 'I couldn't learn anything. No I'm not uneducated,' he added. 'I think self-education is the best kind of education.'

Jobless, he came to Dublin as a teenager and 'messed about'. I asked him how he earned his bread and butter then. But he didn't want to talk about it. 'You shouldn't ask that,' he said. 'Just say I survived.'

In the National Library he discovered a book about casting in bronze. He became very interested in the subject. So he wrote to the German government, who had recently presented the *Bronze Group* which now stands in St Stephen's Green. When he had the address of the group's sculptor, Josef Wacalla [sic], Delaney then wrote to him asking the sculptor to accept him as a pupil. On the strength of having been accepted, he applied to the Arts Council for scholarship. He was given £400 and went off to Munich. The Arts Council subsidised him for a year and a half. For some years after that Delaney remained abroad and continued to learn his craft by winning foreign scholarships.

Though he lives now in Ireland, he says that the environment here does nothing to foster art. 'Kids in school are not allowed to develop as individuals with individual tastes. We have no taste in Ireland: we are taught what we are to like. And that's what's wrong with rural Ireland. The people are like sheep ... waiting for someone to lift them out of the doldrums, instead of developing their own culture. The dance hall has killed rural Ireland.'

That's how Delaney talks. And he talks a lot, throwing out thoughts, often disconnected thoughts. It's difficult to follow his reasoning. But no one can deny that he and his work are highly controversial. And few people in Ireland haven't heard of him. Is he a great artist or just a man who manufactures worthless bronze objects? Everyone has his own theory. For what it's worth, the man and his work fail to communicate with me. Both are enigmas.

The article is at least softened by a photograph of Tone, intact, along with the caption 'an earlier visitor brought a more gentle present – a rose'. And, sure enough, the picture shows a flower in our hero's hand. On the reverse of the page, however – perhaps arranged by a more vengeful editor – was 'Dancehall Scene' and a whole page of showband news. Larry Cunningham was 'storming New York', while a cheesy ballad singer was pictured next to the Emmet statue in Washington, publicising her new version of the 'Bold Robert Emmet'.

But there was some consolation. The Dubliners were expected to have another No. 1 with 'Scorn Not His Simplicity'...

CHAPTER 17

The Long Way Home

In the end, Tone was repaired, much more quickly than expected. You would hardly know he had been bombed at all. Having watched him go over our rooftop the first time, I don't remember him going over it again. Finn Again's Awake and back to the place where he 'was not', as the line goes in *Ulysses*.

One day we were in the Shelbourne Hotel, having just met the Office of Public Works, and Eddie suggested we go over to see Tone. He wanted to see if I could tell him where the 'join' was on the statue. The meeting with the OPW was to discuss the repair of Davis and his 're-unveiling' for the 90th anniversary of the Rising. Tone had already been cleaned and given a wider, repaved plaza. Frail on his legs, this would be Eddie's last trip to Dublin.

What provoked his interest was that he had seen the statue of Saddam Hussein fall apart on TV when he was pulled down by the crowd and he was very disappointed by the cheapness of the cast and the way the join had come loose. This seemed to cause him as much concern as the prospect of Iraqi civil war. Anyway, I couldn't find the join on Tone, so he went around the back to show me. For a moment I thought it was like Davy Byrne's secret 'doorbell' again, but the main join is a solder inside the folds of Tone's coat (He does have a uniform, after all).

Eddie was always on the lookout for falling statues and was much taken with the early 1990s when tyrants and heroes were being toppled all over Eastern Europe, or simply removed and put in storage – a more mature thing to do, as with Victoria. One image was particularly striking. It was a truckful of Lenins on their way to storage. When the sculptor Eamonn O'Doherty was commissioned to do a statue of James Connolly, next to Liberty Hall, Eddie suggested that he should simply get one of the Lenins and swap the head for Connolly's. As it happens, the Connolly statue is indeed standing in a Lenin pose and looking into the mid-distance with his fists at his side. But such a direct transfer might have been a bit too literal for our more bourgeois Labour Party.

The bombing of Tone made him a victim of the Northern Troubles, but unlike most of the human victims, he could be restored. What did Dev think about the attack? Did he ever reflect that maybe the bombing was at least, in part, a consequence of his fiery rhetoric and Southern claims on the North? Or did it just confirm for him the violent effects of British conquest and the Unionist discrimination that the British had allowed to take hold? Unfortunately, we don't know, because the Long Fellow avoided speaking about the Northern conflict.

What would Flanigan have thought: the man who dynamited the original stone for Tone and brought it down from Belfast? Or Kathleen Clarke, who had collected for the statue at football matches? Would they be perhaps impressed at the attack, as proof of the statue's potency and, after restoration, of its endurance? Either way, it certainly enhanced the public's respect for the memorial and from that moment on most of the original criticism disappeared. Getting bombed was the making of him, and on this the otherwise critical Tanis O'Callaghan was correct, 'The rebuilt Tone has been allowed to stand in peace for posterity.'

Today, both statues form part of the city's landscape and reflect the confidence of a state asserting itself and reclaiming its cultural identity after centuries of colonialism. But a statue is easier than an ideology. How easy to put up a Lenin, how much harder to implement his policies. And so with Tone. If the erection of his statue is a national metaphor, then many of the ultimate aims remained unfulfilled. The country's independence may have been enough for most people, but not for Dev. The language was not revived, the British did not leave the entire island and the country is not based on his ideal of small holdings and contented frugality. He lost out just as much as the hippies did. Industrialisation and materialism prevailed, but then it was through such modernity that Ireland gained any meaningful independence.

So it was a strange sort of fulfilment of Emmet's claim that his epitaph 'not be written until Ireland takes her place among the nations of the world'. For decades, it remained unwritten because of partition. But that struggle is over for now, and the people have come to an accommodation with the situation – and freed themselves of Emmet's prescription. Get me out of this straight-jacket of a Republic, as Dev himself had put it. In the way that it was proposed, 'uniting' Ireland seemed like an exhausting and contradictory task, especially when people saw the price, and the violence grinded on into the 1970s and 1980s.

Dev has also lost out in terms of his own reputation. There is, for example, no statue to him in the capital and no road named after him, whereas his bitter rival, Michael Collins, has avenues, roads and busts of himself in Merrion and Parnell Squares. Collins was the sexy one, who died early. He didn't have to stick around to see the disappointments of independence. 'Why is there no road in Dublin named after de Valera?' went the old Fine Gael joke. 'Because they couldn't find a road that was long enough, nor crooked enough, to name after the bastard.'

There is Joycean bite in this, and you can just hear Simon Dedalus spit it out: 'De Valera, the American-born culchie who believed that Dubliners were "flighty". Who did he think he was!' After all, Dev's literary tormentor, James Joyce, also born in 1882, has a whole industry built around him. There is a street named after him, a statue on O'Connell Street, a bridge over the Liffey and blue plaques for his characters, who didn't even exist. Artist's proof and writer's revenge. Meanwhile, Dev floats inside an ether of memory and aspiration, just like his equivalent in *Finnegans Wake*. The revisionists have been overly harsh with his reputation, but it will be a while before he recovers his popular appeal.

Tone meanwhile stands in St Stephen's Green. He is from so far back that his reputation remains unchanged and, for many people, mostly unknown. Whatever about challenging a violent tradition of 80 years ago, challenging the militancy of 1798 seems pointless. This and Tone's humanity and humour ('Huzza, let us drink!') redeem him of blame for this problematic tradition. Critics and public alike are too polite, or indifferent, to delve too much into the real man.

In her catalogue essay for the RHA retrospective, Roisín Kennedy makes the interesting point that there is 'no doubt that both the Davis and Tone projects have as their centrepiece ungainly and awkward historical figures'. She quotes the art historian Judith Hill as saying that Delaney did not treat the statues as 'portraits, but as expressions of life'. They express 'very literally the weight of history and the heroic mantel which Republicanism foisted on them rather than providing the establishment with conventional political symbols'.

'Delaney had major difficulties in reconciling his modernist practices with the conventions of memorial sculpture,' argues Kennedy. 'Both Davis and Tone appear uncomfortable and self-conscious as if their creator was not completely convinced of their heroic status. An important element in Delaney's work is its sense of uncertainty, a quality not normally associated with memorial sculpture.'

This is a fascinating observation: that, in fact, the sculptures represent figures uneasy with the pose expected of them. And is this not also quite an Irish attitude: a down-to-earth self-consciousness and a healthy distrust of pomposity? Like the crowd at the unveiling, standing awkwardly for the dedication. Get me out of this straightjacket of a Republic – and into the cloak of a milder nationalist.

According to Kennedy, this uneasiness was rectified somewhat 'by the inclusion of subsidiary sculptural groups to the monuments, which link the heroic version of history to a much wider narrative of human struggle and triumph. In both sculptural groups, the famine acts as a subtext undermining the dominant egocentric view of history. They also function as key areas for public interaction, with active working fountains … The three emaciated figures behind Tone are a powerful expression of human suffering and dignity. The outstretched arm of the left-hand figure recalls images of torture and even of crucifixion. It also symbolises the triumph of the human spirit. In Irish art, an important precedent for the linking of historical and biblical imagery is found in the work of Andrew O'Connor, such as his war memorial *The Victims* in Merrion Square. It is also an important characteristic of Sheppard's *Cuchulain*, chosen as the official 1916 memorial sculpture in 1934. Delaney expresses the idea in much more universal terms.'

'The animal in the Tone famine group is emblematic of the fundamental cataclysmic nature of the famine,' continues Kennedy. 'Animals and agrarian scenes are prominent in the Davis *bas-reliefs* of the famine. Their presence in these monuments indicates Delaney's unwillingness to embrace modernity uncritically.' Not unlike de Valera himself, of course. 'In one of them, *A Nation Once Again*, an idyllic scene of rural life diametrically opposes the triumph of the Lemass era. The trumpeting heralds surround a pool of strange plants and upturned salmon, a subtle and determined effort on Delaney's part to introduce nature to the centre of modern Dublin.'

Similar observations are made by Peter Murray in the *Irish Arts Review*. 'In nearly all of Delaney's work,' he writes, 'there is the direct appeal to the simplicity of a single human figure, or group of figures gathered easily together. The sense of ease expressed by his figures is perhaps more of a rural than an urban phenomenon. His figures of Tone, Davis and others convey an earthy solidity, a connection with the earth, emphasised by their heavy legs.'

And this is what Davis also suggests: a farmer in from the fields, a man off the bog and onto a pedestal, with his arms hanging down by his side. There is none of the shrill theatre of Grattan, or the arrogant certainty of Burke, with hand on waist, 'reflecting' on the revolution in France. Like them, Tone and Davis were landed

Protestants, but it is as if Eddie has deconstructed their demeanour and turned them into the very peasants they championed. They have been deracinated and democratised. They even look like Eddie himself, labouring to decorate the capital, or the 1960s builders who employed him: self-made, prosperous, on site in a sheepskin coat. As Dev said, Davis could have been one of those 'young scions of nobility, thinking only of themselves and their class'. Instead he's been turned into a farmer and the Bohola mafia. 'The country is theirs,' conceded de Valera, 'and they are of the country.' So this is not a Republic in the full socialist sense, but a place where you can 'get yourself on' and overcome class and religion.

Aidan Dunne agrees about the 'uncertainty' in the public works, but argues that it is this that gives the monuments an appealing, human character. 'This character, a compound toughness and fragility, touches virtually all of Delaney's early work: be they single human figures, close family groupings, and mythical heroes and animals. All have a hard-won, tragic dignity about them and a sense of being frayed by mortality and uncertainty.' This is a line that could describe the atmosphere of the unveiling itself, and especially the line of standing VIPs at the dedication. It is the very quality that all of us have about our everyday lives.

Dunne identifies the paradox of 'an underlying sense of doubt and fragility coming through the intractable, material substance of the figures, be they human, animal or mythical. The most robust forms have an awkwardness, a tenderness about them.' This is presumably the very quality that causes people to come up and touch the statue. The touching of statues is like a religious tradition, of course, invoking solace, seeking connection. It is often an involuntary impulse, which is why children do it even more. They particularly touch Tone's hand at the back, but also the hem of his coat and, of course, his codpiece, where the explosives were later put. They also touch the famine figures and especially the derided dog, making its spine shiny. Kids have no problem with the inclusion of an animal.

Some tour guides mischievously suggest that women rub Tone's codpiece to aid fertility. In Paris, a similar custom exists with Victor Noir's statue in the Père Lachaise cemetery (a custom taken seriously: handwritten notes are tucked inside the statue's cloak). In Paris, flowers are also left by memorials, especially those to the French resistance, and each spring in Dublin children put cherry blossom into the cup of the famine family. Newly married couples, meanwhile, get their photograph taken in front of the famine sculpture, and children similarly come into the Green in their Holy Communion outfits, ordinary Dubliners with their families, and stand before the stricken figures. The Risen People.

Tone appears indifferent to the more official photo opportunities that occur around him, such as the pensive shots of politicians and authors, usually after interviews in nearby hotels (I've done it myself). Or musicians leaning against the granite columns, or pouting fashion models, in among the famine group, and sometimes looking half-starved themselves. In one photo, a heel is perched provocatively on the animal's back like something from Helmut Newton. One can even track the changing fashion styles: from the long-haired 1970s, through to the spiky haired, neon-coloured 1980s. On *Celtic Heartbeat*, a collaboration between Van Morrison and the Chieftains, the album cover shows the musicians mingled in among the sculpture and holding on to the famine figures, just like The Dubliners on *Finnegan's Wake*.

'The feckers,' declared Eddie, who was no longer designing the Chieftain's record sleeves. 'They should be paying for that.'

But Tone's memorial has also been used to promote serious causes, such as suicide awareness, or the Chernobyl Children's Project, where I saw Adi Roche and Ali Hewson pointing towards Tone for reporters, presumably saying that his Republicanism would have included looking after sick children. The space has become a sort of secular shrine. And whereas protest marches begin at the Garden of Remembrance on other side of the city, and pass the GPO, the Tone memorial is reserved for more contained events. It has also been spared the tensions that used to occur at Tone's actual grave when rival groups of nationalists came to pay homage.

Here, in the city centre, there is space and time. Anyone can attend, although Tone would surely have found it amusing that the Knights of Columbanus, from nearby Ely Place, start their prayer walk of the Green at the Tone memorial, and then proceed 'anti-clockwise'.

In the choreography of the space over the years, three images are particularly striking. One is of the Labour Party with all its new TDs crowding around the statue after their big election success in 1992, when they secured a mandate to introduce the long overdue social change that would finally help the country to become a proper secular Republic and less of the Catholic statelet presided over by the other parties. How curious, but perhaps appropriate, that it should fall to James Connolly's Labour Party to achieve this.

The TDs are beside Tone with their leader, Dick Spring, and are then pictured walking away, as if vitalised: *there's work to be done*. Within a few years, divorce was introduced, family planning extended and President Robinson continued her pluralist outreach. After decades of struggle, the secularisation of Ireland was finally underway, a struggle often as rancorous and divisive as that of the 'national question' – John Healy called it 'the second partitioning of Ireland'. In fairness, Garret FitzGerald had launched a constitutional crusade in 1981 to try to achieve these reforms and, in his words, to 'make the Republic a Republic worthy of Tone and Davis'. But his efforts were stymied.

Another image is of Sinn Féin activist Danny Morrison after the IRA ceasefire of 1994. He is pictured pressing his head through the granite columns of Tonehenge: *let us in*, seems to be the message, *we're Republicans too (we're the true Republicans, indeed)*. The long dispute over weapons decommissioning was underway.

The third image is from 1990, when Haughey, as Taoiseach, prepared the capital for the European summit and had spotlights put on Tone, revealing new aspects of the sculpture and stone. Ireland had the presidency of the EU, a bigger deal then than it is now, and in 1990 there was extra significance given the moves towards European Union, and more immediately German reunification. The Irish, and Haughey in particular, were very supportive of German unity, something for which he was profusely thanked when Chancellor Kohl visited Dublin. The Irish saw a parallel with their own divided land and didn't share the uneasiness of the French and British. The Wackerle fountain was an illustration of our different approach to German nationalism.

Alas, not long after the presidency, the lights went off again. And time caught up with Haughey, as did the revelations. And the Tone photos were part of it, for among the allegations which emerged in the late 1990s was the suggestion that Haughey, as Minister for Finance, knew in advance about the impending devaluation of sterling in 1967 but didn't tell the Taoiseach. Haughey claimed that he couldn't tell Lynch because he was busy at a public event. But, in fact, as the photos reveal, they were both at the same event – the Tone unveiling. The implication was Haughey knew in advance about Wilson's move and benefited from currency transactions. However, a further and surely more interesting revelation emerged that the whole government knew about the devaluation and had already decided that Ireland would follow suit. But this was never made public because it would show the people just how little fiscal independence we actually had from the old enemy.

By 1997, Haughey's star had truly fallen, and he was revealed to have taken large sums of money from private donors. In 2003, I wrote an article about my father's work for the Fianna Fáil magazine *The Nation*, but the references to Haughey were deleted. The article even used photos of the two unveilings, but Haughey was not identified, although he is clearly visible, standing there in his French raincoat and determined look. Suddenly, Tone's memorial was the place where the politician 'was not'. The *Sunday Independent* did a front-page story about this crude erasure. It was all a rather sad decline for Haughey, but bound up with his own hubris and overreach. Having been reckless with the economy in the 1980s, he now got it going again and laid the basis for a boom that would transform city and country.

In 2002, in a biography of Patrick Kavanagh, Antoinette Quinn revisited the story of the row. According to his widow, Katherine, the ailing poet had suffered from the minor scuffle and felt 'so humiliated that he went home and cried'. He felt that 'he was still being dishonoured in his adopted city'. This is surely unreasonable. Kavanagh was lauded in his lifetime, and in death even more so. In the Baggot Street area alone, there are three plaques, a canal-bank seat and a lifesize statue, sitting with arms folded and looking so realistic that it startles people at night. Especially if they are night-time revellers, coming from the pubs and clubs. If you want to see an interactive statue, then watch the young women sit beside Kavanagh or even up on his knee, in the way that he might only have wished while alive. *Look, girls, the ideal man: he doesn't talk back!*

Meanwhile, Kavanagh's rival, Brendan Behan, is commemorated with a corresponding statue on the other canal, on the city's northside. Again, the sitting statue is so lifelike that it gets confided to by loquacious drunks and hobos. There's poetic justice: Brendan gets the drinkers, and Kavanagh gets the women. Mind you, people also put broken glass inside Kavanagh's spectacles, lenses fashioned from the lumpy bottoms of bottles and glasses. But at least they are not mangled, as happens with Joyce's spectacles on the many heads of him throughout the town. There is a tyranny in being honoured too. In Joyce's case, he has been co-opted into a 'special Dublin pubs' series, with his head on a metal plaque, grimacing at the activity he is forced to endorse. Here is a case where the subject could have done without a realistic depiction. Better to be sheltered behind an interpretation.

Such has been the ultimate solace for Tone and Davis, since their statues are not realistic depictions at all but just that: interpretations.

'After the singing had died down and the officials had gone home,' wrote Judith Hill, 'Dubliners must have wondered whether they had the statues they had anticipated and how they were going to distinguish between Tone and Davis. Both were broad, be-coated, confident figures with small heads on which their features were briefly sketched, dominating presences rather than recognisable portraits.'

Although 'representations of Tone and Davis had been specified in the brief, the reality is that, for Delaney, both figures were raw material whose scale, proportions and constituent shapes were all elements to be manipulated. Thus, the roughly textured surface of the bronze did not differentiate between body and clothing, and gave the figures their essential vigour.' It would thus be hard to argue with her assertion that 'the statues of Thomas Davis and Wolfe Tone were not treated as portraits but as expressions of life'.

So maybe this is still the place 'where Wolfe Tone's statue was not', as it is in *Ulysses*. And isn't this wonderful? The sculptures are not anybody in particular – they are everybody. It is like a documentary about the famous Falling Man, dropping from the World Trade Centre on 9/11. After much investigation of the grainy image, the film makers couldn't decide who the Falling Man actually was and so, poignantly, they decided that in the end it didn't matter: the Falling Man was many people. The truly powerful thing about the Tomb of the Unknown Soldier in Paris is that the body could be any one of thousands.

Declan Kiberd, our English professor in UCD, used to finish his lecture on *The Playboy of the Western World* by quoting Bertold Brecht – 'Pity the land that has no hero,' to which the class would go 'ahh' knowingly.

'No,' said Kiberd, finishing the quote, 'pity the land that *needs* a hero.' And all the students went from 'ahh' to 'ohh'. ('Pity the teacher who needs an epigram' said a sour scholar afterwards, annoyed to have been caught in such a rhetorical entrapment. 'Or two,' agreed his friend.)

'Gentlemen, you have a country,' Dev told the crowd, but he could have added, 'and so you have no more need of a hero.'

And so just as Davis's lyric is embedded in sculpture and divested of danger, so Tone the rebel is secured by the state and encased in bronze. He is not a patriot any more – he's just a character, and an enduring human being. And it was on this basis I felt free to name my first son after him, when he was born in the Rotunda Hospital on Parnell Square, high up in the building where a short lived Communist Republic was declared in 1916 and where the more mainstream rebels were taken by the British after their surrender from the GPO.

Having been myself emboldened, and burdened, with the names of some of our greatest patriots, I wouldn't dream of denying such a dubious honour to Ciaran Wolfe Delaney. I also thought that I could disentangle myself further from the past, paradoxically by giving Ciaran the name of one of my father's most famous creations. An appropriation to forge a detachment, so to speak. Just as Eddie disentangled himself from the burden of a realistic portrait by taking the idea somewhere else. And, after Tone, he would never do a representational portrait again, which made all those calls for 'realism' particularly ironic.

But he had conquered Dublin and got his way. And yet Peter Murray concludes with a discordant note, 'Like many other serious European sculptors of the 1960s, Delaney ultimately faces the artistic dilemma identified by Rene Huyghe. "Having liberated himself from the past, whose paralyzing effect he dreaded, has the modern artist succumbed to the terror of his new task? Is his ultimate outlet the bitter despair of an essentially human failure, poorly disguised under aesthetic programmes and proclamations?"' Again, one can't but think of the parallel with a struggling state or emerging Republic.

'Delaney found himself in a paradoxical situation,' writes Murray. 'His drawings and sculptures were critically acclaimed, he had received important commissions for public sculpture and yet he steadfastly maintained his "outsider" status in the comfortable Dublin art world, dominated by the Royal Hibernian Academy. Through his art and his personal life, he had established himself as a rebellious spirit, and yet, paradoxically, for many years he was championed by the cultural and political establishment, a paradox in keeping with the self-assertiveness of the 1960s, when a wave of economic prosperity lifted Ireland out of its post-war doldrums.'

Even at the time, this paradox was apparent. Terence Connealy concluded his *Friday Focus* by summarising Eddie as a 'combustible character of apparent contradictions, an avant garde adventurer who cherishes eighteenth-century patriots; a GAA fan who just as blandly holds office as vice-chairman of Seapoint Rugby Club; a dynamic personality whose genius flowers in multiple directions.'

But is this not a paradox at the centre of Irish life and society, a paradox enhanced in recent times? It allows Ireland to project itself conveniently as both rugged and independent, but also ambitious and corporate. In short, it was the spirit of the Celtic Tiger, where 'rebellion' was really all about not letting the rules and conventions hold you back. It was a peculiar 'revolution' we had here: we talk left, but we do right. In 2007, the Shelbourne was bought by native Irish billionaires and completely refurbished. The faded colonial elegance was replaced with a makeover of marble and bright lights. It was, as one critic put it, 'Dubai meets the Galway Races' and a worthy successor to the Hibernian Hotel and the mohair suits of the 1960s. In the plush bar, next to the perma-tanned models, is a mural depicting Tone, and upstairs there is a special suite of rooms overlooking his memorial.

Also in 2007, Merrill Lynch staged a photo opportunity in front of the statue to publicise the expansion of their wealth management operations. 'Wealthy are "more demanding" than overseas', was the headline in the *Irish Independent* and the article described the needs of the 'newly minted Irish millionaires'. The photo shows two young financiers, confident and can-do in their business suits. 'New money tends to be more hands on,' said one of them. Tone is beside them, gazing into the mid-distance. What a long way we've come.

With their coffers flowing, the state was able to refurbish the city's statues. O'Connell had four bullets removed from his head, lodged there since 1916, although not for a moment had it affected his magisterial composure, while Davis was cleaned and repatinated by the OPW and had his fountain restored. To mark the 90th anniversary of the Easter Rising, the Taoiseach, Bertie Ahern, was going to switch the water back on and make a speech from inside Trinity – as opposed to talking *at* Trinity, as Dev did. But the plans changed and instead the event was held on a quiet Sunday, during which Ahern took a break from negotiations at Government Buildings with the Social Partners, where he'd been busy hammering out a new agreement for the industrial peace which had seen the Celtic Tiger flourish. Ahern was a skilful negotiator, who was able to accommodate all sides, and his speech for Davis reflected this. He was, in many ways, the embodiment of the Irish paradox and his text is truly 'all things to all men', as he protects his party's flank from Labour, Sinn Féin and those on the right who wanted an even more free-market Tiger.

But it is also a fine speech, which engages with the past and movingly charts the great changes that have overcome Irish society. In many ways, it is the speech that should have been delivered in 1966, had the state fulfilled more of its potential as a proper Republic. And if it hadn't lost its way in the subsequent decades. Indeed, it is like Groundhog Day, as we again get de Valera's lines from 1966, and even JFK's lines as quoted by Dev on that rainy Saturday.

Opening by describing Davis as 'a great Irish scholar, patriot and statesman', Ahern talks about his influence on subsequent Irish Republicans and about his conviction of the 'enormous potential for progress this country possessed, if freedom could be achieved. At the core of his political being was the belief that a native government was necessary to build up our economy and strengthen its capacity to provide decent livelihoods for all Ireland's people.'

> In our time, our generation has given effect to much of Davis's vision. Economic success and social improvements have unfolded in a context of unprecedented political progress ... Peace is a reality on the island for the first time in our recorded history. As we move Ireland out from beneath the shadow of the gunman, politics must move on and evolve. In shaping a new

politics for a new era of peace and prosperity on this
island, I believe we must always seek to be open, to be
inclusive and remain true to the traditions of our
Republicanism.

Davis believed that the purpose of politics was to
work for all the people and not a privileged elite. In
our time we must guard against the niche politics of
the few and the neo-narrow-mindedness of both the
hard left and rich right [in] reducing all politics to
ideological class-struggle in a world of haves and have-
nots. As Davis did in his time, we must espouse a
politics that looks after all sections and interests of our
people. We must espouse a politics that puts
communities and neighbourhoods to the forefront.
And also a politics too that is built on sound
economics, not reducible to it.

This sounds inclusive but it is also, of course, one of the classic
evasions of Irish politics: we don't do left and right here, we only
do people.

Davis abhorred those who preached politics of a
sectarian hue and this roused his deepest convictions.
In 1844, he wrote: 'I will not be the conscious tool of
bigots. I will not strive to beat down political, in order
to set up religious, ascendancy.' The central tenet of
Irish Republicanism today is that the people are
sovereign. The overwhelming majority of the Irish
people have consistently rejected violence and
sectarianism. Any individual who seeks to use these
methods is not in my view a Republican.

This is absolutely valid, but again it reveals a dichotomy in the Irish
approach. Davis, Pearse and other Republicans all used violence,
and it is debatable whether they had the majority with them when

they did. But by now the Northern nightmare has made the state much more nuanced in its tribute to the armed tradition.

'New politics should learn from old history,' continued Ahern, as if to reinforce the point. He then went on to have a pop at the neo-liberal agenda of raw economics. 'This state's Republican heritage also demands that we never forget the prevailing challenge to remember that there is such a thing as society. That we are part of something that needs us to prosper. To remember that we are not just consumers, we are citizens. And to revitalise the meaning of citizenship for this busy generation. And along the way to work on bringing a new generation into public life.'

There was then a nice passage about change, which echoed de Valera's concerns about materialism in 1966.

> Change has become a commonplace of life in Ireland. We are almost blasé about the scale, pace and range of change. Let there be no mistake about it. Ireland is undergoing the most significant social change in generations. Change is a new thread to our tradition. But so familiar are we with change, that we risk missing the significance of what is happening before our very eyes.

> Davis said that he had one great fear. This was that 'cynics who decry every noble purpose and sneer at every noble effort' might undo the work of patriotic men and women. In our time, we must not be linked by those who see only the next problem, never the last achievement. Because, uniquely in the history of this island, this generation has choices. We are the first generation to enjoy both economic prosperity and peaceful freedom. This means we can choose the kind of future we wish to build. This is a once-in-a-lifetime choice. It is a real windfall from the bough of history.

This is an endearing touch, and gracious too, suggesting that the peace process was not the result of a lot of hard work, not least by the Taoiseach himself, but a gift of fate fallen from the tree of chance, or some such notion. It is an image that would be made real within a year by Paisley's powerful visit South, when Ahern presented him with a bowl carved from a tree felled at the site of the Battle of the Boyne. The gift was actually for Paisley's wedding anniversary, and the Ulsterman was genuinely moved.

Peace has held but, since then, the economy has taken a dramatic downturn, connected to the global situation but the government has been at least partially blamed for overheating the economy and not being cautious. It is interesting then that in the rest of his speech Ahern sounds slightly unclear as to where we're all going with this economic buoyancy.

'I contend,' he says, 'that government must invest not just in physical infrastructure but in social capital. We must invest in the gold standard of identity and allegiance that binds a nation together.' But what exactly does this mean? And as if this wasn't vague enough, he falls back upon some old chestnuts, usually only heard at the Fianna Fáil Ard Fheis: 'We can do this by placing our language and our sporting traditions at the heart of modern life.' It sounded like the government was running out of ideas.

But the Taoiseach quickly returned to the broader picture and the legacy of Davis, as well as de Valera's hippy-like urgings to the young people in 1966 to love their country. 'The single-mindedness of those patriots like Davis who imagined another Ireland into being, in decades blighted by famine and emigration, should inspire us.'

This is an interesting one: Davis as an artist or sculptor, *imagining* another Ireland into being and making his ballad a 'reality'.

It echoes the point made by Roisín Higgins in the book *1916 in 1966, Commemorating the Easter Rising*, about the impetus of the state to have the Davis ballad 'turned into bronze', so to speak, and a fugitive art form institutionalised. But she also makes a more fundamental point that the memorial represented a large paradox at the heart of Davis's teachings, and of Irish society, and it is worth hitting the 'pause' button on Bertie's speech to quote from it.

'The conflict within Davis's own position,' writes Higgins, 'was well illustrated in the recasting of his ballad into bronze. Davis had attempted to create a nationhood that masked the socio-political reality in Ireland. In his construction, sectarianism was a division that could be overcome by an appeal to an inclusive Irish identity. The inclusiveness, however, depended on an exclusion of Englishness. It has been suggested that Davis "was, in a sense, asking Irish society to stand still, perhaps to go into reverse, and retreat from modernisation and Anglicanism".

'However, to argue for his alternative, Davis used the tools of that modern society: literacy, newspapers, industry. The contradictions inherent in the state's position (and indeed in the concept of modernity itself) during the 1916 jubilee were also present in the statue's design. Irishness was presented in a traditional form while the government also attempted to reformulate the country's image as modern. As in the writing of Davis, an appeal to nationhood was used to obscure the structural inequalities in Irish society.'

So here it is, the classic tactic of Irish nationalism, which is to overcome divisions and hard choices by appealing to the mythology of country, history and people. It is inclusive, a 'big tent' philosophy, but it also masks awkward realities. We talk left, but we do right. It has been the prevailing tactic of our mainstream political culture, and especially of Fianna Fáil. And it must be conceded that given what the state inherited in 1921, it has been, in the main, effective.

Hitting the 'play' button again, we hear Ahern quoting de Valera at the original unveiling, who in turn quotes John F. Kennedy: a veritable Matryoshka doll of references. 'We should ask ourselves, not what our country can do for us, but what we can do for our country.' And with that quote, you can hear Dev as he is in the newsclip, his little voice shouting at us again, imploring us to 'love our country', like a mannequin come to life.

Ahern continues:

> In this significant year, when we commemorate the 90th anniversary of 1916, we need to use this time to renew a sense of citizenship: a greater sense of ownership in the life of the country; a greater knowledge and understanding of the values, institutions and rights that citizenship brings to one all. New and old, people of all political persuasions, and of no persuasion, we need to see ourselves not just as individual consumers or investors but together as part of a common project.
>
> Together, we have lifted the shade of poverty and deprivation that has darkened our island history. But this is no cause to be complacent. We must strive to go further and continue our all-out assault on social exclusion wherever it raises its head. Through our targeted anti-poverty policies, we are reaching out like never before to people and places previously neglected: to people who felt rejected by the state; to places where emigration, poverty, unemployment and resentment were the norm.
>
> Thomas Davis inspirationally looked forward to the dawn of a new era of light and hope for Ireland's people. And nothing stirred him more than to imagine the benefits that would flow from an Ireland free of sectarian strife where all our people pulled together. He wrote, 'If we gave up old brawls and bitterness, and came together in love like Christians, in feeling like countrymen, in policy like men having common interests. Tell us, dear countrymen! – can you harden your hearts at the thought of looking on Irishmen joined in commerce, agriculture, art, justice, government, wealth and glory?'

293

In our time, the greatest tribute we can pay to Davis is to ensure every single person on this island – irrespective of class, colour or creed – is given the opportunity to live the dream of freedom and prosperity which the generations before us at home and abroad sacrificed so much to make possible.

And so Bertie pressed the button, and the fountain came back on, and after shaking hands with us and posing for photos and the six o'clock news, he got back into his car and returned to the talks on social partnership. As he left, he handed me his speech – as if he knew it filled a gap in this book, and filled a gap in the story of our emergent republic. It was even marked 'unveiling' as if Davis hadn't been unveiled the first time. That is, properly unveiled. So this was the speech that should have been delivered at the first unveiling, if the country hadn't lost its way.

A lot of quotes come to mind: old chestnuts like '*plus ça change*' or 'those who forget the past are condemned to repeat it'. But I prefer one of my father's favourite quotations, from T.S. Eliot's 'Little Gidding': 'And, at the journey's end, we shall come back to the place where we started and know it for the first time.'

But we can also give the last say to Davis himself and the final verse of 'Tone's Grave', his tribute to his predecessor:

In Bodenstown Churchyard there is a green grave
And freely around it let winter winds rave –
Far better they suit him – the ruin and the gloom –
Till Ireland, a nation, can build him a tomb.

294

Afterword

My father died in September 2009, in a hospital in Galway. It was a short illness, after a bout of pneumonia, but in the last year he had declined considerably, with Alzheimer's, weight loss and immobility. He had spent seven years in Áras Mac Dara nursing home in Carraroe, a good innings considering, sitting there surrounded by the rocks and landscape of Connemara. At one stage, in the hospital, he rallied and sat up and smiled at his children and looked at recent photos of *Wolfe Tone* and the *Famine Group*. He stared at them, clearly thinking of things he might still change. He tried to take the ring off my brother Garech's finger, perhaps thinking he would reshape it. Afterwards, we walked back into Galway city by Nun's Island and the rushing waters of the swollen Corrib, coming down from the upper Connemara, from the mountains and rainy lakes. It was a typical Galway night: stormy and drizzly and yet, paradoxically, mild and soft. We went past Bowling Green near Nora Barnacle's house and the area where, in Joyce's masterful story 'The Dead', the young Michael Furey comes to stand under the window of his lover, catching his death in the pouring rain. It is an audacious story about the mingling of life and death, and the dangers of following your passion.

Walking past the rushing river and the backs of the houses, I thought about *Anna* and the line, inspired by Joyce, about how 'every great river is an old woman and every river on which towns and villages live and grow and die, holds in itself, as old age does, the mystery of simultaneous life and decay.'

I also thought of the Davy Byrne's wall panel and how it was inspired by the Viconian cycles and how Eddie had quoted the first line of *Finnegans Wake* – 'commodicus vicus of recirculation' – but had also invoked the theme of the original bawdy ballad, 'Finnegan's Wake', concerned as it was 'with the revivication of a dead man and the return of the heroic era, "Finn Again".'

In Dublin, at that very moment, *Anna* was sitting in the window of Adams Auctioneers in St Stephen's Green. In the other window were *King and Queen*, with the same cylindrical honeycombed torsos as the Davy Byrne's piece, which the catalogue eloquently describes as 'an evocative embellishment suggestive of organic masses like seaweed, moss or spores, suggesting the fragile and ephemeral nature of life, and yet cast in bronze they seem to strive for permanence'. It was uncanny timing. On the Friday coming, a sister work, *Eve,* was due to be unveiled at IMMA.

My father had rallied, but a few hours later he took a turn and went peacefully. His hands, still warm, took a time to cool just like a cast. It was, indeed, as if he had turned into a sculpture. His body was brought back to Connemara to be waked in Carraroe, and then taken on the long and beautiful car journey up through the mountains back to Mayo, to his home town of Claremorris. It was a journey we had often taken with him late at night in the car, as kids, going through Maam and Cong and watching the moths flying into the headlights and the white flash of sheep caught on the rainy roadside.

Now he was going home, back to Claremorris and to Crossboyne to be buried with his parents and brother. There was a big funeral officiated by his brother Monsignor John and attended by relatives, locals and friends. The Taoiseach sent a military representative, Sean Keane of the Chieftains played the fiddle and soloist Richard Carney gave a powerful rendition of 'There is Treasure in the Fields'. On the altar, I spoke about my father's belief in the Viconian cycles and the extraordinary coincidence that the previous evening, at the very hour we were closing the coffin, *Eve* was being unveiled in Dublin, standing as a symbol of renewal and rebirth after the destruction of war. 'The sculpture outliveth the man,' as Eddie said, but so do his family and children and grandchildren, all of whom walked him to the graveyard. For, as well as being a sculptor, he was a father. And soon he would be a grandfather again, for as we came west we had news that my wife Fiona was pregnant again and that Ciaran Wolfe would have a sibling.

In the end then, I didn't get to finish the book before my son was born, but I did manage to finish it before my father died – except for this final page. Typing these last words, I see on the windowsill his old tools, rusty but still solid: a wrench, spanner and welding goggles. Back in Galway, meanwhile, his steel sculptures remain in the fields, tingling in the sea breeze. After the funeral in Claremorris, we saw photos of Eddie that we had never seen – my father as a child. One of them, taken in a big field, was of a small boy holding on to a small horse and looking at the camera. His life was about to begin.

Index